'James Sedgwick's updating of TA, therapy besides, is a timely, necessar welcome book. The author successfi usual and throwing-the-baby-out-w. field has long paid lip service to the importance of socio-political contexts but Sedgwick attempts to go further by subtle analyses and critical thinking to expose the nature of "horizontal suffering". Whether you share his political analysis or not, Sedgwick potentially offers a seriously game-changing view of therapy in a world that is much more complex and challenging than the first and second waves of theorists of therapy faced. His book deserves a wide readership in the therapy professions.'

Colin Feltham, *Emeritus Professor of Critical Counselling Studies, Sheffield Hallam University, UK*

'This is a timely book, which offers – nay, urgently advocates – a new perspective on transactional analysis psychotherapy, one that reverses the trend towards the focus on the individual and examines what a truly social psychiatry might look like. The author starts from the position that the development of the self, the individual, is a co-creation in and by the environment, with the child as active "learning participant". Furthermore, this is a process that continues at every moment thereafter, as the person shapes and is shaped by the society in which she finds herself, with all its gaps and deficits of possibility. Thus Sedgwick considers "self-and-world" as his client. With this starting premise as a given, he meticulously reviews the theory and methodology of TA to examine how it can best support a therapy that not only addresses what he calls "vertical problems" – those related to an ongoing script – but "horizontal problems" – those that relate to the "force of circumstance and the uncertainty of the world".

This exploration, informed by social theory, contemporary philosophy and a range of psychological theories, involves the deconstruction and critique of all the major concepts of TA. Some of them are defined anew, some are completely revised and reformed. It is a stimulating intellectual journey.

The book is not an "easy read" – it is challenging, thought-provoking and erudite. It is also eloquent and witty, with delightful turns of phrase and pithy metaphors. Many times I found myself smiling in appreciation of Sedgwick's ability to capture a complex idea or summarise a convoluted concept in a few well-chosen words.

It is touching and surprising that a man who writes with such careful, rigorous precision about his ideas, should also come across as a man of passion and compassion. His signposts to the practice of contextual TA are inspiring. I will return to this book often.'

Charlotte Sills, *psychotherapist and supervisor in private practice; teaching and supervising transactional analyst; faculty at Metanoia Institute, UK; Professor of Coaching, Ashridge Business School, UK*

'The main thesis of this book is that certain forms of psychological distress are best addressed through fostering appropriate conditions for greater social and political awareness and identity formation. In presenting this thesis, the author makes a compelling case for a contemporary transactional analysis (TA) that accounts much more for the context of life. In doing so, Sedgwick both acknowledges those authors in TA who have previously argued about the significance of experiences and concepts such as alienation and oppression, and offers his own critical analysis of TA – one that is informed by sociology, historical materialism and class politics, as well as a close reading of some 60 years of TA theory. This is a well-researched and well-informed book that presents complex ideas in accessible and often novel ways, illustrated with clear examples from clinical therapeutic practice. I congratulate Sedgwick on this tour de force and his contribution to what could – and should – be considered to be (to paraphrase a metaphor used by the author) a "good-enough transactional analysis" for the 21st century.'

Keith Tudor, *Professor of Psychotherapy, Auckland University of Technology, New Zealand; Editor of* Psychotherapy and Politics International

CONTEXTUAL TRANSACTIONAL ANALYSIS

Contextual Transactional Analysis: The Inseparability of Self and World offers a novel and comprehensive reworking of key concepts in transactional analysis, offering insight into the causes of psychological distress and closing the gap between training and clinical practice. By providing a bigger picture – as much sociological as psychological – of what it means to be human, the book makes an essential contribution to current debates about how best to account for and work with the social and cultural dimensions of client experience.

James M. Sedgwick captures the ongoing importance of what happens around us and the distinctive kinds of psychological distress that arise from persistent and pervasive environmental disadvantage. Beginning with a view of people as always situated and socialised, the book highlights the many ways that the world always and everywhere constrains or enables thought and action. Ranging through ideas about the kinds of contextual conditions which might make psychological distress more likely and illuminating the complex relationship between socialisation and autonomy, the book suggests what the implications of these conclusions might be for clinical understanding and practice. Sedgwick's insightful and compassionate work revises the theoretical framework, fills a current gap in the clinical literature and points the way to greater practitioner efficacy.

Contextual Transactional Analysis will be an insightful addition to the literature for transactional analysts in practice and in training, for professionals interested in the theory and practice of transactional analysis and anyone seeking to understand the contribution of context to psychological distress.

James M. Sedgwick, PhD, is a certified transactional analyst and senior lecturer in counselling and psychotherapy at Newman University, Birmingham, UK. He continues to practise as a therapist for the National Health Service.

INNOVATIONS IN TRANSACTIONAL ANALYSIS: THEORY AND PRACTICE

Series Editor: William F. Cornell

This book series is founded on the principle of the importance of open discussion, debate, critique, experimentation, and the integration of other models in fostering innovation in all the arenas of transactional analytic theory and practice: psychotherapy, counseling, education, organizational development, health care, and coaching. It will be a home for the work of established authors and new voices.

www.routledge.com/Innovations-in-Transactional-Analysis-Theory-and-Practice/book-series/INNTA

Titles in the series:

Transactional Analysis of Schizophrenia
The Naked Self
Zefiro Mellacqua

Groups in Transactional Analysis, Object Relations, and Family Systems
Studying Ourselves in Collective Life
N. Michel Landaiche, III

Contextual Transactional Analysis
The Inseparability of Self and World
James M. Sedgwick

CONTEXTUAL TRANSACTIONAL ANALYSIS

The Inseparability of Self and World

James M. Sedgwick

Routledge
Taylor & Francis Group

LONDON AND NEW YORK

First published 2021
by Routledge
2 Park Square, Milton Park, Abingdon, Oxon OX14 4RN

and by Routledge
52 Vanderbilt Avenue, New York, NY 10017

Routledge is an imprint of the Taylor & Francis Group, an informa business

© 2021 James M. Sedgwick

British Library Cataloguing-in-Publication Data
A catalogue record for this book is available from the British Library

Library of Congress Cataloging-in-Publication Data
A catalog record has been requested for this book

ISBN: 978-0-367-19287-7 (hbk)
ISBN: 978-0-367-19288-4 (pbk)
ISBN: 978-0-429-20160-8 (ebk)

Typeset in Times New Roman
by Wearset Ltd, Boldon, Tyne and Wear

THIS BOOK IS DEDICATED TO MY
FAMILY WITH LOVE

CONTENTS

CONTENTS

FOREWORD

Contextual Transactional Analysis is the third volume in this new Routledge book series, "Innovations in Transactional Analysis," a series founded to challenge, expand, and deepen the theory and practice of contemporary transactional analysis. With this book, James M. Sedgwick calls transactional analysis back into attending to the crucial relevance of social, political, and economic forces at play in the struggles and concerns that patients bring to psychotherapy and counseling. In so doing, he articulates a perspective that richly fulfils the hopes and visions of this book series. While Sedgwick does not deny the formative forces of personal history and one's nuclear family that is typically the foundation of most theories of psychotherapy, this book takes the reader's head firmly in hand and turns it to look at the outside world, insisting that we see and consider the impact of the socio-economic present and of an all-too-often collapsing future that undermines patients' sense of possibility and promise for themselves and their families.

For the past decade, Sedgwick has worked as a psychotherapist in Birmingham and the Midlands of England. The social and economic realities of the communities within which Sedgwick has worked have made an indelible impression on him and are the cauldron in which the passion that fuels this book was born:

> Fundamental questions of security having been largely settled for a generation, a way of life emerged which was sufficiently at ease with its dissatisfactions to keep social disquiet simmering without boiling over.
>
> This picture changed dramatically in 1979. Against a backdrop of rolling industrial disputes and the Labour party's struggle to manage the public finances, the change in economic policy brought about by the new Conservative government set out, as part of a wider program of deregulation and privatization.... Communities were used to some ebb and flow in the job market but nobody was prepared for the complete and permanent closure of major employers. The factories and mines around which some towns had sprung up and which underpinned a whole way of life closed for good.

I have lived and worked in Pittsburgh, a working-class city much like Bir-mingham, that had thrived through most of its history on the coal and steel industries. The social and economic fabric of Pittsburgh and western Pennsylva-nia was torn asunder by the collapse of those industries in the 1980s, although it has been more fortunate in its recovery than the Midland England that Sedgwick describes. As I worked with Sedgwick over the past year, watching this book come to fruition, I thought often of my own clients, the history of my city, and of my many neighbors in the historically marginalized (African-American) com-munity in which I live – facing the ways in which their personal psychologies have been shaped by the social and economic realities within which they have lived. As I sit to write this preface, the impeachment trial of Donald Trump is unfolding. Since Trump's election, the social and political world has flooded into my office and those of my colleagues; despair, uncertainty, and fury are a daily presence in my therapeutic practice. I hear from my British colleagues of the constant anxiety and uncertainty that fills their consulting rooms in the midst of the utter chaos of the Brexit process. So too, I hear the despair of European col-leagues in the midst of the rising nationalist forces transforming the political dia-logue and economic landscapes. To look to the Middle East and the East, we witness the rise of totalitarian governments and the marginalization of entire populations.

Since the earliest years of the development of psychoanalysis, there has been a tension, one could say a profound ambivalence, between an emphasis on the forces of personal history and consequent psychological defences on the one hand and attention to the impact of social, cultural, economic, and political con-ditions on the other. Freud struggled throughout his life with a pained recogni-tion of social and cultural factors and the seeming inevitability of the violence inherent in humankind (1913, 1915, 1921, 1930, 1933). But after his death, those followers who most dearly claimed to follow the Freudian canon – Anna Freud, Melanie Klein, and Heinz Hartmann and the ego psychologists – focused with near total exclusivity on the role of family history, fantasy, and intrapsychic defenses as the domain and terrain of psychoanalytic treatment. Contemporary with Freud, there was Wilhelm Reich (1935/1962, 1946/1970, 1972), whose work was passionately grounded in the confrontation of social, cultural, and political forces, but he was rapidly marginalized and almost erased from the history of psychoanalysis. While Erich Fromm's books (1941, 1955) were widely received by the public at the time of his writing, they too have had little influence on the theory and practice of psychodynamic models. A similar fate has been afforded to much of the work of Erik Erikson (1963). Within cotempo-rary psychoanalytic thinking, there is a significant resurgence of the recognition and repositioning of social, cultural and political factors that must be considered in psychodynamic methodologies – Samuels (1993), Dimen (2003, 2012), Moss (2003), Harris and Botticelli (2010), Dahlal (2013), and Govrin (2015), to name a few particularly articulate voices. Most recently, Nancy Chodorow (2020) brings together her two professional identities of sociologist and psychoanalyst to create a compelling argument for the synthesis of the intrapsychic and the sociological. It is a compelling question as to how and why it is that self and world are so often bifurcated in our clinical theories. It is a question with no easy answers, but it is a question with which Sedgwick wrestles mightily in this book.

It is within this sea change of theoretical perspectives, that Sedgwick brings these questions to the foreground of theory and practice in transactional analysis. Although there have been others in transactional analysis who have addressed similar issues, Sedgwick offers us what is by far the most systematic and articulate argument on behalf of the synthesis of the intrapsychic and the social, insisting that self and world are inseparable.

In his first chapter Sedgwick addresses the paucity of TA literature systematically addressing social and political forces, in part a result of the founder Eric Berne's insistence that the practice of transactional analysis be apolitical. He writes,

> Speculations about Berne's personal reasons for this position, including revelations of his unnerving brushes with government forces determined to snuff out dissident thinking (see Cornell, 2016; Steiner, 2009) are certainly intriguing. Whatever the personal history behind their adoption, these ideas have outlived their initial formative circumstances and remain a core part of our theory.

Here the facts of Berne's social and political history are highly relevant and underscore a fundamental premise in Sedgwick's argument.

Berne was a psychiatrist during World War II tasked with evaluating the fitness of inductees to serve in the war. That task and the war itself left an enduring impact on Berne, as evidenced by a number of unpublished articles written post-war on the impact of the war on the minds and functioning of returning soldiers. He then went on during the late 1940s and early 1950s to travel internationally on his own, unaccompanied and self-funded, to study the practice of psychiatry in other cultures, producing a series of articles published in psychiatric journals based on his cross-cultural studies. This was during the infamous McCarthy era of the relentless "anti-Communist" investigations undertaken by the U.S. federal government. The FBI investigated Berne for his alleged anti-American activities, as evidenced to the U.S. government by his international travel and studies. His passport was seized and all of his correspondence and papers confiscated by the FBI. In his lifetime, Berne never wrote about this, but it did indeed result in his insistence that transactional analysis remain apolitical. Having been involved in the TA community for 50 years now, this piece of history needs to be known and understood for yet another example of why and how psychotherapists and psychoanalysts have so often turned their backs on social and political realities. There are real risks in questioning and transgressing social norms. Berne's traumatic reaction to the aggression of the federal government was a formative factor in transactional analysis, rendered an even more powerful one by his silence as to its history and meaning. Berne's adamant insistence that transactional analysis be apolitical, with its dissociated history, had an enduring impact on many first and second generation TA practitioners, a compelling example of transgenerational haunting (Apprey, 2003, 2019) within a professional community.

Among those students closest to Berne before his death at age 60 was Claude Steiner, who often crossed swords with Berne with regard to politics. Steiner (1975), Hoagie Wykoff, and a band of colleagues formed a movement known as "radical psychiatry," in which they endeavored to bring the experiences of alienation and oppression into transactional analysis. Theirs was an effort polemical and righteous in spirit but lacking a clinical depth, so it did not succeed in having a lasting effect in transactional analysis. Leonard Campos (2014, 2018), a first-generation transactional analysis, has maintained a political voice throughout his career, but his work has never made it to center stage in the development of TA theory. But for the most part, the socio-political landscape within TA remained largely a desert for decades. More recently, Keith Tudor (2017) and myself (Cornell, 2018) (among others) have sought to bring social, cultural, and economic concerns to the center of TA theory and practice; a 2018 volume of the *Transactional Analysis Journal* was devoted to the theme of "social responsibility in a vengeful world." *Contextual Transactional Analysis* represents a landmark contribution to our evolving theory.

In these pages, Sedgwick undertakes a thorough review, critique, and re-conceptualization of major areas of transactional analysis theory, challenging and expanding the standard TA canon with perspectives drawn from sociology and philosophy. For those readers familiar with transactional analysis, this book affords an opportunity for a substantial revisiting of such central concepts as ego-states, the Parent ego-state in particular, frames of reference, games, and script. While it is beyond the scope and purpose of a preface, I do want to highlight Sedgwick's re-evaluation of the Parent ego-state, both because the ideas themselves are exciting but also because this chapter is a wonderfully rich example of critical thinking that, as he puts it, "I need to unbolt and pull apart some cherished assumptions about [the Parent ego-state] before reassembling the theory from the ground up." In his reassembly he questions the emphasis on the role of internalization and turns our attention to the centrality of socialization.

To quote Sedgwick at some length:

> We never quite stop being parented even when we are past the ages of dependence. The psychic organ exteropsyche (Berne, 1966) – literally "outside mind", quite different from just parent – is not a filing cabinet in which we store our family dramas before sealing it against other influences. It needs to be thought of figuratively as an open space, an ever-shifting constellation of outside influences of varying prominence and strength, sometimes complimentary sometimes discordant. This entails a rather different definition of maturation's peak than separation

from others. It acknowledges that autonomy is always balanced with ongoing dependence and co-operation.

For those readers unfamiliar with transactional analysis, you will find both an excellent introduction to contemporary TA and an argument of urgent relevance to our clinical and social worlds of today.

William F. Cornell
Series Editor

References

Apprey, M. (2003). Repairing History: Reworking Transgenerational Trauma. In (D. Moss, Ed.) *Hating in the First Person Plural*, 3–28. New York: Other Press.

Apprey, M. (2019). "Scripting" Inhabitations of Unwelcome Guests, Hosts, and Ghosts: Unpacking Elements that Constitute Transgenerational Haunting. *Transactional Analysis Journal, 49*(4), 339–351.

Campos, L.P. (2014). A Transactional Analytic View of War and Peace. *Transactional Analysis Journal, 44*(1), 68–70.

Campos, L.P. (2018). Meeting the Challenges of a Vengeful World with a Socially Responsible Transactional Analysis. *Transactional Analysis Journal, 48*(2), 126.

Chodorow, N.J. (2020). *The Psychoanalytic Ear and the Sociological Eye*. New York: Routledge.

Cornell, W.F. (2016). In Conflict and Community: A Century of Turbulence Working and Living in Groups. *Transactional Analysis Journal, 37*(2), 136–148.

Cornell, W.F. (2018). If it is Not for All, it is Not for Us: Reflections on Racism, Nationalism, and Populism in the United States. *Transactional Analysis Journal, 48*(2), 97–110.

Dalal, F. (2013). *Race, Colour, and the Process of racialization: New Perspectives in Group Analysis, Psychoanalysis, and Sociology*. London: Routledge.

Dimen, M. (2003). *Sexuality Intimacy Power*. New York: Routledge.

Dimen, M. (Ed.), (2012). *With Culture in Mind: Psychoanalytic stories*. New York: Routledge.

Erikson, E.H. (1963). *Childhood and Society. 2nd edition*. New York: W.W. Norton & Co.

Freud, S. (1913). Totem and Taboo. *Standard Edition*, 13: 1–162. London: Hogarth Press.

Freud, S. (1915). Thoughts for the Times on War and Death. *Standard Edition*, 14: 273–300. London: Hogarth Press.

Freud, S. (1921). Group Psychology and the Analysis of the Ego. *Standard Edition*, 18: 65–144.

Freud, S. (1930). Civilization and its Discontents. *Standard Edition*, 21: 57–146. London: Hogarth Press.

Freud, S. (1933). Why War? *Standard Edition*, 22: 203–215. London: Hogarth Press.

Fromm, E. (1941). *Escape from Freedom*. New York: Farrar & Rinehart, Inc.

Fromm, E. (1955). *The Sane Society*. New York: Henry Holt & Co.

Govrin, A. (2015). *Conservative and Radical Perspectives on Psychoanalytic Knowledge: The Fascinated and the Disenchanted*. New York: Routledge.

Harris, A. & Botticelli, S. (Eds.) (2010). *First Do No Harm: The Paradoxical Encounters of Psychoanalysis, Warmaking, and Resistance*. New York: Routledge.

Moss, D. (Ed.). (2003). *Hating in the First Person Plural*. New York: Other Press.

Reich, W. (1962). *The Sexual Revolution: Toward a Self-governing Character Structure*. New York: Farrar, Straus & Giroux.

Reich, W. (1970). *The Mass Psychology of Fascism*. New York: Farrar, Straus & Giroux.

Reich, W. (Ed. L. Baxandall) (1972). *Sex-Pol Essays, 1929–1934*. New York: Random House.

Samuels, A. (1993). *The Political Psyche*. London: Routledge.

Steiner, C., Wyckoff, H., Goldstine, D., Lariviere, P., Schwebel, R. & Marcus, J. et al. (1975). *Readings in radical psychiatry*. New York: Grove Press.

Tudor, K. (2017). *Conscience and Critic: The Selected Works of Keith Tudor*. London: Routledge.

ACKNOWLEDGEMENTS

This book argues that what we take to be our view alone always rests upon what we have borrowed and learnt from others. The influential thinkers I have encountered solely in print are gratefully recognised and thanked through the customary means of appropriate citation. The gratitude that I owe to the many stimulating conversations with colleagues, trainers, friends and fellow travellers across the years is harder to register for the debts are great and my time short. None the less a few notable individuals stand out for honourable mention.

I would like to thank my colleagues at Birmingham Healthy Minds and Newman University for generously granting me the sabbatical time necessary to complete the writing of this book.

Colleagues and friends Helen Rowland, Mo Felton, Ruth Roberts and Romey Sylvester volunteered some of their precious time to read and comment upon early drafts of the manuscript. Their shrewd and warmly delivered feedback has both sharpened the thrust of my argument and guided me towards finding my audience. It would have been a poorer book without their efforts. Clinical colleagues Dani Curtis and Mark Pulley have been an endless source of informal support. Their grassroots experience in and enthusiasm for reaching those clients that therapy sometimes leaves behind has been a great encouragement.

Bill Cornell's faith in this book has not wavered from its earliest conception to the final draft. Alongside his theoretical acumen and editorial experience, he has kept the project on the rails and turned what often seemed like an unmanageable task into a completable one.

Nicky James was the 'Vygoskian Parent' I needed as I was assembling my initial ideas. Her huge passion for and knowledge of sociology were so often my light in unfamiliar places, her challenges the spur to the further work that I needed to extend my argument in the right directions. Without her initial guidance and tireless support this project would never have progressed further than undisciplined speculation.

Finally, this book necessarily acknowledges a debt to my clients from who I always have more to learn and for whom I always hope for better times.

Part I

CONTEXT INTRODUCED

INTRODUCTION

Making a place for the contextual

This book offers a new way to understand some types of suffering that our clients experience. In doing so, it questions assumptions shared by both clients and therapists[1] about the nature and origin of that suffering and about how we understand people to be. These new ways of thinking became necessary as I struggled to close the gap between the transactional analysis in which I was trained and the novel demands of the clinical situation. I suspect this feeling that our theories don't fully explain some of our client's stories is a familiar one to many experienced, committed and open-minded clinicians. What I had not anticipated is how far down the revisions of transactional analysis theory needed to go before the answers I sought began to take form.

The ideas I settled on are sufficiently unorthodox within the field to require an extended retracing of the chain of reconsiderations by which they were reached. Those coming to the book seeking a compendium of road-tested technical adjustments or modest polishings of sturdy conclusions are less likely to find answers to existing questions than they are a call to substitute their old questions for new ones. Eric Berne memorably and provocatively stated that therapists should write only about how to cure patients (Berne, 1971). I accept Berne's challenge to be optimistic whilst adding a cautionary note: before we think we about 'curing' people we have to understand what it is we think we are curing them of. This is by no means as simple a question as it might initially appear. Psychological distress can be seen and felt without announcing its origin or revealing its workings. Some problems become fully visible only when we have gained the means to see them.

The particular kind of suffering I propose to describe arises under circumstances of persistent and pervasive environmental disadvantage. Not all aspects of this specific kind of distress have been fully recognised either within transactional analysis or within the wider therapy world. If the existence of such a distinct kind of problem is acceptable to my readers then I take it that the reworking of established ways of thinking volunteered here will necessarily follow.

Since this book offers solutions to theoretical blindspots that transactional analysts (and sympathetic fellow travellers) may not yet know they have, it is incumbent on me to disclose what I think we have collectively failed to see. It may seem peculiar to suggest that the external sources of distress are not immediately apparent when we are confronted with lives blighted by political and social oppression, poverty, worklessness, crime, violence in the home and on the street, widespread drug and alcohol misuse, poor living conditions and commonplace health difficulties. Many outside our profession might conclude that the unhappiness associated with existing in such circumstances is so readily comprehensible that a psychological theory of such misery will be little more than professionalised common sense. Those who feel that psychological theories add something crucial and additional to our understanding of people's responses to difficult circumstances will adopt the view that there will be something in the way the person thinks, feels or act in the situation which magnifies their misery. It is this purported individual response which is thought ripe for psychological exploration and change, even if the explanation offered varies according to the therapist's theoretical orientation: so far, so uncontentious.

Initially this was my view too. When I began my work as a therapist over a decade ago in socially and economically deprived areas of post-industrial cities, I took myself to be merely stating the obvious when I identified my clients' circumstances as the primary source of their unhappiness. I hoped, in line with my training but often without dramatic success, that I could find something within them which might not have quite surrendered to the brute realities of their predicament. I became and remain convinced that for many of my clients, a change in circumstance would offer a fuller relief than therapy can grant them.

However, the more people I met, the more I began to notice common features of each story which both went beyond the understandable impact of their unhappy circumstances and yet lacked the bright flashes of a unique, resourceful subjectivity which therapy often seeks out. I was struck again and again by the fact that my clients seemed to have only a limited awareness that life could be different in a way that seemed quite distinct from both stoic acceptance or weary resignation. I often noticed myself experiencing an outrage at the routine casting aside of human hope and dignity which my clients did not share. If I disclosed my view it felt like crass imposition on the process, if I stayed silent it felt like a betrayal.

Transactional analysis theory is likely to guide us to certain answers to the questions posed here. Script theory would place responsibility for suffering at the feet of a complex mingling of defence and deficit. We might imagine we could find a hidden, vibrant Child ego-state kicking and screaming to be released from the historic chains of an early decision. Attention to the transference might uncover early feelings and needs, barely formed and never yet met but still reaching forth, craving a recognition which would allow them to rejoin and nourish a stronger more integrated self.

As useful as such ideas can be, they didn't seem to be the right answers here. Rarely did I find a Child ego-state up to the task of change. And whilst clients responded positively to empathic attunement it often felt as though they could take in the warmth of my responses whilst the meaning I hoped to communicate

4

passed right through them bringing neither vitality nor enlightenment. Sometimes I felt as though there was no gap between self and circumstance, as though the world around them had gone right down to their roots taking with it all hope of things being different. From my vantage point outside their situation I took myself to be perceiving a gap in their understanding and identity that I didn't quite understand how to name or respond to.

From conversations with colleagues, I suspect most therapists feel similarly adrift when confronted with clients raised in such disadvantage. Although we acknowledge this too rarely, therapy was not pioneered and developed in places where these life experiences were common. Whilst state and charitable provision of therapy sometimes extends its reach into different communities, a disproportionate amount of our clinical literature continues to be based on the sliver of individuals who have the means and willingness to pay privately for open-ended therapy. Few have seriously contemplated the possibility that theories based on work with affluent, educated, psychologically-minded, cultural-majority clients doesn't automatically generalise outwards to provide either a universal understanding of human experience or treatment practices that will help everyone uniformly (notable exceptions are, Kearney, 1996; Minuchin et al., 1967).

Without the opportunity to regularly contend with clients born and raised in collective struggle, we are left with a pool of clients who swim with life's tide more often than not, who rarely want for opportunity and have a sense of agency that naturally accompanies this. Their suffering is atypical amidst their general good fortune. Confronted with such difficulties, our learned tendency as therapists is to look 'inside' the person to find what sets them apart and holds them back. By way of explanation we are likely to turn to the overlooked details of their minds, the legacy of their early family history, their particular, individual tendencies to respond to things in unhelpful ways. We need only change the person and then return them to their relatively benign circumstances.

The frequent success of these ideas notwithstanding, they presume that a highly individual pathway into suffering must be traced. The question which asserted itself repeatedly to me is what happens when suffering is not ours alone, when whole communities, everyone you know, has been pulled down in the same way? Should we approach client work in the same way when misery and hopelessness congeal into a collective way of life? Distress would no longer be something that separated you from the world, but something which joined you with others. The problem would no longer be just inside us but also around us, a common rather than individual predicament handed down from parent to child and shared with your community.

Alongside the obvious injuries and indignities of circumstance, I sensed a secondary wound becoming visible. If a whole collective experience become problematic in this way, the possibility of dreaming of a better tomorrow might begin to disappear. The terrible would simply be the normal, horrifying life events wouldn't be an abrupt and shocking departure from routine existence, they would be a continuation of it. People might collectively lose a sense of what they could have been if the world had been different. Deprived of a voice and the power to make it count, a collective mood of powerlessness and apathy might descend. Their horizons limited to coping with today, people might never learn social and political dimensions of being necessary for efficacy and optimism. They weren't and never had been the people they could have become if life had been different and therefore couldn't fully grasp what was missing.

Initially my improvised ideas for responding took it as a given that whilst these problems I was encountering might be different, the transactional analysis picture of human functioning that I used to formulate my response would remain largely unchanged. Whatever their circumstances, people are still people. Old tools can be used to complete new jobs. Moreover, as a self-proclaimed 'social psychiatry' (Berne, 1961, p. 12), transactional analysis seemed well placed to account for contextual difficulties. It talked about the interdependence between what happened between people and what happened inside them (Berne, 1961; Clarkson, 1992) which held out at least the promise of enhancing my under-standing and guiding my work in the right direction.

Unfortunately, as I am by no means the first to suggest, some parts of transac-tional analysis theory look rather better at a distance than up close. I had initially hoped that a modest revision of the theory of the Parent ego-state was all that would be necessary since this is the part of ego-state structure which lets the outside world in. Yet my clients rarely manifested distinctly observable parts of themselves which self-prohibited or instructed in the way that Berne proposed (Berne, 1961). They did, however, often talk in ways which carried the clear imprint of place and people sometimes to the point where taking positions outside their cultural beliefs appeared only fleetingly. Using our customary theory, it was hard to tell where the Parent ended and the Adult began. If your theory of change tells you that unlocking and integrating different parts of the mind will bring forth new meanings and strengths then this is something of a problem. If your theory also tells you that Adult reality testing can overthrow inherited limitation then you are equally stumped if no counterpoint position presents itself.

I wondered what the distinction between Parent and Adult ego-states was sup-posed to look like in a place where viewpoints converged without serious chal-lenge. Things just were as they were so there is no need for the Parent to suppress dissenting opinion. The distinction between 'I' and 'Us', a collective and individual viewpoint, also didn't seem to exist in the same way. In com-munities where circumstances are static and belief is handed down as tradition, adulthood is achieved precisely by becoming like those who have come before you not by differing from them. It felt unhelpful to think in terms of parents sending their children discrete 'messages' about the world which were then internalised. A more plausible story is that those children had been inducted wholesale into a worldview which now constituted the unbreachable horizon of their understanding. As a concept the Parent Ego-state was a starting point but one which would require considerable reform to address these questions.

6

Having cut and reshaped the Parent ego-state to make it fit for purpose in a way I describe in Chapter 3, I then found the concept couldn't be slotted back into its usual place in the theory. Having tugged at a loose theoretical thread, it then felt as though I had accidentally unravelled the whole transactional analysis sweater. Further key parts of the theory including ego-states, games, frame of reference, scripts, autonomy and transactions had to be similarly unbolted, stripped down and, in some cases, put back together in an effort to make them compatible with my burgeoning sense of the irreducible primacy of the social. This book is the product of that rethinking process.

This final reassembling of newly modified theoretical components, comprehensive enough to warrant a new designation – contextual transactional analysis – rests on two significant challenges to familiar ways of thinking. The first is an inversion of usual priorities between the psychological and the social so that what happens 'inside' us is understood primarily in terms of what happens 'between' us and others. The second, related challenge is a suggestion that sometimes we need to prioritise the Parent and Adult ego-states over the Child in our efforts to understand and help people.

It's not unprecedented within transactional analysis to place greater emphasis upon the social (Kreyenberg, 2005; Massey, 1985, 1989, 1996), but this book goes further than previous authors in subjecting our core concepts of ego-states, games, scripts and frame of reference to penetrating revision in the light of sociological ideas. Since these concepts have had something to say about the social, we have too often presumed that by using them we have said enough about it and that revisions to our theory are not necessary.

Not only do I believe there are crucial aspects of collective social functioning that our current theories are unable to capture, we also need to acknowledge that psychotherapy and sociology produce knowledge that may sometimes coincide but will begin from quite different starting assumptions about how best to understand people. They cannot be completely merged without loss and inconsistency. We do not yet know how to see people both individually and collectively from the same starting point. Depending on what kinds of things we are trying to comprehend we have to jump to one side of the line or the other. This book allows us to make that jump as required though it does not deny that sometimes we will need to jump back and re-embrace psychological explanation.

Transactional analysis has always started from psychological inwardness and tries to work outwards to the social. Even at its most socially aware, it always eventually loops back either to ground explanation in the things people think and feel or to consider the social purely in terms of its impact on thought and feeling. It treats the social as a kind of secondary byproduct which we can explain as the cumulative meshing of the thoughts, feelings and actions of the individuals who comprise it. The social itself, the aggregate product of our interactions which transcends specific interactions, isn't thought to require a separate kind of explanation. By contrast, sociology will tend to see the influence working the other way. Starting from the recurring, large-scale structures or patterns of interactions which comprise the social, it works inwards from the collective to show how our individual thoughts, feelings and actions are shaped and rendered possible by the collective. Contextual transactional analysis is an outside-in theory: it starts with the social and works back to the individual – with all the conceptual gains and inevitable sacrifices this entails.

Our theory has strained to reach this point because our basic unit of the social remains either two people in mutual interaction or else the contracted therapy group. Transactions and transference constrain our sense of the social to parent and child, therapist and client. As the number of people increase beyond two, we are forced to amalgamate people into a static, generalised other or cultural Parent (Drego, 1983) so we can repeat the trick, forcing the social relationship between self and society into the existent psychological framework of self and other. Personifying the social in this way fails because large-scale social systems can't be understood in the same way individual people can. Human intentions are only one ingredient in social patterns. Their laws and regularities are often unplanned and emergent. Social artefacts may start out as products of our intentions before swinging free and exerting a reverse influence on their makers. Therapy groups fall short in a different way for they are such artificial, particular entities that they offer only limited guidance on naturally occurring social phenomena. There seems to been an almost stubborn insistence on stretching our concepts to explain the social at all costs.

Contextual transactional analysis starts with 'we' of the social and work backwards to the individual 'I' because sometimes we understand individuals best when we know what is happening around them and where they have come from. It starts with the view that people are the partially unique, emergent products of general social patterns and structure. Individual viewpoints are thought to rise out of our immersion in collective knowing. We all cut a unique path through the common world which means our identities will be simultaneously individual and shared. The common tongue of belief and language we are initiated into both shapes and enables our identity and thought, it does not merely express it.

An outside-in account of the psyche suggests that the most important parts of ourselves are inseparable from the social from the word go. The inside-out, by contrast, regards our most precious parts as pre-social and only added to the world subsequently. Contextual transactional analysis denies that either early non-verbal experience or untutored biological givens (retained in the Child) are somehow more 'authentic' and vital than what was first borrowed from others and goes on to become central to our sense of self in the course of living. It takes the theory that a child is born free and then placed in chains by contact with the world as a story it may be appropriate to tell some clients with particular life experiences, but not a good general account of how we come to be how we are or how we can change. I have come to call latter position a 'shouldn't-have-happened-but-did' theory of human development.

Contextual transactional analysis presupposes a theory of socialisation (introduced fully in Chapter 3) as a compliment to more commonly cited theories of individual development. Socialisation accounts for the development of competence and how successfully the person takes their place in the world around them. Such a theory makes a larger place for learning and the mastery of shared concepts at the heart of both development and the therapeutic enterprise. As socialised beings, we are inducted via co-operative learning into a social world which precedes us and surrounds us at every step. The initiation process can be done better or worse – and the social world we are inducted into can also be locally better or worse at supporting human flourishing (to use Aristotle's phrase (Aristotle, 1999)) depending on whether ongoing contextual conditions are in place to let us become who we need to be.

We achieve ourselves in interaction, participation, learning and opening out to experience. In addition to the more familiar developmental needs for love and security, if the world fails to teach us what we need to know and give us what we need to have then we arrive in our lives unprepared and confused. The hidden dimension of social oppression is not just that it knocks us down but that it deprives us of the means to understand fully that rising again is possible. Here is a social counter-part to what we might call 'should-have-happened-but-didn't' developmental accounts of the relational and integrative schools within transactional analysis where the formative years may not be characterised by traumatic incidents but there is a pervasive sense that something precious and necessary was lacking (Moursund & Erskine, 2004; Hargaden & Sills, 2002).

This reversal of pre-eminence between the psychological and the social leads on to the second startling inversion in our way of thinking – that the mature Parent and Adult ego-states (P2 and A2 in the structural model, see Stewart & Joines, 2012) are more central for understanding some aspects of human experience than the Child. Transactional analysis has always been a very 'Child-centric' therapy. Either we presume that the source of present distress is the persistent recurrence of challenges in early development or we take the Child to be a wellspring of untapped vitality, innate wisdom and change potential (a view which I will challenge in Chapter 4).

We need to give this mature psychological structure its due for I believe it is in the immediate interface of our present selves and world that the origin of some problems can be best understood. Whilst insight will sometimes remain essential, it is the faculties that are best suited to 'facing outwards' and those parts of our experience where we make good use of shared and inherited ideas which hold most promise for developing 'outsight', the capacity to perceive the external world clearly. If we need to penetrate the top layer of the present rather than dig into the secrets of our individual past, it is the resources of the mature psyche which may prove our best allies. They are the receptacle for our best hopes of getting to grips with the world.

Properly reconceptualised so their individual attributes and relationship with each other are reformulated, the Parent and Adult ego-states can lead to a new account of how we get a grip on the world. Berne argued that Parent contaminations, the tendency to confuse someone else's worldview with our own, can usually be countered by leveraging the reality testing powers of the Adult. All we need to see things clearly is for the Parent and Child to get out of the way. Transactional analysis generally continues to perpetuate Berne's related assertion that Adult reality testing is quick and easy (if superficial) whilst the deconfusion of the Child is long, hard and more rewarding.

I don't find this a satisfactory answer. There is far more to understanding what is happening around us than simply opening our eyes. The complex hidden order of things uncovered by social scientists of all persuasions, the forces guiding us out of awareness are not self-evident any more than the molecular structure of a chair will present itself to us without the aid of a microscope. The social is endlessly complex, profuse and opaque: it is no less mysterious than the unconscious substructures of the mind (Lippman & Curtis, 1991). Oppression and other social difficulties don't simply present themselves as a sensory object might, we have to learn to see them – sometimes when they are actively evading our efforts to perceive them. Here socialisation announces its virtue, for what I can know on the basis of direct experience will rarely be enough. It is the shared tapestry of experiences, beliefs, stories and languages appropriately offered to us which raises us up to achieve this 'outsightful' penetration.

When Berne subdivided autonomy into awareness, spontaneity and intimacy (Berne, 1964) he was saying that we become our best selves when we understand the world around us and our place within it, when we are completely and fully ourselves without internal restriction and when we can build loving, constructive relationships with others. Contextual transactional analysis reminds us of a lesson we are in danger of losing sight of – we can only come to understand and be ourselves in tandem with understanding the world and the opportunities and constraints which it brings. Awareness as something more than mere cognition needs to be reasserted here. Spontaneity and intimacy without workable awareness of the world are blind and vulnerable. Sending people back out into their lives at the end of therapy without an enhanced understanding of how things are going wrong means the world will continue to bend them out of shape in the same old ways it did before. The introduction of political and social awareness into our practice and our client's lives represents the best response to this challenge.

Therapy and politics

My intention is easily misunderstood. I have no wish to turn therapy into the kind of unproductive conversation about how terrible the world is which we might have with our friends in a bar. The impression I gain from talking to experienced practitioners is that many of them already discuss social and political realities with their clients, particularly when not to do so would seem to be discounting the obvious. Yet they tend to present such moments as a temporary aside from what really matters: a quick spot of normalising then back to 'real therapy'. There seems to be no awareness of how to usefully bridge these dimensions. The advantage of rethinking things contextually is that not only does it gifts us greater sociological know-how for talking about how things are going wrong in the world but it renders apparent how progressively enhancing social and political awareness alongside insight, integration and personal accept-ance can complement each other.

The distinguished tradition of 'critical therapies' (for example, Halleck, 1971; Steiner et al., 1975; Newman & Holzman, 1996) has not been entirely successful at providing this bridge. In their haste to get their politics right and entirely radical, these approaches risk shredding some of therapy's useful caution and compassion. A flight into professional apostasy, denouncing therapy's com-plicity with power structures, often occurs. Critical approaches are also prone to seeing therapy as a conduit for the delivery of established (usually leftist) polit-ical ideas whose legitimacy is presumed not argued for. In a profession which, if my personal experience is in anyway representative, is somewhat monocultur-ally leftist, critical psychotherapy may be guilty of a well-meaning though undis-criminating embrace of certain political ideas and the benign indoctrination of unsuspecting clients.

My hope is that contextual transactional analysis will strike a fine balance between introducing new ways of seeing things as a necessary precondition of building or reclaiming an autonomous political identity and the reparenting trap door of just telling people what to think. There are many conceptions of the good life and a politically sensitive therapy therefore should not rest purely on an expectation of the practitioner holding the 'right' political views. Contextual transactional analysis aspires at points to be neutral about what a good world should look like whilst simultaneously being highly partisan about clients having the opportunity to form a considered, passionate, workable picture of how things might be. It is pro-politics in general, not pro a particular political vision. The task of therapy is to identify the ways in which the formation of a political iden-tity rather than just political belief has been contextually stymied so that con-ditions for its acquisition can be created, as far as possible, in the therapeutic space.

There is a further risk of my argument being absorbed into the burgeoning therapy literature on the modification of theory and practice necessary to work with minority identity client groups. Stung by fair accusations of indifference to the specific needs of minority communities, the profession is now making amends for its historic negligence in a widespread pleading for an increase in therapist awareness of the key issues with corresponding modifications to prac-tice. I cautiously welcome some of these developments whilst remaining mindful of their limitations. First, the kinds of contextual difficulties I will outline here can be found in surprisingly advantaged places – or in unexpected ways in dis-advantaged places. The whole point about the difficulties I am identifying here is that they are often not obvious to those they are happening to. That we so often defer to an approved list of minority identity categories is itself evidence that these groups have already achieved a robust political identity, public recognition of their plight and institutional support. They can already name their problems and articulate their wants. This does not mean that everything has been accomplished, but disadvantage is both a slippery and a movable feast. Our map of inequalities and problems shift constantly as the world changes. If we approach our clinical challenges with an open mind we may be better positioned to discern new blind spots in collective awareness.

We also risk shrinking the political and social to fit inside the psychological so that we might carry on using old concepts for new purposes. Since we are disposed to seeing critical and neglectful close relationships as the driving force behind psychological distressed it is perhaps only natural that we are drawn to a type of 'therapeutic' politics which seems to closely mirror these assumptions. A good deal of our professional literature addressing questions of difference and diversity consequently risks adopting a superficial version of what Nancy Fraser calls 'the politics of recognition' (Fraser, 1997). We focus on the painful feelings which result from being poorly regarded, excluded and persecuted because these are the aspects of social disadvantage which we see most readily.

We do not yet know how to bring into the therapy room the more dispersed, abstract social forces which invisibly shape both the occurrence and experience of social disadvantage because we often have not yet learned to see these things or how they might meaningfully connect to our narratives about ourselves. Looking to the client's own experience as the best starting point for whatever needs to come forth, we don't know how to begin dialogue about factors which shape them without leaving productive traces in their experience. We are drawn to the politics of recognition as a comfortable road into the political because we cannot conceive of how to talk about disadvantage that does not somehow wear a human face. We need to expand our ways of thinking and talking about how people come to be as they are so that wider web of social forces, usually shrouded in obscurity and incomprehension, can be integrated into their sense of how things are. Once their impact on the available possibilities for thinking and being have come to light then new options and understandings may result.

The notion of political identity which guides this book is lightly sketched to better include differing political convictions and circumstances of practice. It's designed to take on whatever local flavour is required. Political identity is equal parts knowledge, ability and optimism. No more substantial a definition is needed than that a person should possess a sufficiently advanced sense of how things currently fit together around them. They should come to understand themselves as constantly in mutual – though usually unequal – interchange of various kinds with the world around them. To this should be added a sense of how things might currently fit together around them if people's enlightened wishes were better reflected in what happens next. The world of people is not an unchangeable given, and that it sometimes seems so is a problematic illusion. The social world is created and recreated again as the cumulative product of human intention and action. Once this is understood things can sometimes be questioned and changed.

The political individual acts purposefully and creatively through solidarity and participation in the world, finding themselves in the impact they can have. Andrew Samuels similarly writes of 'political energy', the enervating fizz that accompanies meaningful action and impact (Samuels, 2015, p. 5). I'm OK – You're OK is understood here in terms of what we might call (following Kant) a regulative ideal. It's an act of faith, a commitment to working towards the versions of ourselves individually and collectively revealed by our better purposes. It invites us to see people and ourselves as we could be rather than as we are. Without first learning to see clearly and act capably the attempts to tend to the inner life in isolation will be cast onto stony ground.

The structure of the book

The changes to our understanding that I have promised cannot be delivered plausibly in one motion. Understanding and agreement must be earned step by step. Each chapter here offers a particular piece which contributes to that whole jigsaw. Chapter 5 and the second part of Chapter 4 are addressed to readers who may want to submit the underlying assumptions of the book to detailed scrutiny. Those who are happy to take my conclusions at face value can skip these chapters without getting lost in the remainder of the book.

Chapter 1 defines the particular problems associated with persistent and pervasive environmental disadvantage and suggests several useful subcategories of the definition. The viability of this definition demands a reconfiguration of the relationship between self and world. Drawing upon a detailed case study of post-industrial cities in the Midlands of England, Chapter 2 argues that autonomy can only exist in what I call a 'good enough world'. I propose four minimal conditions that any social context must achieve to be good enough.

Chapter 3 establishes a new definition of the Parent ego-state and, by extension, the Adult which takes into account this revised relationship between self and world. Expanding the notion of development as socialisation, I argue that some dependence upon shared ideas and experience are an unavoidable aspect of life. The distinction between Adult and Parent ego-states is found to be based around the degree of authority we have achieved over the ideas which we use to navigate through life.

Likely disquiet resulting from some of my proposed revisions must be anticipated and addressed respectfully. Chapter 4 starts by arguing against the commonplace therapeutic assumption that clients already have enough innate capacity for change and that detailed talk of the social is therefore a distraction or an irrelevance. The second half responds to imagined philosophical resistance, particularly from quarters sympathetic to postmodernism, who are likely to be troubled by my emphasis upon increasing client awareness as insensitive to viewpoint pluralism. The chapter ends by sketching a new ethos for contextual therapy rooted in pragmatist philosophy.

Chapter 5 shows how we can achieve individual autonomy from a starting point in the shared language into which we have been initiated. Drawing further upon ideas from pragmatism, it suggests that speaking a word presupposes knowing how to use it properly. The chapter concludes by considering how we might think of therapy as a way of expanding someone's expressive capacity, building on their current understanding so that new and better ways of seeing things become available. Learning to make the common rules of language work for better for ourselves provides the necessary pathway from what *is* meant to what *could be* meant.

Chapter 6 revisits the concept of the frame of reference, posing the questions how do we come to know – both individually and collectively – what we know, how do our horizons become limited and under what circumstances might we change our mind about things. Suggesting that our seemingly coherent world-view is actually a messy patchwork of knowledge loosely held together by various ordering principles, I conclude that changing our minds is a gradual, piecemeal and open-minded process of learning and reform.

Chapter 7 shows how at least some games are brought about by limitations of a collective frame of reference rather than script or unconscious processes, The absence of relevant knowledge and experience prevents people from escaping the unhelpful social patterns they were raised into. The specific contextual conditions necessary for games to take root are described.

Bringing together the book's overall emphasis on acquiring the outsight, hopefulness and capacity necessary to achieve a fully adequate social and political identity, Chapter 8 briefly considers what kind of modifications to practice might be called for to achieve this. Reconsiderations of our ethical stance are followed by an outline of a learning focused approach to therapy fit for the problems outlined in the book. Chapter 9 offers some final thoughts on the social context in which therapy takes place and the impact this has on the activity itself. Arguments in favour of a programme of ongoing reform to better respond to the needs of a changing world are offered in light of the book's wider conclusions.

Conclusion

Since therapy of any kind is a contingent activity the most important words when writing a book on it are 'maybe' and 'sometimes'. My hope is that I will extend the reader's horizons to encompass new ways of thinking about and responding to the struggles of our clients. Though I will venture committed arguments against certain ideas, I am not offering a comprehensive stand-alone theory intended to sweep away all that came before. Varieties of transactional analysis which dedicate careful, empathetic attention to our subtle interiors will remain as indispensable for the well-rounded practitioner as they continue to be for me. I take it to be an uncontentious statement to say that certain therapeutic ideas are better tools for different jobs. My aim is supplementation not replacement. I don't ask that a socially literate way of using our ideas drives out our psychological ones, more than they sit in parallel, chosen and adopted as the moment requires. If the book focuses on ideas needing improvement or renewal, this does not mean genuine appreciation for the contribution of our forbearers and contemporaries is not quietly felt. My hope is that I have left the theories in better condition than I found them.

The persistent call to look again at familiar theory may frustrate those who are hoping purely for clinical instruction, but it would be inconsistent for me to argue in favour of clients acquiring the authority necessary to use ideas whilst not giving my readers the opportunity to retrace my every step. This book doesn't aim at the transmission of ideas, it seeks instead to create the active, engaged learners who will share ownership of them. I want peers and reform-minded critics, not followers. At times this will make demands on the reader as familiar theoretical landmarks disappear from view but I believe if you take the time to teach people *how* to think about things then they have less need to be told *what* to think. Sometimes it may seem I have gone a long way round for only modest adjustments, but the persistent reader will hopefully find themselves reflecting at the end that this was the right way to come after all.

Note

1 In this book I shall use the terms therapist or therapy as generic ways of referring to any talking therapy practitioner including and the field of talking therapy respectively. Where I refer to transactional analysis or transactional analysts I am making reference either to the theory and practice of transactional analysis and those who identify their professional identities primarily by reference to these ideas.

References

Aristotle (1999) *Nicomachean Ethics*. Translated by T. Irwin. 2nd edn. Indianapolis: Hacking.

Berne, E. (1961) *Transactional Analysis in Psychotherapy: a Systematic Individual and Social Psychiatry*. London: Souvenir Press.

Berne, E. (1964) *Games People Play*. London: Penguin Books.

Berne, E. (1971) Away from a Theory of the Impact of Interpersonal Interaction on Non-Verbal Participation. *Transactional Analysis Journal*. 1 (1), 6–13.

Clarkson, P. (1992) *Transactional Analysis Psychotherapy: An Integrative Approach*. London: Routledge.

Drego, P. (1983) The Cultural Parent. *Transactional Analysis Journal*. 13 (4), 224–227.

Fraser, N. (1997) *Justice Interruptus: Critical Reflections on the 'Postsocialist' Condition*. New York: Routledge.

Hargaden, H., Sills, C. (2002) *Transactional Analysis: a Relational Approach*. Hove: Routledge.

Halleck, S.L. (1971) *The Politics of Therapy*. New York: Science House.

Kearney, A. (1996) *Counselling, Class & Politics: Undeclared Influences in Therapy*. Manchester, PCCS.

Kreyenberg, J. (2005) Transactional Analysis in Organizations as a Systemic Constructivist Approach. *Transactional Analysis Journal*. 35 (4), 300–310.

Lippman, W., Curtis, M. (1991) *Public Opinion*. New Brunswick: Transaction Publishers.

Massey, R.F. (1985) Transactional Analysis as Family Systems Therapy. *Transactional Analysis Journal*. 15 (2), 120–141.

Massey, R.F. (1989) Script Theory Synthesized Systemically. *Transactional Analysis Journal*. 19 (1), 14–25.

Massey, R.F. (1996) Transactional Analysis as a Social Psychology. *Transactional Analysis Journal*. 26 (1), 91–99.

Minuchin, T., Montalvo, B. Guerney Jr., B.G., Rosman, B.L., Schumer, F. (1967) *Families of the Slums: an Exploration of their Structure and Treatment*. New York: Basic Books.

Moursund, J.P., Erskine, R.G. (2004) *Integrative Psychotherapy: The Art and Science of Relationship*. Pacific Grove, CA: Brooks-Cole.

Newman, F., Holzman, L. (1996) *Unscientific Psychology: a Cultural-Performatory Approach to Understanding Human Life*. Westport: Praegar.

Samuels, A. (2015) *A New Therapy for Politics?* London: Karnac.

Steiner, C., Wyckoff, H., Goldstine, D., Lariviere, P., Schwebel, R., Marcus, J. et al. (1975) *Readings in Radical Psychiatry*. New York: Grove Press.

Stewart, I., Joines, V. (2012) *TA Today*. 2nd edn. Melton Mowbray: Lifespace Publishing.

1

SELF-AND-WORLD AND HORIZONTAL PROBLEMS

Vertical and horizontal problems

It is usual practice in therapy literature to assemble a picture of how people are, then ask what has gone wrong in this picture in order to explain a client's distress. I intend to start by describing a problem and then work backwards to suggest what this problem tells us more generally about people. To bring problems resulting from persistent and pervasive environmental disadvantage fully into view, I will need both to identify the ways in which those problems are distinctive and then to present an argument which suggests that the world gets into the self in a more subtle, comprehensive and penetrating way than our current ideas allow. Redrawing the relationship between the self and the world provides the means to revise the understanding of ego-states, autonomy, frames of reference and games which will be offered in subsequent chapters.

In my imagining, unnecessary psychological distress can be divided along two axes, the first of which I will call vertical-axis problems (from here on abbreviated to vertical problems). The term vertical problems presses together two axioms which often appear conjoined in our thinking. The first is that psychological problems are best understood by reference to a person's interior, their subjective or individuated disposition to think, feel and respond in certain ways. The second is that psychological individuation is formed and reformed across time. This assumption sometimes distracts us from adequately recognising that people are also spatially organised through participation in collectives. Exemplifying what Lynn Hoffman calls 'linear thinking' (Hoffman, 1981, p. 5), a vertical perspective focuses on the separate individual across time. It highlights the relative continuity of individual dispositions to think, feel and act and the ongoing relevance of individual history to these dispositions. These are explanations centred around individuals with collectives playing a bystander role.

Clinically, vertical problems lead to a view of suffering which presupposes what have been called 'therapies of isolation' where the self is separated out from its social context (Epston & White, 1995, p. 341). Few therapists will deny that the wider world plays some role in either triggering the distress or shaping the response but they are always trying to sniff out the distinctive and the singular. They seek to figuratively cut the shape of the isolated person out of the world around them to better discern what has happened. Whatever our guiding metaphors, whether we think of troubled minds as broken machines, internal wars, blocked strivings or unintegrated parts, unpacking the individual response is thought to lead to a better understanding of the suffering and show the path to recovery.

Individuated selves are the taken to be the site of the problem and the source of the solution. We are trained to pursue 'what is means for the client' thereby assuming that the influence of the world is somehow merely advisory, that it stops at the skin and something interior that is uniquely 'us' takes over to process, interpret, shape and sort the experience. We sift out self and world into separate components because we presume to understand people best in producing the most complete picture of their psychological surface and private depths. The psychological problem reveals itself in the act of gradually unearthing, recognising and describing what is already there in the client. Thinking vertically seems self-evident because once we have located the difficulty 'inside' the person it helps us to understand how the problem follows the person around between locations. If we are unhappy wherever and whenever we are, no matter how benign the surroundings, then the thinking goes that the person themselves must be the source.

Each model of therapy has its own set of assumptions about how vertical problems come about. Candidates can include defence against awareness, internal conflict, developmental deficits including attachment disorders, the thwarting of our innate potential, distorted thinking patterns or the failure to accept or integrate parts of our experience, all of them united in describing an individual psychological *response*. Transactional analysis has historically placed a strong emphasis on locating these difficulties in the Child ego-state. Berne's stack of pennies metaphor (Berne, 1961, p. 53) implied if you want to understand what is going wrong in the present then look for what went wrong in the past. If you want to understand why the surface is so troubled then you need to look behind it. These are the usually productive guiding assumptions of our profession.

Therapies tailored to the alleviation of vertical problems are interested in the relationship of the self to itself, the fostering of insight, integration and acceptance, the dissolving of inhibitions to improve thinking, feeling and behaving. These kinds of therapies are more likely to be facilitative and non-directive, believing that the client needs only the lightest of touch from the therapist to achieve the change they seek. Most people will indeed respond positively to the ministrations of a careful, unobtrusive listener but whether this is enough to build the changes that are needed is another matter. Sometimes we need to turn our attention outwards and to understand the self as part of a more complete picture of the world. We may need to achieve ourselves by way of learning and interaction, an active, open involvement with something beyond the border of the self.

Thinking vertically about our clients overlooks the factors necessary to understand horizontal-axis problems (hereafter horizontal problems). These occur when the person's current or historic context either deliberately withholds or fails to provide something necessary for the person to understand the nature and origin of their problems and to resolve them autonomously. The isolated self simply doesn't hold the answer no matter how deeply we probe. Horizontal problems presuppose that in order to be an autonomous individual, the world must positively co-operate in our efforts to act and understand. Without this help, the person will suffer without a full understanding of why or may misidentify the problem because some essential aspect of the world has not been disclosed. Thinking horizontally opens up a spatial orientation whereby we come to understand the individual as always inseparable from their relationships and the inevitable opportunities, constraints and mishaps that living in a world with others entails. Horizontal problems sit across the self and the world rather than inside the self alone.

My argument will seem unusual if we persist in thinking that the main barriers to understanding and action are internally motivated (the presence of obvious external barriers notwithstanding). Recognising horizontal problems brings us to acknowledge that our grip on our lives is fragile and that a great many things outside of our control need to go right in order for us to fully know and become ourselves. We often take the smooth working of our social order somewhat for granted if we are fortunate enough to live in peaceful, prosperous and politically benign societies. Horizontal problems appear most often in contexts characterised by oppression, significant social change and the break down or violation of the social and political order. The marks that contextual turmoil leave on individual lives can be both glaringly obvious and invisible to the untutored eye at the same time. The notion of horizontal problems was designed to make the whole visible.

If vertical problems are best understood psychologically then horizontal problems are most clearly viewed from a vantage point somewhere between psychology and sociology. We move our exclusive attention from what happens 'inside' of people to favour what happens between them and around them. Within transactional analysis, horizontal problems have been best understood as what Clarkson calls 'confusion', an externally generated impediment to Adult awareness (Clarkson, 1992). The formation of a frame of reference adequately resourceful for social and political identity formation either does not occur or is torn down.

That practitioners often unwittingly assimilate horizontal problems to vertical ones is not solely a matter of theoretical bias for our clients often inadvertently lead us in the wrong direction by adopting what I will call a 'partial-explanation' for their difficulties. A partial-explanation for psychological distress is an account which is vague or platitudinous. It offers the satisfaction of basic understanding whilst inadvertently obscuring a more enlightened viewpoint. Since people always try to make sense of their struggles and often interact with others who may have ideas about what is going wrong, experiencing psychological pain and having a story about that pain usually go hand in hand. So often when I meet individuals whose difficulties are best understood horizontally, they will describe themselves as depressed, lacking in self-esteem or confidence. It's not that these descriptions are wrong, more that they often don't really seem to go anywhere. Their suffering lacks the means to speak a clearer truth. Partial-explanations never open a door into a more meaningful story. They stand in the way of true outsight and autonomy.

Since the person has been deprived of the means to fully know themselves, horizontal problems can only be fully comprehended when a more advantaged position becomes available. As a concept, horizontal problems shares some features with Marxist-inspired theories of psychological 'alienation' (see Laing, 1967; Steiner, 1974). An alienated individual is thought to have been separated from full and healthy expression of their true nature and denied understanding of the world through calculated misinformation (mystification). Steiner would later refer to this as 'mindlessness', the purposeful discounting of our Adult and Little Professor in the hidden service of illegitimate social control (Steiner, 1974). Yet it's crucial to appreciate that not all horizontal problems can be understood as instances of oppression. They can spring from both unwitting ignorance or the unintended consequences of social action and interaction (see for example Watzlawick, Bavelas & Jackson, 2011). The insufficiency of our Adult to achieve outsight is sometimes a compound impairment, neither traceable to one source nor resolvable by a single means.

Horizontal and vertical problems are not mutually exclusive. It would be incredible to think that a lifetime of adversity hadn't left the kind of vertical wounds that most therapies seek to heal. A therapeutic approach able to embrace both axes will often be necessary. My argument is simply that horizontal problems require a separate and sometimes predominant resolution within the course of therapy. When general circumstance has been stable, benign and co-operative but the individual remains in distress, then therapy aimed at the vertical axis will emerge as the most productive path. When the anguish of the self is inseparable from the wider failures of the world around the person then the solution must sometimes be learning which leads to social awakening. We must sometimes understand our world better as the precondition for improving our lives within it.

Two paths with different assumptions confront us: the vertical path seeks to distinguish the self from the world, looking inwards for answers. The horizontal path leads our attention outwards to the place we hold in the world. It sees the interior as always inseparable from what has been learnt and provided by the world. Its aim is critical awareness of context and its means is engaged learning about the world as much as inward reflection.

Transactional analysis and the social

The suffering which accompanies horizontal problems is experienced no less subjectively than that of vertical problems, but their genesis lies in the intersection between self and world. In order for my account of horizontal problems to

20

be persuasive, I need to establish an understanding of the relationship between self and world which is rather different than the one we are used to. Rather than thinking of the self and the world as separate things that go on to be combined, I propose that we consider them as always inseparable. The 'we' and the 'I' are never quite as distinguishable as we have been led to think. This state of perpetual inseparability – without total merger – will be referred to as self-and-world.

Introducing such an idea into an unreformed transactional analysis is challenging, for so much of our existing theoretical apparatus stands opposed to the move. Berne's writings left us with a legacy of conflicting attitudes towards the social. Whilst demonstrating an empirically-informed curiosity about cultural variations in psychiatric practices (Berne, 1949, 1956, 1960), his later writings unmistakeably concluded that social differences were only skin deep, that sociology was an unhealthy preoccupation with the trivial and transient (Berne, 1970) and that what is universally and invariantly true of all people is what is most important about them. At the same time, Berne considered environmental influence as crucial; few figures within psychotherapy have done more to chase down the many insidious ways in which unfavourable happenings can shape us for the worse. Berne's initial favourability towards adaptation to current reality as a pathway to flourishing (Cornell, 2010) gave way in his later writings on script to the sour conclusion that being plunged into the world will only ever erode your potential. In this Berne remained a good Freudian, seeing the eternal conflict between the self and the world as our inescapable and defining predicament (Rieff, 1959).

Events were not excuses for Berne. As he embraced existential defiance of the world as the path to script-free living (Heiller & Sills, 2010), he correspondingly shrunk the social to a resistible influence. He remained unforgiving in his refusal to allow people to justify their actions by reference to circumstance (see Steiner, 1974, p. 99). Speculations about Berne's personal reasons for this position, including revelations of his unnerving brushes with government forces determined to snuff out dissident thinking (see Cornell, 2016; Steiner, 2009) are certainly intriguing. Whatever the personal history behind their adoption, these ideas have outlived their initial formative circumstances and remain a core part of our theory.

Perhaps it is inevitable that clinicians who bear witness to their client's stories will be confronted with daily evidence of the world at its most damaging. It's easy to see how a picture of Manichean struggle between self and others has captured the imagination of generations of transactional analysts. Whatever its instinctive appeal, the picture has limits: it is silent about the changeability of circumstance and fails to understand that the world is also always a constituent part of the self rather than just a series of assaults and obstructions coming from outside. It also paints a regrettably egocentric picture of life, identity and development. There is little sense in Berne that societies rather than just people can change for the better and that large-scale social co-operation may expand options for living. There is scant acknowledgement that others bequeath to us their cumulative wisdom and experience to spare us the grind of starting from scratch, a feature of our minds derogated to basic 'messages' and 'information' within transactional analysis (Berne, 1972). There is little sense that we are more fully ourselves in collectives than we are apart.

If all we knew of things was transactional analysis then, at worst, we would be limited to seeing the social world as a cage that imprisons our better natures. At best, we would reduce other people to the status of emotional fertilizer, doling out strokes for our personal growth, taking what we need to become ourselves whilst simultaneously denying others their dignified status as people in their own right. There is little sense in our theory that our lives oblige us to think beyond the question about whether the world meets our needs. A cynical note of 'take what you need and get out' lingers as though obligation were always just a compromise. If we adhere to this collection of ideas then the concept of self-and-world as an inseparable whole will be both inconceivable and intolerable. My job now is to show that a new way of thinking about our relationship to the world is both possible and desirable.

Context and contextual explanation

Understanding self-and-world requires that we adopt what Mills calls a 'sociological imagination' (Mills, 2000). The term 'world' here is derived indirectly from Heidegger to indicate our surroundings in their meaning for us (see Taylor, 2016). To this I add that it may be possible for others to perceive significances in our world that we as yet do not. Talking of the world in this way draws attention to what matters for our understanding of how people are and what configuration of opportunities and constraints they emerge from. Significance isn't always self-evident nor is it unchanging. We can be blind to some forces guiding our minds and actions though alternative possibilities sometimes come into view, however fleetingly.

Contextual transactional analysis therefore presumes that the best way to understand an individual is to look 'around' them as well as 'inside' them. It ranges across and integrates different kinds of explanation, psychological and sociological, into a meaningful whole. Contextual explanations arise when we notice something about a person that we either do not fully understand or think could be different. Our curiosity takes the form 'why is this person the way they are and not some other way?'. If we ask this question with our attention turned both outwards and inwards, a process of drawing previously unconsidered elements into our explanatory frame commences. Contextual explanation makes use of our general background sense of how we take things to be in the world so that we can make some aspects of the individual's predicament clearer. Social breadth and psychological depth must partially align for complete understanding.

We ask why someone is some way and not another way because we recognise from our vantage point that things can change. The art of a good contextual explanation is to balance accuracy and relevance about what is the case with informed hopefulness about what *might* be the case. Analysis is not a detached scalpel but an engaged and fully human effort to stir, re-engage and free up imaginative transformation of social possibility. How much of the world is significant enough to be included in an explanation at any given time will vary. Contexts can be as small as two people and as large as the globe taking in family, community and society in between. Perhaps we could imagine context as concentric circles expanding outwards with the individual at their centre: if the circle gets too large the person vanishes into the background: if the circle is too small then not enough is admitted for a satisfactory explanation.

The scope of our contextual explanations will be dictated by the kind of questions our therapeutic work is raising. We aim for *enough* context, the point at which a new explanation for what is happening with a person emerges but does not move so far past their immediate experience into abstraction that the possibility of new, situated thought and action is lost. Contextual transactional analysis typically finds its range in the local, a mid-point between the merely interpersonal and the whole society. Communities often serve as a ready-made unit of analysis, the sum total of recurring happenings and interactions both intimate and casual which make up a daily existence. As new details coalesce into hopeful possibilities, our sense of 'how things are' makes way for pictures of 'how things might be'. This enlightened sense of possibility is exactly what is missing in horizontal problems.

Contexts have both physical and social dimensions. Materially, they will encompass fixed, invariant aspects of the physical universe that we are largely powerless to alter and objects, buildings and tools we have collectively fashioned to suit our purposes (Searle, 1995). The social world of language, belief, customs, art and literature, laws, administrative systems, societies and nation states are made and maintained by people both deliberately and habitually. Unlike the given physical world, the social would not exist if human beings had not been here to invent it. However imperfectly, the social expresses our collective intentions and values. They are not inevitable, however frozen in place they may seem at the level of our experience. The key issue is always the extent to which existing social forms meet our individual and collective needs. Fully formed social and political identities emerge as an attempt to wrestle with this question.

The social world is best understood as a process rather than an object. Words like 'society', 'capitalism', 'culture', 'power' and 'patriarchy' refer not to static things but to ways of talking about the cumulative effect on our lives of complex, multi-strand relational patterns played out across thousands of instances which ultimately aggregate into an overall direction of the world (see Tilly, 2002, 2005). We use these terms to pick out consistencies and generalities which can be traced through particular instances. Since such vast processes won't change course as a result of solitary human endeavour, they can sometimes be experienced as fixed, unresponsive and permanent. Relational social processes, which seem as unresponsive to our wishes as the rising of the sun, can generate a sense of unqualified resignation. Fortunately, the possibility of changing *our* world rather than *the* world can sometimes be enough. Many local happenings wriggle free from the grip of general patterns (Unger, 2004) providing the necessary breathing space for independence, idiosyncrasy and alternative viewpoints.

If we take the world to be a cage not a home then we collapse back into Berne's pessimistic vision of the world as something which takes away from us rather than something which also adds to us. The materials of a common world provide the essential backdrop to social co-operation, opening up options whilst keeping others away from awareness and action. As Giddens notes (Giddens, 1984) we are both made by the world and make it through our collective daily actions and intentions, we are users and participants in culture and society not merely their products, dupes and victims. In practice not all contexts and societies grant its participants equal opportunities to determine the overall course of their collective lives. It will be those instances where constraint begins to outweigh opportunity that will concern us in this book.

The contextual self-and-world

Talk of looking both inside and around people are metaphors I've adopted as a usefully familiar beginning, yet this language carries with it assumptions that I wish to dissolve. Claiming that a clear point can be found where we end and the world begins is neither possible nor necessary to understand ourselves even as the deeply ingrained habits of clinical theory may make it seem so. Western thought has come to take separation and individuation to be the preconditions of personal autonomy and responsibility (Taylor, 1989). Sweep away the idea of borders and we have to understand autonomy differently. This is a subtly different point to the one made by intersubjective theorists (Storolow & Atwood, 1992), for where they speak of doing away with the borders of selfhood, contextual transactional analysis instead explores the interpenetration of worldviews.

To talk of self-and-world means then the distinction between what is mine alone and what belong to world will start to blur. It will still make sense to talk about subjective experience, but not to think of subjectivity in the language of inside and outside. Subjective experience is made from the social, it does not precede or escape it. Our minds are socialised all the way down. I call for a break with the developmental story that imagines a preformed yet undeveloped OK self, added to the world and always holding back something pristine and original even during social immersion. This picture will not be relinquished easily because it seems intuitively correct. Clients tells stories about the people and events which have knocked them down and kept them low. We listen out for their particular individual responses in the hope of uncovering an aspect of their response to them that the person themselves has missed. We slip without effort into dividing the story into external happenings and internal, subjective responses. In doing so we slip back into the language of vertical problems.

24

More than just a series of foregrounded events, the world is also the background, the atmosphere, the horizon against which these events occur. The world is not merely what happens to us, it also the socially-derived language and concepts we use to formulate our response: there is no outside here. If we continue to think of the world as a series of specific events 'having an influence' on an individuated self then we might compare the interrelation of self and world to the relationship a fish has to the ocean. The fish's will is shaped and thwarted by the ocean's wash, flows and currents, the availability of food and safety from predators drawing it inevitably in certain directions. The fish will sometimes have a tangible sense of the world pushing back against how it might want things to be, forcing certain choices upon it. Sometimes it has no choice but to swim with the tide.

Irreducible borders none the less remain. Fishes are individuated by virtue of their distinct physical bodies and separate awareness. The ocean's influence may overpower its will, but the fish always retains this physical separateness and private experience: whatever happens, these cannot be taken away. If we take the relationship between the fish and the ocean as illustrative of the position of human selves in the world, then we are committing ourselves to a picture of a mutual pushing and pulling between always-separate entities. The boundaries between self and world remain inviolate no matter how one-sided the influence.

This is still not the whole picture; the fish can dream of better times *within* the ocean, but it can't imagine life outside of it. It has no experience to tell it there may be places where currents don't shape destiny. The ocean is both the things that happen to the fish and the unchanging, background world in which those happenings occur. It's both the object of its thought and the environmental preconditions which enable and shape that thought. Here the distinction between self and world starts to seem less clear.

In the theory of the Parent ego-state, transactional analysis cracks the distinction between self and world by suggesting that people who once influenced us can go on to become a distinct part of our minds. Yet Parent ego-states have tourist visas, but not citizenship; they are never fully 'us', that is an honour we reserve for our Child and Adult. Parent ego-states are treated in the theory as a historic legacy, a once necessary and now compromising alien invasion of reclaimable territory. Transactional analysis therefore moves the border between self and world within the psyche but does not erase it. The fantasy remains that once maturity has been achieved, we then shut the doors on further influence. Having climbed the ladder to development's peak provided by our parent's teachings we can kick it away, make autonomous choices, turn the base lead of Parental messages into the gold of ethos. We return as adults to the condition of unsullied autonomy that we lost in the process of growing up, finally becoming ourselves alone.

I would argue that there is never a point at which the world stops penetrating our borders. Our Adult is socialised as thoroughly, though differently, than our Parent. Throughout life we remain dependent upon others, periodically hostage

25

to fortune, unknowingly swayed by the currents of common opinion. We can no more fully separate from the influence of the world than the fish can refuse to admit water into its gills. Common language and shared thought are the oxygen of subjectivity. Even once we achieve maturity, the Parent ego-state will continue being replenished and updated throughout life by fresh influences. This argument will be revisited and enlarged in Chapter 3.

If we switch metaphors, we might better understand self-and-world in terms of the relationship between a wave and the ocean rather than a fish. Whilst identifiably distinct, it would not be possible to imagine waves existing apart from the ocean. We could not trace the line where the wave ended and the ocean began. (A reader acquainted with Gestalt theory will have encountered similar conclusions before (see Philippson, 2009; Wollants, 2012).) Notice that our minds are assembled from the common ideas of the world. If we embrace inseparability it makes little sense to form hard borders between where we end and the world begins. We might think of minds and waves alike as *emergent*, things that rise out of the background of life without fully separating. Individuation would be seen as enabled by the world rather than compromised by it.

This is the early stages of a longer argument. What I am inching towards across the book in talking of self-and-world is ultimately a plea to drop questions of selfhood in favour of more useful concerns about whether there more autonomous ways to be, believe and act. We can readily accept that everyone possesses a pre-reflexive sense of their own conscious experience (see Zahavi, 2014) which the social cannot fully own without drawing further conclusions from this. As Harré has argued, the term self simply designates our cumulative ongoing sense of seeing the world from a point of view, as experiencing ourselves as largely continuous and as having a sense that we are both distinct from and part of the world around us (Harré, 1998). Identifying a quiet, pre-social core which is 'originally us' just isn't that important for my purposes. It has no resources to tap. It explains less than we might hope.

Dropping talk of selfhood and accepting that we emerge but don't separate from our contexts should not unleash fatalism. It may be impossible for us to imagine ourselves apart from the particular course of our life experiences, the culture and place in which we arrived and the challenges it has presented, but none of this is inconsistent with a sense of autonomy. We are still individuals, but we are individuals of a recognisable kind. We bear the marks of time and place. Heidegger wrote of the 'thrownness' of existence, that that we arrive in a world in motion, already made by others and that we necessarily fall into responding to how things are from our first breath (Heidegger, 1962). The inescapable work of responding to the world around us means there is no exit, but not that we cannot be more or less at home there.

That this book is written in English is an accident of my being thrown into the world at a point where this is the common tongue. To arrive here and speak as I do was not my choice, nor the choice of those who came before. I cannot step outside of being an English speaker for the very thought to do so would be uttered in the same language. I have abstract knowledge that there are parts of the world where English is not spoken, but no lived experience of what this might be like. My thrown predicament is experienced neither as consciously chosen nor problematically impeding, it is simply the climate in which my life moves. I experience myself as being able to think creatively and autonomously in English even as I am aware that complete originality is not possible. English is the ocean from which my mind emerges. If I decide to learn Japanese, it would require complete immersion before I stop being an English person mouthing a second language. It would take many years of living dedication before I dream in Japanese, before it becomes the tongue of my soul.

Particular events bring the usually sleeping background of our lives into sharp focus. If I were suddenly transported to a country where nobody spoke English then a previously unreflective, settled, background part of my ongoing existence would be changed into a difficulty which pressed itself upon my present attention to demand action. Even here what occurs is partial reform, not complete escape. Struggles will foreground some aspects of our world against the endless horizon of a complacently unnoticed pre-given world that is always the backdrop to present focus.

Emergence and autonomy

Our emergence from the ocean of the world is made possible by the world itself. Like Heidegger, John Dewey also thought that we arrive in a world already in motion, but he was more positive that we are able to make use of what is already there to engage purposively with the tasks of living as we find them (Dewey, 1922). Dewey encourages us to move past the distinction between subject and object, to abandon the view that we are detached, investigative spectators on the world in favour of one where we are always active participants. In this optimistic vision, we become ourselves in the course of our living, experiencing and responding to the world as the course of life unfolds. We simply start from where we start from and grab what is available. The language I speak as an unreflective part of my experience can also be thought of as an inherited tool for getting by alongside the beliefs, knowledge, collective experiences, individual stories, customs and laws which I encounter in the course of living.

The common world can be a resource. It allows me to communicate with and co-ordinate my actions with others, it enables me to know and describe myself, to receive information about the world vital for my current and future prosperity. It is indivisible from my sense of my own strengths. The tools of the world, the bequest made, remade and handed down to me by those who came before enable my autonomy. The world presents itself to our attention as a stream of opportunity and, where the tools don't seem to work so well, constraint. Autonomy is therefore never complete freedom, the availability of all options for living at our fingertips simultaneously but as long as we have the wit and vision to make necessary reforms, that should suffice.

This how it works in happy times. The problem remains that not all contextual 'oceans' are equally enabling. The more fortunate will find themselves arriving in parts of the world where a legacy of material prosperity, peace, social stability, cumulative wisdom and pervasive love and respect are so abundant that a contented life seems readily graspable. For those born in times and places where experiences of deprivation, lack or oppression are all that has been known then the individuals that emerge from such waters cannot but take on and recreate something of this collective impoverishment. Pierre Bourdieu writes of our 'habitus', the cumulative, unreflective sense of ourselves which we inherit from others and perpetuate through our actions making how we will be tomorrow seem inevitably no different from how we were today (Bourdieu, 1977; Bourdieu & Wacquant, 1992). Sometimes 'could be different' has no chance to break through 'just the way it is'.

Describing the predicament of the African American community in the year preceding the signing of the civil rights act, President Lyndon Johnson stated:

> You do not take a person who, for years, has been hobbled by chains and liberate him, bring him up to the starting line of a race and then say, 'You are free to compete with all the others,' and still justly believe that you have been completely fair. Thus it is not enough just to open the gates of opportunity. All our citizens must have the ability to walk through those gates.
>
> (Johnson, 1965)

Sometimes the failures of the world are comprehensive and total. This is quite different from fundamentally benign contexts in which a single devastating event erupts for here there is a remembered equilibrium which can be restored. It's an entire condition of being which deprives people of the chance to know who they might otherwise have been – a collective horizontal problem. It requires a recovery which goes beyond healing specific wounds towards a gradual reform of the whole sense of things. The alternative is to stay an emergent wave of stagnant waters.

Varieties of horizontal problems

Initially I believed that horizontal problems only occurred in the particular social and political conditions which characterise deprived communities. Clearly there is a strong and complex correlation between material deprivation and other forms of disadvantage but the relationship is not exclusive. As my attention moved from the more material difficulties of those communities to the invisible deficits of hope, opportunity and comprehension which shadow them, the more I noticed that a debilitating blindness to undergirding social realities was sometimes present in what appeared at least superficially to be highly functioning and

28

resourceful social contexts. Contextual transactional analysis had a potentially broader range of application than I had first imagined.

I have identified three different kinds of contextual configurations which I presume increase the likelihood of horizontal difficulties by depleting, confusing or fragmenting the self-and-world. I do not claim that this is an exhaustive list or that additional processes might not be identified in future. In preparation for the larger argument to follow in subsequent chapters and in keeping with my definition of horizontal problems, I intend to link each of these processes to particular configurations of the Parent and Adult ego-states. I have named these configurations oppression, overlap and chaos.

Oppression

Oppression is usually defined as social conditions where the powerful unjustly exploit, control or persecute another group of people within the same society. Since I am interested more in the psychological workings of oppression than its material precipitants, I intend to coin a narrower definition: a set of circumstances where the oppressed person or group has no choice but to adopt a description of the world enforced by the powerful. Oppression can aim simply at the infliction of suffering though often there is an undisclosed aim to illegitimately hoard resources, prestige and power. Historically the term has been used to describe authoritarian and totalitarian political regimes which exploit state control of the political system, media, financial system and the military to terrorise and confuse their citizens into compliance and to delegitimise and undermine political contestation (Scott, 1990).

After Marx, we cannot fail to be aware that more insidious, whispering strains of oppression can be present even in purportedly advanced democracies. Here oppression can be traced to subterranean processes, the subtle erosion of democratic accountability, media reporting which misleads by omission rather than mis-representation and violence against citizens performed under the guise of legal legitimacy. Political movements promoting the rights and dignities of oppressed minority groups will trace oppression through the seemingly innocent details of daily life, the innocuous misunderstandings, restrictions and prejudices which are so ever-present they turn the unjust into the normal. There are common features to oppression at cultural, institutional and interpersonal levels.

Successful oppression does not merely terrorise the body, it drains hope and understanding from the mind. The means by which this is achieved are varied. In authoritarian states, people are aware of what is being done to them but dare not mobilise openly to resist. In open societies, oppression hides in plain sight working through everyday action to sow confusion and bury the sense that things can be different. It seeks to turn victims into accomplices by persuading people to become their own willing jailors (Lukes, 2004). Oppression differs from social exclusion for the latter may be both more transparent and lacks the rationale of exploitation. The oppressor may need something from the oppressed and this is made easier by a social inclusion which manipulating them into subjugation.

Transactional analysis already offers two accounts of the psychology of oppression – the writings of Claude Steiner, in particular his participation in the radical psychiatry movement, and the cathexis school. Each approaches the problem from somewhat different starting points but I believe that, brought together, they can combine into a coherent and persuasive take on how oppression produces horizontal problems.

Both theories stress how power is grabbed within interpersonal relationships by those who control the description of reality. Steiner and colleagues, who are more attuned to societal-level oppression, begin from the assumption that the relationship between the world and the self can be modelled on transactions between the Parent and the Child respectively (Steiner & Wycroft, 1975). Having aligned the social and the Parental, oppression is then readily conceived as an onslaught of negative 'messages' which force their way into the psyche. The radical psychiatrists document the various ways in which culture, state, community and family contexts act in concert to indoctrinate people into their description of things. This description prevents the person from knowing and articulating their own wants and needs resulting in the condition of alienation. Oppression works by virtue of its relentlessness and the Parent's presumption of moral righteousness. Psychological oppression is overcome in the radical psychiatry tradition by an act of internal rebellion, calling the Child ego-state back from its exile in alienation to overthrow the Parent and reconnect with its innate wisdom.

Cathexis theory is only sensitive to domestic oppression. It is interested in showing how people perpetuate the disadvantages of their early upbringing through an interlocking series of psychological and interpersonal mechanisms (Schiff et al., 1975). It traces a persuasive link between how the person needs to maintain a rigidly consistent worldview (frame of reference) and manoeuvre others into concurring with it in order to recreate the familiar but deeply damaging relationships they have been used to surviving. Having started life being oppressed by their family, the person goes on to oppress themselves by actively restructuring their perceptions so that better ways to meet their needs never reach awareness.

Since an oppressive frame of reference will not consistently match the consensus definition of reality, oppressed persons must resort to striking acts of distortion and emotional manipulation to eliminate discrepancies between perception and world. Cathexis theory emphasises the way in which the capabilities of the self and alternative options for action are discounted instrumentally to engineer predictable outcomes. This is not dishonesty as such for the discounter has told the same useful lie about themselves so frequently they may have quite forgotten what the truth is. A discounter wields the power of the powerless, pressing others to do what they claim not to be capable of. Over time this will come to seem like the only way to live.

Concerned solely with discounting as a mechanism for masochistic disempowerment, cathexis theory lacks a corresponding account of how the powerful discount the powerless: fortunately, it leaves us with the materials to easily assemble one. Oppressive forces discount the existence, importance, worth, and equality of others (for an intriguing argument in a similar vein, see Karpman, 2019). Oppressive discounting of the powerless does not work just by Parental messages. It also generates a fundamental confusion about who one is and what is happening: it is equal parts lies and absurdity. Oppression produces an environment designed to keep the oppressed reeling in shock and fear so that orientation and mobilisation become impossible. Political imagination and will surrender and die. Our internal compass shattered, we cannot know who we are or which way the world is. Horizontal problems result when we collapse, exhausted and defeated, the cruel absurdity of circumstance facilitating the takeover of our view by theirs. They win in ways we can no longer fully recognise.

Oppressive regimes have been swift to learn that lies alone won't work and that destroying the very possibility of sense is paramount. Abusive families can work in much the same way. A parent that openly criticises a child as bad or worthless has at least stated something that can be grasped, understood and resisted. The parent that punishes without obvious sense or reason, that selectively ignores what a child says or withholds information from them will progressively erode the child's capacity for autonomous thought. These invisible injuries creep up unnoticed alongside the painful blows and injurious comments. In this way the Parental takeover of the Adult leaves us as little more than the mouthpiece for malign absurdity.

Clinical vignette

Polly came to therapy seeking help with a life-long fear of vomiting. 30 years old and a new mum, she could no longer rely on avoidance to manage. Her child needed Polly to cope when she was sick; she didn't intend to let him down. Polly had previously sought behavioural therapy for her difficulties and reported that her symptoms had reduced to nothing within a few sessions only to spring back up within days of completing treatment. Both of us were confused as to why.

In our second meeting, Polly remembered that her mother also had a fear of vomiting. As a child her mother would often hide when Polly was unwell. She recalled several memories where her mother was staring directly into her eyes, reciting the words over and again, 'you won't be sick … you won't be sick'. When Polly became distressed by this, her mother would encourage the rest of the family to mock Polly for not coping. As Polly made friends outside the family home, her mother would let other parents know that Polly didn't cope with vomiting. Everyone treated Polly as having a fear of vomiting – and over time she came to believe it herself.

I struggled to understand why Polly's difficulties had persisted into adulthood until I found out that she and her partner now lived only four houses away from her parents. At the first sign of her son being unwell she would call her mother and

31

ask her to come around. Her mother would appear but hang back, supposedly offering support, but subtly criticising Polly for not coping better. Crisis over, her mother would then call Polly's partner and father to say how once again Polly had not coped. Family gatherings often featured talk of her failure which made her anxious and upset about future incidents.

Polly took her mother to be merely concerned about her and believed their relationship was close. I heard a different story running alongside this, that she had spent her life trapped in occupying a role assigned by her mother's perpetual redescribing of the world. I speculated that perhaps this allowed her mother to mask her own fear and inadequacy under a veneer of concern. To no great surprise, when Polly's mother went on holiday for a week, Polly suddenly found herself able to cope with her son without anxiety.

The theory of symbiosis, defined as a close, interpersonal situation where two people are thought to selectively decathect ego-states so that between them they form a single, whole psychological structure, provides a better model for understanding oppression than script (Schiff et al., 1975). Where a symbiosis is forced on one party rather than entered into for mutual benefit, the oppressor's description of the world forces out the Adult of the oppressed and in doing so compels them to play a supporting role in the oppressor's script drama (a phenomenon increasingly referred to as 'gaslighting' (Abramson, 2014)). The self-imposed limitations of script alone cannot explain the compliance of the oppressed. To do so would be to discount how hard the oppressor is working to keep them there. There may be minor script predispositions which render people more vulnerable to collusion with their oppression but the tangible imbalances of power and resources which undergird an oppressive symbiosis make the suggestion of an equal share of responsibility both psychologically naïve and politically reprehensible. Co-creation is not equivalent creation.

Canny oppressors can gull all but the most script-free individuals. Domestic violence often replicates socially oppressive processes in miniature. Perpetrators deploy an interlocking set of strategies designed to progressively isolate the victim from friends and family, persuade them that they are to blame for the violence and undermine their confidence in their capacity to leave for a better life. Finally, when the usual coercion fails to persuade, a temporarily sincere show of tears and heart-felt contrition accompanied by a promise that it will never happen again offers just enough to keep the whole show going. The abuse works on all ego-states simultaneously, taking over the Parent, driving out the Adult and stirring the early Child disturbances in the script.

Overlap

There is some comfort to be had from categorising all social disadvantage as oppression. Imputing a unified, malign intention to harsh circumstances (Roy &

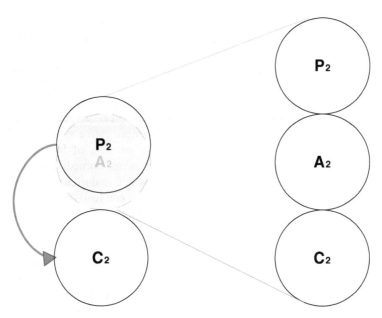

Figure 1.1 Oppression.

Steiner, 1997) may conveniently psychologise the social in a way which stokes the white heat of indignation, but it risks oversimplification and a corrosive splitting where everything wrong is projected onto the world. Teaching people that oppression penetrates every part of their world, often considered a necessary step in consciousness-raising and mobilisation, may itself constitute a form of oppression if it misrepresents the nature of the problem, the changeability of circumstances and the complex humanity of those identified as oppressors (Boltanski, 2011). Fortunately, a reconciliation with, rather than rejection of, the world is sometimes possible. If oppression is only a partial account then there is a need for supplementary explanations.

The world around us changes. Rather than thinking of societies or cultures as permanent artefacts like cultural Parents (Berne, 1963; Drego, 1983, 1996) the world we emerge from is always in motion (Margolis, 1995, Unger & Smolin, 2015). As the world changes our ideas about it often lag behind. Within that space between old ways of seeing things and new circumstances, horizontal problems may flourish. The world will move between being frozen or fluid in different ways at different times. Whilst the shifting of tectonic plates will take countless millennia thereby seeming permanent when measured against a brief human lifespan, the airy social worlds that we make and unmake amongst ourselves can change much more rapidly. This has been particularly evident in post-traditional Western societies since the middle of the last century. Sweeping economic, political, social and technological changes have torn holes in settled ways of living. Some changes are shockingly swift and dramatic whilst others happen gradually beneath the threshold of our noticing, leaving us subject to a creeping incremental alteration.

Some social changes are desired and actively pursued whilst others arrive accidentally and unbidden. Human societies are complex and changes in one area can ripple out into 'unintended consequences' elsewhere (Merton, 1936). Changes can begin in material resources, technological advances, geopolitical realignments, transformations in political and administrative systems, and alteration in culturally commonplace attitudes and patterns of beliefs. Once in motion, they set off a chain reaction in the wider ethos. Immediate experience is a limited vantage point from which to anticipate and understand these changes for the interconnectedness of the world is vast. This can lend the changing world a surprising, fluid quality which leave us feeling unsettled, uncertain and conflicted as we struggle to keep up (Gadamer, 1996).

Where striking changes in a collective worldview occur, people experience something I will call an overlap. This term refers to a particular state of social transition when two whole yet quite distinct senses of how the world is will be simultaneously present. The new has arrived and cannot be ignored but the old has not yet given up its place. Comfortable certainties are thrown into the air and we cannot yet know how they will land.

Overlaps are themselves in motion, with the older, established view progressively conceding ground to a less familiar, emergent one in a constant process of negotiation. In the case of colonialism or globalisation, the split in ethos can be both temporal and spatial, between a pre-existing local sense of how things are and a new perspective imposed from outside. In my clinical practice I notice striking overlaps in second generation immigrants who are often divided between the more traditional values of their home and community and the way of life offered by the wider world. They cannot yet reconcile these competing senses of things into a new whole and therefore flip internally between unintegrated realities. At the social level, overlaps are often pauses before a new zone of consensus restores equilibrium. They are a limbo where we cannot yet easily see how things will work out.

Overlaps profoundly disturb our sense of what is possible, what is permissible and what is important. Whilst some will enthusiastically reach for the new and some cling to the old, often these changes are greeted with ambivalence and uncertainty. People will feel split across both old and new senses of the world and between desiring and rejecting the changes. Writing on social circumstances which increase criminal behaviour, Jock Young argues that when people are split between a general sense that they are entitled to society's freedoms whilst simultaneously lacking the material opportunity to act on them, then this split is likely to bubble over into indignant lawlessness (Young, 1999, 2007). What is permissible exceeds what is possible. Ian Hacking argues that in the contrary situation, when we have the material opportunity to live as we please but do not yet have the cultural permission to embrace it, then disinhibiting psychological disorder can result (Hacking, 1998): people can only be free by losing their inhibiting minds. Overlaps will therefore often engender a sense of loss. When the new worldview erodes possibility, permission and opportunity, discontent at and defiance of the old order will ferment and take root.

Transactional analysis bears the imprint of having been born at the apex of a recent overlap where a new, prosperous and socially liberal worldview was beginning to establish its ascendancy. Ronald Inglehart makes an empirically-supported argument that in the mid-twentieth century, Western societies began shifting from materialist values which placed a strong emphasis upon economic and physical security to post-materialist values which prize free choice and self-expression (Inglehart, 2018). Inglehart notes that it takes peace and economic prosperity to become settled, complacent facts of existence before self-expression becomes the dominant force, a gradual transition which can take decades. In the interregnum, in homes, workplaces and community spaces, this creeping change is played out in social encounters – often intergenerational in nature – characterised by curiosity, confusion, heated disagreement, and incredulity at the viewpoints on the other side of the divide.

Bringing this background of our professional history to light allows us to see why early transactional analysts talked so often about clients sharply conflicted about new freedoms. They encountered people struggling with guilt and anxiety from breaking with the increasingly objectionable constraints imposed by the previous generation's values. These conflicts were being enacted in their daily lives, not just played privately in their heads. It is also no surprise that those early clients were quite receptive to a clinical theory that often told them that they were experiencing an impasse between the censorious introjects of their Parent ego-state and the surging, unused promise of their Child. Perhaps transactional analysis worked in part because the psychological story it told had immediate social plausibility and provided a soothing therapeutic alibi for people to embrace the new without regret.

Since all parts of the ego-state structure are inseparable from the world, sometimes overlaps institute a split *within* ego-states as much as *between* them. Curiously, Berne described encountering such split in what he took to be an atypical clinical case (Berne, 1961). Acknowledging an unexpected challenge to his thinking, Berne traced the split to the ego-state being divided between the competing 'programming' demands of biology, autonomy and society. However, he did not consider that conflict could occur between two distinct social programmings because he treated the social as an indivisible, coherent whole rather than a complex constellation of processes which are sometimes in harmony and sometimes at war. He also did not appreciate that supposed Child yearnings for expression, far from being pre-socially 'natural', were themselves formed, articulated and made possible by the culture of self-expression that was gaining ascendancy. These were conflicts between different senses of the world in which the self is snared, not conflicts between self and world.

35

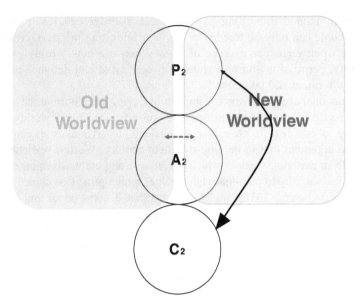

Figure 1.2 Overlap.

Clinical vignette

Yufeng informs me that he and his brother both used their English first names for most of their life. Since he moved from his home city, he has started using his Chinese second name. He doesn't know why but says it somehow felt right. He was raised in the Chinese quarter of a northern city to first generation immigrant parents. His family hung close to other Chinese immigrants and even though he went to a local school attended mainly by white students, Yufeng spent most of his time outside within the Chinese community. As he entered adolescence, he felt an increasing distance from his family and community. He didn't do well at school and began to hang out with the kids who did drugs. He couldn't picture himself working in the family business. When he decided to take a post as a support worker with a homeless charity in another city his parents, as was their way, neither openly approved nor protested.

Yufeng feels anxious all the time but doesn't know why. His mother calls him twice a day and speaks of everything and nothing. His colleagues are friendly and invite him for drinks but he finds their lives strange and unenlivening, as though he is both there and not there when they talk about them. He gets drunk and dances on his own in clubs. He likes the look of a white girl he has seen there often but never approaches her and says he had always imagined he would marry a Chinese girl. Yufeng asks me if he should return home for although he knows a part of him wanted to embrace the unapologetic wildness he found in his white class mates, he hadn't realised how strange it would feel when he got there. He half-jokingly suggests that it was no coincidence that he ended up working with homeless people for he feels he belongs nowhere.

Chaos

The flux of the world has gathered pace. In the West, technological change has accelerated, unfolding possibilities for personal and collective interchange with people across the globe and bringing about the breakneck dismantling of social mores (Harvey, 1989). The final triumph of post-materialist over materialist values has arrived. We experience both the thrill and the peril of collective lives speeded into a blur, overloaded by change to the point where we are uncertain who we are and confused about where we are going (Huyssen, 2011). Chaos is characterised by precisely this ceaseless profusion of options and possibilities and the absence of shared signposts. It is the curdling of personal freedom, leaving the self over-stretched and confused, overwhelmed with the individual responsibility to choose a way through (Schwarz, 2004).

A range of thinkers have usefully described the unpredicted consequences of our drive for prosperity, self-expression and technological mastery. We have seen our collective lives become 'liquid' (Bauman, 2000), abandoning permanence and tradition in favour of the ever-fluid present, have become 'saturated' (Gergen, 2000) and overloaded with a kaleidoscope of information and perspectives. In its infancy, transactional analysis naturally dedicated its energies to the immediate task of unshackling us from prohibiting and discredited forms of life. We are now in a position to see what the freedoms we have sought taste like and the traces they have left on the selves we have become. Some have flourished in the new openness; others are flailing. I am not the first within transactional analysis to suggest that these changes have brought a subtly different kind of client to our clinic waiting rooms (Hargarden & Sills, 2002) though I think the resulting changes to the structure of the Parent ego-state have gone unnoticed. We are starting to see clients whose Parent is all permission and no prohibition, rootless opinion but no tradition (Bauman, 1993). Every option can seem available but no way of life feels solid under foot.

I am wary of adopting the view that our liquid world has only left us mired in confusion and uncertainty. Chaos has been accompanied by many positive changes and I have no wish to open the door to a reactionary restoration of socially conservative mores. I am simply concerned that we have not yet developed an adequate social and clinical understanding of the challenges of this brave new world. I have come to see the pure permission of some Parent ego-state as leading to 'disorders of opportunity', a neologism which names the potential negative consequences of general affluence and near-limitless freedom. It tends to strike down those who have the most, turning their strengths against them. Han states that in what he calls 'burn out society' the freedom to do anything quickly turns into a compulsion that you should do everything. The biggest sin is now regret and the urgent call of the next moment to be seized never quiets (Han, 2015, 2017). Chained to the runaway horses of our liberated wants and fearful of falling behind, we dare not stop even if we knew how to.

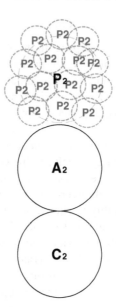

Figure 1.3 Chaos.

Clinical vignette

Sophie asks me if she should carry on training as a solicitor. She asks my advice on everything from her romantic relationships to decisions about how to spend her leisure time. She burns with shame because she asks these questions of everyone. Sometimes they answer. She feels temporarily reassured before doubts emerge. Top of her class from the very beginning, popular, sporty and strikingly attractive, Sophie could and would do everything except do nothing. She describes a loving family, go getters all of them, accomplished in all things they attempt. She claims she has always wanted to be a lawyer. Her life was a picture of unblemished serenity until she began to wonder if there was something better she had overlooked.

I attempt to discern the nature of Sophie's dissatisfaction with her training post and discover nothing but the gnawing disquiet that perhaps there is a career out there that she might enjoy more. She paces her flat at night similarly undecided about how to spend the evening. Is it better to visit friends? To exercise? To take up another hobby? Her boyfriend is attractive and makes her laugh but she isn't sure that he is husband material. She's not sure what husband material really means or what she feels about him. When I invite her to think about what she wants she says it changes. She fears she might want something else tomorrow. Sophie binge drinks to quiet her racing mind. She has begun to take time off sick from work to lie in bed and watch TV. Anything to bring the thinking to a stop, to slow her world down. Her quick intellect gobbles up my words without chewing, every comment sends her mind spinning in different directions, looking for answers in a time when there are only questions.

Clients who experience disorders of opportunity like Sophie find themselves empty, exhausted, spread too thin, consuming everything and savouring nothing, their daily actions carried out by an increasingly machinic sense of compulsion which has come to replace want and need. It is relatively easy to misunderstand disorders of chaos as vertical problems linked to early developmental disturbances. Yet as Verhaeghe notes, such clients typically lack the unconscious depth you would have expected to find in yesteryear: their difficulties are all on the surface, unthinkingly acting through the body in a way which is devoid of psychological depth to work with (Verhaeghe, 2008). In the era of chao, it isn't that our sense of self is any more fragile, defective or split than it would have been in previous generations, it is that few people can manage to develop the kind of optimum, capable selves sufficient to keep up with the aspirations they have been encouraged to have.

Chaos is also easy to misrecognise as prohibition. It is tempting to see contemporary client's self-condemnation as the eruption of a disapproving parental introject when it is in fact simply the self turning on itself. When everything is permitted there is no-one left to blame but yourself. In times of chaos, 'I'm not good enough for you' is slowly giving way to the torment of 'I'm never enough for me'. My younger depressed clients are increasingly partitioned into those devoid of opportunities and those who are overburdened with them. The former mark us with an impression of stagnant hopeless and lethargy which can leave the therapist soporific whilst the latter seem taut with energy, radiating a desperation born of failure to keep pace with their bright hopes (Ehrenberg, 2016).

Each of the three social contextual configurations identified here provide fertile grounds for the production and maintenance of horizontal problems though inevitably individual histories are also necessary to fully explain particular susceptibility. In oppression the particular interests of the dominant powers and their consequent slanting of the social order are concealed in a way which can lead to confusion amongst people about the nature and source of their unhappiness. In times of overlap a settled way of being is overturned by a new order which leads to an enforced, elongated and unsettling re-evaluation of forms of life and the redistribution of opportunities and constraints. We are not quite sure where we are, who we are or how to speak cogently about our condition. I share Frederic Jameson's concern that we have not yet developed the language necessary to comprehend the unprecedented predicament of chaos, what he calls a failure of 'cognitive mapping' (Jameson, 1990). Conceptually we are struggling with an unbridgeable divide between our abstract picture of the world and our immediate local experience. We have run out of road and have not yet grasped that we are suspended in mid-air, waiting either to crash or for grounding wisdom to catch up. We must forge not merely a new therapeutic sensibility to meet the difficulties resulting from chaos, overlaps and oppression but new political and social ways of thinking to meet the contemporary challenges of our shared predicament.

References

Abramson, K. (2014) Turning up the Lights on Gaslighting. *Philosophical Perspectives*, 28, 1–31.

Bauman, Z. (1993) *Postmodern Ethics*. Malden, MA: Blackwell.

Bauman, Z. (2000) *Liquid Modernity*. Cambridge: Polity.

Berne, E. (1949). Some oriental mental hospitals. *American Journal of Psychiatry*, 106, 376–383.

Berne, E. (1956) Comparative psychiatry and tropical psychiatry. *American Journal of Psychiatry*, 113, 193–200.

Berne, E. (1960) The cultural problem: Psychopathology in Tahiti. *American Journal of Psychiatry*, 116, 1076–1081.

Berne, E. (1961) *Transactional Analysis in Psychotherapy*. London: Souvenir Press.

Berne, E. (1963) *The Structure and Dynamics of Organisations and Groups*. New York: Grove Press.

Berne, E. (1970) *Sex in Human Loving*. Harmondsworth: Penguin.

Berne, E. (1972) *What Do you Say After you Say Hello?* London: Corgi.

Boltanski, L. (2011) *On Critique: A Sociology of Emancipation*. Translated from French by G. Elliot. Malden, MA: Polity.

Bourdieu, P. (1977) *Outline of a Theory of Practice*. Translate from French by R. Nice, Cambridge: Cambridge University Press.

Bourdieu, P., Wacquant, J.D. (1992) *An Invitation to Reflexive Sociology*. Chicago: University of Chicago Press.

Clarkson, P. (1992) *Transactional Analysis Psychotherapy: an Integrated Approach*. London: Routledge.

Cornell, W.F. (2010) Aspiration or Adaptation?: An Unresolved Tension in Eric Berne's Basic Beliefs. *Transactional Analysis Journal*, 40 (3–4), 243–253.

Cornell, W.F. (2016) Eric Berne and politics – a brief history and reflection. *The Transactional Analyst*, 6 (4), 6–8.

Dewey, J. (1922) *Human Nature and Conduct: An Introduction to Social Psychology*. Reprint 2007. New York: Cosimo.

Drego, P. (1983) The Cultural Parent. *Transactional Analysis Journal*, 13 (4), 224–227.

Drego, P. (1996) Cultural Parent Oppression and Regeneration. *Transactional Analysis Journal*, 26 (1), 58–77.

Ehrenberg, A. (2016) *The Weariness of the Self: Diagnosing the History of Depression in the Contemporary Age*. Translated from French by D. Homel, E. Caouette, J. Homel, D. Winkler. Quebec: McGill-Queens University Press.

Epston, D., White, M. (1995) Termination as a Rite of Passage: Questioning Strategies for a Therapy of Inclusion. In R.A. Neimeyer & M.J. Mahoney, Eds, *Constructivism in Psychotherapy*. Washington D.C.: American Psychological Association, 339–356.

Gadamer, H.G. (1996) *The Enigma of Health: The Art of Healing in a Scientific Age*. Translated from German by J. Gaiger & N. Walker. Cambridge: Polity Press.

Gergen, K. (2000) *The Saturated Self: Dilemmas of Identity in Contemporary Life*. New York: Basic Books.

Giddens, A. (1984) *The Constitution of Society*. Cambridge: Polity.

Hacking, I. (1998) *Mad Travellers: Reflections on the Reality of Transient Mental Illness*. Cambridge, MA: Harvard University Press.

Hargarden, H., Sills, C. (2002) *Transactional Analysis: A Relational Perspective*. Hove: Routledge.

Harré, R. (1998) *The Singular Self: An Introduction to the Psychology of Personhood.* London: Sage.

Han, Byung-Chul (2015) *The Burnout Society.* Translated from German by E. Butler, Stanford: Stanford University Press.

Han, Byung-Chul (2017) *Psycho-politics: Neoliberalism and New Technologies of Power.* Translated from German by E. Butler. London: Verso.

Harvey, D. (1989) *The Condition of Postmodernity: An Inquiry into the Origin of Cultural Change.* Oxford: Blackwell.

Heidegger, M. (1962) *Being and Time.* Translated from German by. J. Macquarrie & E. Robinson. Oxford: Blackwell.

Heiller, B., Sills, C. (2010) Life Scripts: an existential perspective. In R.G. Erskine, Ed. *Life Scripts: a Transactional Analysis of Unconscious Relational Patterns.* London: Karnac, 239–268.

Hoffman, L. (1981) *Foundations of Family Therapy: A Conceptual Framework for Systems Change.* New York: Basic Books.

Huyssen, A. (2011) excerpt from 'Present Pasts: Media, Politics, Amnesia'. in J.K. Olick, V. Vinitzky-Seroussi, D. Levys Eds, *The Collective Memory Reader.* Oxford: Oxford University Press, 430–436.

Inglehart, R.F. (2018) *Cultural Evolution: People's Motivations are Changing, and Reshaping the World.* Cambridge: Cambridge University Press.

Jameson, F. (1990) Cognitive Mapping. in: C. Nelson, L. Grossberg, Eds, M*arxism and the Interpretation of Culture.* Chicago: University of Illinois Press, 347–360.

Johnson, L.B. (1965) *To Fulfil These Rights.* 4 June. Commencement Address at Howard University, Washington D.C.

Karpman, S.B. (2019) Discounting of Person, Meaning and Motive. *International Journal of Transactional Analysis Research & Practice,* 10 (1), 40–49.

Laing, R.D. (1967) *The Politics of Experience and the Bird of Paradise.* Harmondsworth: Penguin.

Lukes, S. (2004) *Power: A Radical View.* 2nd edn. London: Red Globe Press.

Margolis, J. (1995) *Historied Thought, Constructed World: a Conceptual Primer for the Turn of the Millennium.* Berkeley: University of California Press.

Merton, R.K. (1936) The Unanticipated Consequences of Purposive Social Action. *American Sociological Review,* 1 (6), 894–904.

Mills, C.W. (2000) *The Sociological Imagination.* Afterword by T. Gitlin. Oxford: Oxford University Press.

Philippson, P. (2009) *The Emergent Self; an Existential-Gestalt Approach.* London: Karnac.

Rieff, P. (1959) *Freud: The Mind of the Moralist.* London: Victor Gollancz Ltd.

Roy, B., Steiner, C. (1997) *Radical Psychiatry: The Second Decade.* 3rd edn. Unpublished Manuscript. Available at: http://radicaltherapy.org/uploads/Second_Decade_Part1.pdf. Accessed 26 November 2018.

Schiff, J.L. Schiff, A., Mellor, K., Schiff, E., Fishman, J., Wolz, L., Fishman, C., Mombs, D. (1975) *Cathexis Reader: Transactional Analysis Treatment of Psychosis.* New York: Harper and Row.

Schwarz, B. (2004) *The Paradox of Choice: Why More is Less.* New York: Harper Collins.

Scott, J.C. (1990) *Domination and the Arts of Resistance: Hidden Transcripts.* New Haven: Yale University Press.

41

Searle, J.R. (1995) *The Construction of Social Reality.* London: Penguin.

Steiner, C. (1974) *Scripts People Live.* New York: Grove Press.

Steiner, C. Wycroft, H. (1975) 'Alienation' in C. Steiner, H. Wyckoff, D. Goldstine, P. Lariviere, R. Schwebel, J. Marcus, Eds, *Readings in Radical Psychiatry.* New York: Grove Press, 17–27.

Steiner, C. (2009) *The Heart of the Matter: Love, Information and Transactional analysis.* Pleasanton, CA: TA Press.

Storolow, R.D., Atwood, G.E. (1992) *The Intersubjective Foundations of Psychological Life.* Hillsdale, NJ: The Analytic Press.

Taylor, C. (1989) *Sources of the Self: The Making of the Modern Identity.* Cambridge: Cambridge University Press.

Taylor, C. (2016) *The Language Animal: The Full Shape of Human Linguistic Capacity.* Cambridge, MA: Harvard University Press.

Tilly, C. (2002) *Stories, Identities and Political Change.* Lanham, ML: Rowman & Littlefield.

Tilly, C. (2005) *Identities, Boundaries and Social Ties.* Abingdon: Routledge.

Unger, R.M. (2004) *False Necessity: Anti-Necessitarian Social Theory in the Service of Radical Democracy.* 2nd edn. London: Verso.

Unger, R.M., Smolin, L. (2015) *The Singular Universe and the Reality of Time: A Proposal in Natural Philosophy.* Cambridge: Cambridge University Press.

Wollants, G. (2012) *Gestalt Therapy: Therapy of the Situation.* Los Angeles: Sage.

Verhaeghe, P. (2008) 'A combination that has to fail: new patients, old therapists', Lecture in Dublin, EISTEACH, accessed at: www.paulverhaeghe.com/lecturesand interviews/Dublineisteach2008.pdf [Accessed 6 October 2017]

Watzlawick, P., Bavelas, J.B., Jackson, D.D. (2011) *Pragmatics of Human Communication: a Study of Interactional Patterns, Pathologies and Paradoxes.* New York: Norton.

Young, J. (1999) *The Exclusive Society: Social Exclusion, Crime and Difference in Late Modernity.* London: Sage.

Young, J. (2007) *The Vertigo of Late Modernity.* Los Angeles: Sage.

Zahavi, D. (2014) *Self and Other: Exploring Subjectivity, Empathy and Shame.* Oxford: Oxford University Press.

2

THE GOOD ENOUGH WORLD

We are emergently self-and-world and therefore any picture of our capabilities and shortcomings must take account of our social context. Since the social world is assembled by people to serve their collective interests, how things are and what we need should ideally be in sync. Experience suggests this happens only infrequently! In extreme cases, the world's capacity to enable and support us breaks down so badly that it fractures people's experience of themselves as autonomous, self-aware and capable of living a purposeful, responsible life. In happier times, the contribution the world makes to this comforting illusion is often banked without gratitude. Immediately available, conscious awareness of our ability to think, choose, act and influence the course of our lives inevitably tilts us towards explaining their trajectories by reference to our initiatives, choices and efforts. The painful eruption of difficult circumstances humbles us into periodic recognition that a good deal needs to fall into place for this impression of capable selfhood to be maintained. Distress is always experienced subjectively, but the cause sometimes lies across the self and the world.

Specific happenings in the world which either stand in our way or lift us up are immediately apparent. Everyone can point to poverty, violence, crime, unemployment etc. as bad events that command attention, foregrounding themselves against the general horizon of the world. My interest here is in what else might be going wrong in the background without standing out, hiding in plain sight if you will. These barely visible deficits and defects are where horizontal problems ferment. In Chapter 1, I outlined several kinds of contextual configurations which may injure us without leaving an obvious mark, evading the awareness of those denied appropriate social and political awakening. These configurations erode the foundational conditions which need to be in place in order for the world to work as it should. This chapter brings these conditions into the light so that they might be better understood.

Successful societies can vary enormously in composition, but I take it that under this surface diversity certain basic contextual conditions are always in place which enable people to live autonomous, co-operative, functional lives. These conditions don't have to be met perfectly, they just have to be good enough. I have called these four conditions of the good enough world resourcefulness, responsiveness, truthfulness and integrity and they will be out-lined carefully in the remainder of the chapter. Since we tend either to take these conditions for granted or claim undue credit for their contribution, when things start to go wrong we are often confused about what is happening, blame our-selves for want of an alternative or lash out at others in instances of gross con-spiracism. Lacking a breakthrough in social awareness, we stumble on blindly in the hope that the old order will be restored.

The notion of a good enough world gratefully borrows from Winnicott's theory of the 'good enough mother'. He argued that in order for a child to express and act on its innate dispositions, the parent figure must step in to antici-pate and supplement its still-forming mind. The parent uses their own body to do for the child what its own limbs won't yet support, their mind to give shape to the child's inarticulate thoughts and their words to say what the child does not yet know how to communicate (Winnicott 1960, 1971). The parent is both mirror and exoskeleton: when parenting is good enough, the child feels understood and enabled. The mirror and the exoskeleton are a scaffolding from which the well-formed, capable child will eventually free itself when these supports are out-grown. Winnicott believed that failure to provide these conditions would crush the child's burgeoning, fragile sense of self and force them into cramped over-adaptation. In becoming what is needed rather than what is wanted, a self-made to fit the world rather than a self capable of transforming the world in light of its own needs, the child's future ability to form an identity and act in accord with their legitimate wants is grossly impeded. A self so under-formed will lack the necessary ability to name their own hurt and act to alleviate it.

Even after psychological maturation is complete, we continue to need the world to be good enough in a way which imperceptibly extends and compli-ments our individual capabilities. If we were suddenly transported to a place where those around us did not share our language and we were deprived of money, communication technology or any transferable knowledge about how to get on there, then at a stroke we would find ourselves helpless and regressed. We would be entirely dependent on the know-how and goodwill of strangers. For most of us this is an extreme possibility, several worlds away from our daily experience, but more subtle deficits can be detected if we learn to see them. The basic capability to get on in the world that we take to be uncomplicatedly 'ours' is, in reality, an achievement of our collective co-operative intention, our shared history, culture and social mores from which we draw and in whose benign tidal flow we are carried.

Since we are more likely to appreciate these four conditions by their absence, I need to introduce what a context that does not meet the threshold for 'good enough' looks like. My argument will unfold through a detailed picture of eco-nomically and socially deprived communities in post-industrial cities located in the Midlands of the United Kingdom. There are many contexts which might act perfectly well as illustrative examples, these are simply the ones with which I am most familiar. The particular historical line traced by my story reflects my belief in the salience of materialism and class politics as a starting point: inevitably this means other potential starting points, particularly the experience of minority and immigrant communities which played a huge part in reshaping these cities during this time, are not represented here. I have done my best to ensure that the conclusions I have reached are sufficiently general to apply beyond the circumstances of their discovery, but short of an equally intimate familiarity with other parts of the world, I cannot be certain that different experiences would not have yielded different conclusions.

I appreciate that in introducing general ideas through the concrete specifics of place and person I risk drawing the reader's eye to the visible social ills and away from the partially concealed preconditions which are my main focus. I am keen for my argument not to be mistaken for a familiar kind of critical barb against the failings of the contemporary west (see James, 2007; Prilleltensky & Nelson, 2002; Smail, 1993; Verhaeghe, 2012). Appropriate criticism of specific injustices and failings has its place as a precondition of reform but we should also acknowledge that utopia is no more than an invigorating mirage. No known society has been entirely free of injustice, unnecessary suffering or social malaise. The risk of specific criticism is that it lets general lessons slip away. I am more concerned about the basic preconditions of successful societies than evaluating the particular kinds of societies that people go on to make. I implore the reader to look through the material indignities and unnecessary hardship I am about to portray and perceive the deeper failings of social integration, collective efficacy and hopefulness which run alongside and partially explain the creation and trajectory of the surface problems.

I am mindful that in speaking of these contexts as impoverished in fundamental regards, I may be accused of heaping further scorn on communities who are already familiar with the daily experience of unjustified contempt. Clinicians spend their time solely with those who seek help so I acknowledge from the outset that the voices of therapy clients are not always representative of entire communities and that successful and rewarding lives which go unmentioned in my story can also happen. There will always be individual cases that escape the general trends, though specific counter-examples don't disprove the existence of the typical. I have emphasised the worst of these communities not to say that this is all they are or could be (see Haylett, 2003) but to honour their potential to becoming better if the problems identified are addressed.

It must be possible to acknowledge simultaneously that a community can possess both supreme social competence and unaddressed blind spots. It must be acceptable to see cultures and societies as the wellspring of pride, strength and meaning whilst recognising that they have still fallen short of providing a good enough world in other ways. There is no contradiction here though I appreciate it risks controversy amongst those likely to recoil from the very possibility that the benign intention of outside observers will inevitably result in crass meddling and incomprehension. These concerns will receive a detailed and careful response in Chapters 4 and 5.

Resourcefulness

Many aspects of the story I must tell about the Midlands cities will be broadly recognisable (with local adjustments) to those acquainted with urban decline elsewhere in the West. It is a story which combines elements of both oppression and overlap with additional factors as yet unnamed. In the early twentieth century, these cities were home to a thriving manufacturing sector. Large factories gave rise both to stable communities of workers and an ecosystem of smaller businesses and services that sprang up alongside them. The lives lived in these communities were tough and often unrewarding both in the workplace and at home, yet tangible improvements were arriving. Based on the recommendation of the Beveridge report of 1942 (Beveridge, 1942), the post-war welfare settlement had introduced universal health care, improved national insurance and established a related range of social safety nets. These ensured that even though your working life may offer only dirty, dangerous and poorly remunerated work, you could go to sleep at night secure that you would only ever be allowed to fall so far before society caught you.

Basic security and minimal prosperity were guaranteed for the first time by health care free at the point of access, a state pension and public housing. A little extra money clawed back from employers by unionised workforce representation and favourable labour market conditions which drove up worker's bargaining power enabled working people to buy a fresh range of consumer luxuries for the first time. Driving many of these changes was the Labour party which gave political expression to the hopes and wants of working people. Fundamental questions of security having been largely settled for a generation, a way of life emerged which was sufficiently at ease with its dissatisfactions to keep social disquiet simmering without boiling over.

This picture changed dramatically in 1979. Against a backdrop of rolling industrial disputes and the Labour government's struggle to manage the public finances, the change in economic policy brought about by the new Conservative government set out, as part of a wider programme of deregulation and privatisation, to render the manufacturing sector more lean through competition, to reduce the political power of organised labour and to increase tertiary sector employment (Elliott & Atkinson, 1998; Seabrook, 2013; Harris, 1987; Hobsbawm, 1994). Nearly 20 per cent of British industry disappeared over five years, disproportionately from the Midlands, North and Wales. There followed across the subsequent decade a steady loss of manufacturing jobs to both automation and countries offering labour at cheaper rates.

Communities were used to some ebb and flow in the job market but nobody was prepared for the permanent closure of major employers. The factories and mines around which some towns had sprung up closed for good. If jobs returned at all, they came back with poorer pay and conditions. The burgeoning service sector largely orbited London in the south so these regions were consigned to neglect and decline. Larger cities that were host to several industries survived the blow better than smaller towns for whom the closure of a single large employer deprived them of their animating purpose. In a further upheaval, the Housing Act of 1980 permitted tenants who rented from the state to buy their houses at a competitive rate, an initially popular move with long-standing tenants. Over the longer term, the depletion of social housing stock made it harder for younger people to gain independence, placed them at the mercy of private landlords and ensured that the remaining housing stock was assigned on the basis of need. This often resulted in a high concentration of vulnerable, struggling individuals within the same geographical area (Sibley, 1995).

Losing role and revenue simultaneously often set off a devastating chain reaction in the domestic sphere with many of my clients who lived through these times reporting daily and often violent arguments about money managed with spiralling alcohol consumption. Supported by prevalent ideas from second-wave feminism, women entered further education and filled service sector jobs in greater numbers. They left violent and unhappy homes and increasingly raised their children alone or with the support of their extended family. In what Jock Young identifies as 'an almost universal criminological law' (Young, 1999, p. 12), young men forced from their customary and expected life path, often fell back on their physical strength – the last remaining stronghold of their presence and dignity – to embrace a culture of street crime, steroid-enhanced machismo and jocular contempt for respectability. Whilst they often sneer at the thought of consulting a therapist, these men are awfully good at driving other people there in a traumatised state. Whilst I perceive most of my clients to remain fiercely dedicated to their children, the changes of the last 40 years now mean that romantic relationships are entered into more in hope than expectation.

These communities, in which around 30 per cent of the UK's population are thought to live (Hutton, 1996), suffer ongoing deficits in the condition of resourcefulness, defined as the capacity of the world to provide for people the things they need to live successfully. Sufficient resourcefulness begins when a required level of security and satisfaction can be individually achieved with a level of effort that falls within the spectrum of general human capability. Increased resourcefulness is the central aim of social co-operation. It begins with the knowledge that working together ensures outcomes than can be achieved alone.

Advanced societies will have achieved and maintained basic plentifulness of food, shelter and protection. This hardly exhausts the sense of the resourcefulness we might hope the world makes available. New wants and needs start to break through once security has been achieved. Most of my clients have enough money to survive but not to live. Transient employment and draconian benefits cultures means they often dangle above destitution by a slender thread. They cannot fail to realise that the riches on offer elsewhere are being withheld.

The concept of resourcefulness also applies to a society's capacity to grant a meaningful role. Poverty is frequently accompanied by losses of social position, personal dignity, loving connection and just treatment. I am not denying that individual effort plays no part in achieving these aims, I'm simply noting that people cannot conjure up a world in which to prosper and belong solely through their own actions. The failure of context to provide people with meaningful occupation, a chance to earn their bread and shelter rather than have it begrudgingly given, and a say in how their lives are run erodes the purpose and healthy self-regard necessary to contribute. As Emile Durkheim discovered over a century ago, when people are deprived of a worthwhile place amongst others and can see no way to achieve it, then this 'social death' too often leads to actual suicide (Durkheim & Simpson, 1951). Those who soldier on may show admirable persistence and resilience but, lacking opportunity, will never know themselves as the people they could have been.

Linked to role deprivation is the scarcity of the resourcefulness of 'strokes' (Berne, 1972) or what philosophy after Hegel calls 'recognition' (Honneth, 1995, 2012; Fraser & Honneth, 2003). Recognition denotes the positive acknowledgement by society of our innate dignity, capability and social worth. It recalls Kohut's developmental theory of the selfobject need to be mirrored by others. According to Kohut, we cannot experience ourselves as whole and capable unless we are witnessed and responded to by others in the light of those qualities (Kohut, 1977, 1984). The specific ways we want to be recognised and available opportunities for achieving this are particular to time and place and inseparable from the wider ethos. I still take it we are on safe ground if we assume this to be a case of minor variations on a universal theme. Since recognition is a prerequisite for full social participation then its absence will cascade down into a range of further difficulties (Pickett & Wilkinson, 2010). Too often what results is a crumbling of dignity and the human spirit, suffocating for lack of acknowledgement and grasping at unsatisfying compensations.

Due to the increasingly transient, low paid nature of work, many of my clients are dependent upon state financial support even whilst employed. In a deliberate attempt to erode the post-war welfare settlement, government policies have presumed that worklessness indicates recalcitrance. Claimants find themselves being treated as naughty children requiring reform rather than responsible citizens in need. In recent years this has resulted in a precarious existence for many where a subsistence level income can be cut off overnight upon the perceived violation of increasingly demanding administrative requests. As Charles Karelis argues, under such circumstances the tendency of the poor to seek solace in sugary food, alcohol and cigarettes, far from being a failing of character, is a perfectly rational coping behaviour. If you have no prospect of solving the really big problems in your life then short-term relief is the best you can hope for even if in the long run it shreds your dignity whilst confirming people's suspicion that you just aren't trying hard enough (Karelis, 2007). Recognition linked to the role of parenting is often the sole foundation for joy and hope in these communities yet rooting your identity in one thing is precarious. The almost inevitable struggles of their children can prove a shattering blow.

A shared culture is also a kind of resourcefulness, however intangible, upon which we draw to enrich our daily lives. The unofficial, emergent summation of

48

our collective experiences, stories, decisions and memories, cultures can generate a momentum that propels people along with a sense of hope, purpose and meaning. Social network theory describes how when everyone we know also knows each other and everyone has similar life experience, individual lives aggregate and calcify into a dense, monochrome worldview (MacDonald et al., 2005; Christakis & Fowler, 2009). When whole streets are under the care of mental health professionals, when joblessness is prevalent and domestic violence a nightly occurrence behind every door then horizons narrow and circumstance becomes destiny. Too many failed, unhappy lives in close proximity congeal into an ethos marked by pessimism, change-aversion and resignation (see Cronqvist, Siegel & Yu, 2015; Malmendier & Nagel, 2011).

There are too few happy endings around to leaven the despondency. More capable children from such places so often leave for want of opportunity and do not return, a bittersweet achievement which further shrinks the available range of shared experience. Clients will often describe themselves to me as 'lacking in confidence', as though confidence were like fuel that they had run low on. In fact what we call confidence is simply the experience of having lived successfully to this point and the expectation that one will carry on doing so. Collective success, available role models of what life can be here often clear pathways for others to follow. The truth that life can be different is hidden from you by sheer density of similar defeats.

Responsiveness

Whilst deficits of resourcefulness will always provide the larger part of any explanation for suffering, they are not sufficient to account for horizontal problems in isolation. Communities which believe change is possible, desirable and just can and will mobilise to make political claims on the wider society. By the late 1970s, the Labour party had represented working-class communities for 80 years whilst also providing a route for working people to enter politics via local associations and trade unions. The Conservative party's attempt to make British industry more 'competitive' depended upon eliminating the unions' contestatory role. Unionisation of the workforce used to ensure that occupation and politics took place within the same building. After work, the pubs, libraries and working mens' clubs nearby acted as incubators for an aspirational, politicised class consciousness. This meant politics was threaded through daily life for a critical mass of people. A worldview which linked local action with a national picture and allowed people to join movements aimed at articulating their interests provided a vehicle for purpose and hope.

Political engagement has never been universal but a gradual seeping away of class consciousness had already begun by the 1980s. As Hobsbawm notes, in the post-war period working-class people tended to spend their evenings in pubs and clubs talking politics because their homes were too cramped for socialising at night (Hobsbawm, 1994). At work they would have been members of trade unions. The simultaneous improvement of housing quality, rising living standards and the emergence of a burgeoning consumer culture allowed working-class people to conclude what Oscar Wilde reportedly said many years before: socialism takes too many evenings. The balance of people's lives began to tilt from politics towards leisure.

The decline of mass political involvement amongst the working poor coincided with a simultaneous rise of left-wing political consciousness amongst university students. The decimation of British industry in the early 1980s drastically reduced the size of the working-class voting block which over time made it politically expedient for the Labour party to find common ground between its industrial heartlands and a growing constituent of socially liberal, middle class, often state-employed professionals (Hobsbawm, 1994). The combination of de-unionisation and the takeover of the Labour party by a middle-class, university educated, professionalised political class decreased both opportunities for political influence and ensured that the political voice of working people grew more silent and more unheard (Cadwalladr, 2014). This has resulted in a growing sense of hopelessness, powerlessness and corrosive cynicism amongst communities that were once committed to meaningfully reshaping the country. The frequent lament that politicians are 'all the same' is so often another way of saying 'no longer one of us'.

By an unhappy combination of intention and accident, these developments reduced what I call contextual **responsiveness**. This is defined by the capacity and willingness to recognise the legitimacy of identified wants and to respond appropriately to them at an individual or collective level. Responsiveness presumes a level of resourcefulness for you cannot give what you do not have. It also presupposes a material substrata of administrative and infrastructural connections. People cannot voice their claims without public spaces to be heard, newspapers to report on them, wireless networks to communicate through and local branches of state administrative systems. You cannot send material resources to remote regions without road or rail. Disconnected places easily become forgotten places, and the more one is forgotten the less one tries to connect.

Attitudinal responsiveness proceeds naturally from valuing and respecting general social co-operation. It matches a sense of obligation to others with a willingness to treat them as members of a common community both capable of articulating their wants and entitled to do so. Under optimum democratic conditions, responsiveness offers not merely opportunities for participation in a common life but the scope to transform it through collective will. Of course, in principle, non-democratic societies can be responsive where those in power take an attitude of care and responsibility for the wider social group, although clearly there are an abundance of examples where this is not the case. Responsiveness may actually decline as resourcefulness increases, particularly where those resources are held by the few. The rich and powerful usually surrender their advantages only begrudgingly. In resource rich societies, poverty is a choice, something that one group of people does to another group by attacking political responsiveness.

Since brute persecution of the populace or the overt devaluation of citizenship often leads to civil unrest, the hoarding of wealth and power can only be achieved in advanced democratic societies through the furtive discounting of recognition and a restriction on transformative political options. Confusion, misdirection, broken promises and an administrative dragging of feet – all diseases of responsiveness – can achieve a similar preservation of the status quo that brute opposition used to produce. Such political conditions can induce torpor in the general population, a sense of fatalism and cynicism which periodically breaks out into ugly waves of unconstructive and misdirected anger.

As my story so far testifies, the breakdown of responsiveness is not all about hidden interests acting in the shadows. Seeing the decline of responsiveness as the primary malaise of complex post-industrial Western societies, Jürgen Habermas argues that the political and economic administrative subsystems run by specialist groups on the basis of expert rationality have become progressively more detached from the wider collective imperatives and democratic accountability from which they first sprang (Habermas, 1976). Initially intended as a means to efficiency, the administrative systems begin to generate their own priorities which obscure their original purpose. Initial good intentions mutate over time into unsatisfactory outcomes.

Remote administrative systems became increasingly indifferent to people's collective sense of what is wanted: technocratic assumptions about 'what works' tend to prevent discussion of 'what's right' (Habermas, 1976, 1987; Cooke, 1994). Habermas and others speculate that this crisis leads to a sense of personal apathy and detachment, a shrivelling of our identities as citizens, a narrowing of politics down to a thin menu of choices with transformative options ruled out (Laclau & Mouffe, 1985; Mouffe, C., 2005; Brown, W., 2015). A conviction takes hold that things are wrong without us being able to collectively articulate a workable vision of what being 'right' might look like. Citizen apathy and system remoteness mutually reinforce each other, breaking the social order apart until discontent, violence or breakdown emerge (Mair, 2013).

Failings of responsiveness can also happen at the interpersonal level. In addition to using language to communicate information about ourselves, we can also perform a whole host of verbal actions including asking questions, making requests, giving orders, promising to do something etc. These linguistic actions initiate local social co-operation (see Austin, 1962; Searle, 1969). They all presume the attentive co-operation of another person who is invited to respond or act in some way. Yet speaking words alone doesn't always guarantee the hoped-for response. The identity, role, power and social position of the people speaking and responding will also play a central role in determining whether the action is completed as hoped (Bourdieu, 1991). Responsiveness is unequally distributed.

When we discount people we no longer have to act responsively towards them; as a result they may cease engaging with us. Complete absence of responsiveness might lead to the disintegration of personal autonomy. When our voice isn't heard and we lack the social power to influence others, then the Adult capacity to act on the world through open communication evaporates. We have been insufficiently attentive within transactional analysis to this vital question of how we step out of the Victim position (Karpman, 1968) when others are not willing to acknowledge our existence and significance. Claiming power amongst others requires acknowledgement, not just assertion. If we continue to see efficacy and power as innate qualities which flow from our Adult rather than something which must also be granted by a good enough world then we will miss the irreducible contribution that others make to our ongoing sense of capability.

When protestations of hardship necessary for welfare claims are treated with automatic suspicion, then people become the victims of what Miranda Fricker calls 'testimonial injustice'. This is a credibility deficit in the eyes of others which erases the space for us to speak on our own behalf (Fricker, 2007). When managing executives make clandestine, opaque decisions *about* workers rather than *with* them protest dwindles and bottom-up contribution stops. When politicians answer the question they think you should have asked rather than the one you actually did a familiar sense of impotence and defeat descends. I am aware that many of my clients have to dance a particular dance with services in order to get their welfare payments, a weekly ritual of shame and tactical communication excusing their failure to find work where there are no jobs to be had. This absurd and cynical ritual takes the place that constructive, responsive and respectful engagement should occupy.

Living in a more responsive, co-operative social context provides the background conditions for people to become ourselves through purposive action. It seems apparent to me that my middle-class clients have an expectation that the world will respond to them affirmatively in a way that my working-class clients do not. Whilst deficits in political responsiveness now seem to be reaching the shores of the somewhat affluent, my experience of working with middle class clients is that in spite of their increasing anxiety and anger at a perceived dwindling of control over things, they retain a sense of themselves as resourceful because the world has generally met their actions half way. When they sense responsiveness crumbling, they fight to restore it by pulling the levers of complaint, exploiting their social resources and joining political movements. The sense we can and are entitled to act meaningfully is an essential accompaniment to the belief that things can change. Without it, change is something we wait to be delivered, not something we make with our own hands.

Those who have lived in the absence of responsiveness long enough for it to become all they can remember will come to experience the world around them as a static, impassive thing, entirely detached from their actions. People accustomed to responsive worlds can be conceived of as 'I think' people since they presume both the general significance of their opinion and the changeability of the world. The disenfranchised are 'it is' people for the world is so unresponsive to their views that circumstance is destiny. The longer-term psychological

THE GOOD ENOUGH WORLD

consequences of this are clear for, as Charlesworth notes, the collective energies of the working class are dedicated in their entirety to coping with how things are, to building a tough, gnarly identity as a buffer against inevitable cynicism and hopelessness (Charlesworth, 2000). The trouble is this kind of resistance and coping renounces the possibility of transformation. Without responsiveness and the faith in people, institutions and governments it requires, the collective capacity for imagining different worlds dwindles.

Truthfulness

The privacy of the therapy space allows people to say things that they could not say anywhere else. Yet if the kinds of things our client can't say to others are also the kinds of things those other people can't themselves say, then over time a whole way of talking about things begins to disappear for want of use and acknowledgement. An accidental or unofficial conspiracy of silence develops. What starts as unsayable will eventually become unthinkable.

The decline of working-class communities from the 1980s onwards was experienced (and arguably intended) as an attack on them and their political claims. Since events were understood to be a class battle that was fought and lost, a mood of collective disgrace followed. So much of the domestic violence, drunkenness and depression which emerged in the aftermath can be plausibly described as the distal result of a community unable to contain and process the scale of the loss. Political solidarity begins when you discover that you are not alone, that people like you have common experiences and a shared thirst for change. Collective shame attacks solidarity like a virus for what needs to be shared remains shrouded in silence.

Truthfulness, the third condition of a good enough world, needs to be understood as a sufficient level of both accuracy and sincerity in interactions necessary for people to understand themselves, others and the world (see Coetzee & Kurtz, 2015). A social context will begin to fragment when need and truth can no longer be reconciled. When we begin lying to ourselves in order to cope then we are on the path to being lost, although public dishonesty and private truthfulness can be valued routes to survival under certain conditions. James C. Scott describes how dominated communities can develop 'weapons of the weak', a coordinated performance of public compliance which conceals, in Goffman's words, a 'back stage' political awareness which thrives secretly whilst not speaking openly (Scott, 1990; Goffman, 1959).

Svetlana Alexievich's oral history of Russian citizens who lived through the collapse of Soviet Union reveals the clear importance of secluded, kitchen table gatherings with like-minded souls away from watchful eyes of the authorities (Alexievich, 2016). Having others bear witness to your perspective allows you to keep a grip on your sanity in the midst of terror and disorientation. In the 1970s, at the instigation of the feminist movements, victims of domestic violence emerged blinking into a more truthful sense of the world by discovering for the first time that many other women they knew were also being beaten by their husbands behind closed doors. Stepping out of the shadows into a shared predicament provided the truthful preconditions for the transformation of personal and collective identities and the forging of new viewpoints.

Genuine solidarity and collective efficacy can't break through until people can have truthful conversations about how things are, about what matters to them and about how they would like things to be. This is not an insensitively unconditional demand. As therapists we understand how such grievous injuries to dignity, respect and identity can sometimes feel impossible to voice openly. Too much truthfulness in a life would be unsparing. We all need our moments of quiet solitude to heal and mourn before returning strengthened to the world, but too little corrodes our ability to collectively orient ourselves. Stanley Milgram's notorious psychological experiments can be understood as confirming how much all of us depend upon others moment by moment to confirm our view of things. Milgram created a fake scenario where a person was ordered to administer what they took to be electric shocks to a person in another room. They repeatedly complied against their misgivings even as the screams of pain intensified. His subjects overruled their misgivings because it did not fit with their sense that seemingly reputable professionals would not ask them to do anything wrong. Milgram's chilling lesson is how easily we can become unlike ourselves when we trust where we should not (Milgram, 2010).

In communities where toughness and resilience are prized above all else there is no place where the shame of having failed to fight harder can be voiced. That people can see how hard overburdened friends and families are trying to cope on scarce resources often compounds the guilt. Younger men in particular simply have neither the language to express their pain nor lived experience of political and social optimism. They rarely cry not so much because it is prohibited (though this plays its part) but because sadness makes no sense in the official worldview that people share with each other. This finds a compliment in Fanita English's theory of rackets, the work of moulding one's feelings into more socially acceptable ways and covering up less permitted ones (English, 1972). The key difference is that here the distinction is between more commonly expressed, familiar and worked out emotional responses and underdeveloped ones.

Rackets remain useful tools for understanding individual deformities of response, but they cannot quite capture what happens to a community if everyone is excluding the same feelings in the same way. You can't be sad if you have forgotten what has been lost. This results in what has been called a 'spiral of silence' – the less something is said, the more it become progressively unsayable, alien and unreal (Noelle-Neumann, 1991). Once people wore protective masks of untruthful feeling. Over time they forget what they were defending against. The mask becomes the new real. Deficits in truthfulness eventually result in deficits in understanding.

Truthfulness establishes basic level of trusts which are essential for individuals to co-operate. There is an intersection between truthfulness and resourcefulness because the pooling of knowledge allows us to know more collectively than we would individually: everyone chips in what they have found out. Bernard Williams and Edward Craig both tell a similar 'state of nature' story which invites us to imagine the conditions under which human co-operation might have begun. The story goes that if collective survival once depended upon knowing where to find food and shelter then someone testifying truthfully that they have located such resources was a matter of life or death (Williams, 2002; Craig, 1990). Truth mattered because the stakes were high. Craig even proposes that more general preoccupations with truth and truthfulness may originally derive from this needing to trust some people as reliable sources of information: a relational theory of truth, if you will.

Truthfulness isn't just something we are, it's something we do. It is more than just principled abstention from deceit, it has an active dimension. Plato understood that knowledge had to be sought, we can't just wait for it to turn up (Plato, 1987). It calls upon us to explore, to find things out, to commit time and energy to valuable inquiries. Truthfulness presumes committed investment. The precious gains of science didn't just turn up because people were honest. They are the fruits of a willingness to experiment, an openness to new ideas, risk-taking and strenuous effort. Truthfulness calls us beyond the current limits of complacent understanding. Our relationship with the world needs constant renewal and the duty of inquiry won't allow for resting. Communities that don't talk about the things that matter let truthfulness decline at their peril.

State sabotage of truthfulness is the blunt instrument of oppressive societies. Authoritarian states secretly recruit informants from the civilian population knowing that this attacks the bond of trust between people. Clients who have escaped such countries tell me they trust no-one because they understand that a loose word to the wrong person can be fatal. Oppressors in open societies lack such options and must instead beguile us more covertly. Obvious lies may be easy to spot, but this is not the same thing as being able to concretely imagine the whole unobscured truth. Open societies with an abundant media culture are now experiencing what has been called 'hypernormalisation' (Kakutani, 2018) which is where the sheer relentlessness of half-truths and misinformation so saturates our collective consciousness that the impossibility of sifting truth from lies causes us to sink into defeat (Davis, 2017). The omnipresence of 'infotainment', news content tailored to generate hits online and stir the passions rather than inform the mind erases the distinction between what we should believe and what we want to believe. These conditions are ripe for demagogues to displace dissatisfaction onto marginalised and misunderstood social groups. Starved of truthfulness, political consciousness shrivels to a cynical, anxious and outraged husk, hooked on the cheap thrill of lashing out or withdrawing into cynicism and paralysis.

Advanced societies can become idle about truthfulness once collective security is taken for granted. As neoliberalism has progressively restructured all aspects of our lives along market lines, fierce competition for jobs, relationships and social esteem become the norm. Anyone who has attempted to meet a partner online will understand the irresistible pull of exaggerating their best points just to keep up. Anxious comparisons with others become commonplace. Even when we suspect that exaggeration is the norm we dare not risk acting on our convictions. The era of chaos (see Chapter 1) replaces the notion of self as something with respectful obligations to the wider whole with the notion of self as a kind of project, something you plan and invest in (Brown, 2015). Believe what you choose comes to replace believe what you ought. If you live for long enough in a climate where truthfulness has been abandoned and convenient deceptions stalk unopposed then it is hard not to let the mind get swept along by tides of unrooted and emotive consensus. More than not knowing what to believe or not to believe, we lose the sense of ourselves as people disciplined and capable enough of rising above the convenience of mere opinion.

Integrity

The destruction of Britain's industrial heartlands was a short and brutal affair lasting a handful of years. It was far more abrupt than most previous changes in labour patterns which could take decades (Seabrook, 2013). Wholesale, instantaneous adjustment would be a tough ask for even the most resourceful and optimistic communities: it was largely beyond a people whose mindset had been forced to acclimatise to what they took to be a permanent way of life handed down from parent to child. Ultimately conceding the immovability of the neoliberal economic consensus, left-wing politics ceased trying to reshape the world to better fit the interests of working people and began trying to reshape working people to better fit the interests of the world.

As jobs and class politics disappeared from post-industrial communities, the reforming state increased its presence. People would now be subject to ongoing efforts to have their lives reformed, buffed and polished by an army of professionals. Often queasily uncomfortable with being asked to overlook the material causes of distress in favour of morale-boosting talk of upskilling and character-building, most of these professionals quickly resigned themselves to working within the system. Today there are doctors exhorting their patients to give up sugary foods, alcohol and cigarettes, social workers overseeing their parenting, welfare advisers prodding them off benefits and schools preparing them for the world of work. Therapists working in such communities may similarly feel compelled to join this chorus in favour of the benefits of getting on better in the world as it is.

Conversations between people and professionals end up conducted in a superficially respectful yet jargonated 'statespeak' which presumes personal responsibility for ongoing efforts at self-management. There is no space for acknowledging the possibility that the world itself might need to change. Re-describing struggling people as problems in need of a solution, an oppressive description, sinks in precisely because its stinging accusation chimes with people's Child ego-state recollection of themselves as once proudly self-reliant. Over time the pre-existing tapestry of their collective worldview has been partially replaced with dependence upon the expertise of professionals (Furedi, 2004). People talk less amongst themselves about their lives, they talk more about their defects with paid helpers.

There were some fairly obvious objections to trying to put communities back on their feet in this way. Investigating the lives of working-class boys in the late 1970s, Paul Willis showed that the anti-authoritarianism and anti-intellectualism they displayed were actually intelligible responses to the patronising attitudes of their teachers and future employers (Willis, 1978). Favouring dignity over getting-on, defiance over compliance and loyalty to their existing way of life over admiration for middle-class respectability, boys like these were most unlikely to offer anything other than clenched resistance to efforts to reshape them. This attitude was not universal and many of their peers were much more interested in quiet respectability, keeping a good home and getting on at work. None the less, it seems that a deep reservation about leaving place and people behind cuts across these intragroup divisions: the ties of class runs deep. It often seems as if the key predicament for working-class people remains how to succeed in a world run by the middle-classes without having to become like them.

The material and cultural changes described so far in this chapter damaged what I will call the **integrity** of the community. Integrity is harder to define than the other three conditions since it is an emergent property, hard to trace back to tangible acts, material objects or processes. It refers to the ecological coherence, character and intelligibility of a community or social context, the product of countless daily transactions which congeal into traditions, stories, colloquialisms, local knowledge and collective memory. It comes close to the sum total of what Berne described as the technics, etiquette and character of a social system, the 'how to do it', 'why to do it' and 'what we do, but can't quite put into words' (Berne, 1963; Napper, 2010), though cultures are inevitably more complex than the sum of their parts.

Quite apart from its functional benefits in providing the background ethos for co-operative action, integrity leads to a sense of being at home, of being somewhere rather than anywhere. Rooted in place and history, our actions feel like part of a meaningful whole (Bracken, 2002). Integrity functions as a kind of resourcefulness. This allows the collective life to be the recipient of our love and loyalty (Richards, 2018). Integrity allows the world to perform what Kohut called a self-object function, the things around us that we invest with our need for stability, coherence, meaning and identity (Kohut, 1977). Without it an imperceptible loss, hard to name but impossible to ignore, creeps over us. Although the notion flirts with conservatism and nostalgia, the value of integrity has become clear under conditions of chaos (described in Chapter 1). Prior to the onset of rapid social change, the emergent meaning of social continuity would simply have been presumed. Tearing up tradition in the name of progress we have come to love integrity in the instance of losing it.

Integrity can be a double-edged sword. When a sense of purpose and meaning is based on continuity then it's understandable that people will sometimes cling to what they know. On the other hand, cultural stagnation or stifling nostalgia can be as undesirable as social unravelling, particularly for those pushed to the margins of current social arrangements. There is a meaningful distinction between a people voluntarily tearing down their way of life knowing what they plan to erect in its place and an ethos unthinkingly dismantled by disinterested outsiders. Integrity allows us to know who we are and who we are not. It provides a vital ballast to weather times of change but is not itself a call for things to remain as they are.

For communities under siege, the urge to protect their threatened way of life can become all consuming. Under conditions of perpetual domination, people's ability to know themselves as they might have been is drowned out by the daily need to maintain boundaries, to protect 'us' from being swallowed up by 'them'. Opposition can feel as though it has become an end in itself rather than a means to a higher purpose. In working-class communities, this sometimes appears as an inverted prejudice not to appear 'posh', a gesture which carries with it a cumulative dismissal of a middle-class ethos. These are not always helpful assumptions to cling to, yet they are sometimes felt necessary. A strong sense of who they are can seem more precious than the alternative. If the price of integrity is that sometimes it freezes life so that we cannot see what lies beyond our current horizons, it none the less ensures that when change is initiated that it is firmly rooted in and guided by a rooted sense of our identity and shared history.

Conclusion

The inevitably simplified picture of post-industrial working-class communities I have painted here has attempted to illuminate the kinds of underlying difficulties which make horizontal problems more likely to occur. Many of these deficits were the result of actions taken against the communities from the outside. The failure to plan a future for these regions after deindustrialisation continues to have a devastating impact on the resourcefulness of those areas, their ability to provide the material and social conditions where occupation, love and self-respect can blossom. The decline of responsiveness remains mostly the responsibility of wider powers intent on maintaining a state of political and social oppression by engineering apathy and the withdrawal of opportunities for political participation. The narcotic effect of consumerism was a chance development with unfortunate effects here (see Hall, Winlow & Ancrum, 2008). I have also suggested that a complete account will acknowledge the ways in which communities themselves have, often with the best intentions, co-operated in their depoliticisation at points where other options may have been available.

The decline of truthfulness also did not well up from a single source. Democratic deficits in national politics and media culture reinforced the raw inability of people to articulate their pain, sense of loss and future hopes. This has stood in the way of the first steps necessary for a constructive revival in spirit and solidarity if not in wider fortunes. Necessary conversations about the interlocking ways that things went wrong and how they might go right in future could provide a new substance to community integrity and a people's sense of themselves beyond defeat and defiance. The intentional vandalism inflicted from above which left the community feeling that it's sense of itself had been sliced in half, a stark overlap between past and current senses of things.

The alleviation of horizontal problems depends upon durable increases in the levels of resourcefulness, responsiveness, truthfulness and integrity which a person can partially recover through co-operative interaction with the world around them. Therapy will succeed to the extent that it can assist this process. Realism is essential: we cannot change the whole world on the basis of two people talking in a room. Therapy, in the end, is only therapy. We must be clear-sighted about what can be accomplished for the larger forces swaying local circumstances will persist unimpeded. We must be content doing what we can to resource people with outsight, to show them the cracks in the existing order that can be widened and remind them of the value of doing so.

It's crucial to understand how often horizontal problems are evolving, compound injuries which start with one difficulty and then add others. We must address each of the four conditions identified here. Enhancing resourcefulness through knowledge and learning may help to lift the fog of confusion (see Bourdieu et al., 1999). Helping people to recognise their shared condition may lay the foundations for local solidarity. Assisting people to live truthfully will not merely entail the therapeutic diktat to 'know thyself' but will also encourage a responsibility for the accuracy of their thinking about the world, and encourage a willingness to explore and try out different ideas. Integrity can be an effective partner to truthfulness. It must be respected as the starting point of any conclusions the person reaches about things whilst also being re-explored and rediscovered for the roads not taken. Its main lesson may be that things didn't have to end up this way.

We have seen how much needs to go right in the world for anything to work with us. Starting with the world and working inwards has opened up new options for thinking about people and their problems. We are now in a position to focus on how these conditions, or their absence, turn up in the texture and structure of individual experience.

References

Alexievich, S. (2016) *Second Hand Time*. Translated from Russian by B. Shayevich. London: Fitzcarraldo Editions.

Austin, J.L. (1962) *How to Do Things with Words*. Oxford: Clarendon Press.

Berne, E. (1963) *The Structure and Dynamics of Organisations and Groups*. New York: Grove Press.

Berne, E. (1972) *What Do You Say After You Say Hello?* London: Corgi.

Beveridge, W. (1942) *Social Insurance and Allied Services*. London: His Majesty's Stationery Office.

Bourdieu, P. (1991) *Language and Symbolic Power*. Edited by J.B. Thompson. Translated from French by. G. Raymond & M. Adamson. Cambridge: Polity Press.

Bourdieu, P., Accardo, A., Balazs, G., Beaud, S., Bonvin, F., Bourdieu, E., Bourgois, P., Broccolichi, S., Champagne, P., Christin, R., Faguer, J.P., Garcia, S., Lenoir, R., Œuvrard, F., Pialoux, M., Pinto, L, Podalydès, D., Abdelmalek, S., Soulié, C., Wacquant, L.J.D. (1999) *The Weight of the World: Social Suffering in Contemporary Society*. Translated from French by P.P. Ferguson, S. Emanuel, J. Johnson, S.T. Waryn. Cambridge: Polity.

Bracken, P. (2002) *Trauma: Culture, Meaning & Philosophy*. London: Whurr.

Brown, W. (2015) *Undoing the Demos: Neoliberalism's Stealth Revolution*. New York: Zone Books.

Cadwalladr, C. (2014) How Passion has been Purged from Politics – along with ordinary people. *Guardian*, Sunday 28th September 2014. available at: www.theguardian.com/politics/2014/sep/28/how-passion-purged-politics-ordinary-people-labour-conference. Accessed 31.10.2019.

Charlesworth, S.J. (2000) *A Phenomenology of Working-Class Experience*. Cambridge: Cambridge University Press.

Coetzee, J.M., Kurtz, A. (2015) *The Good Story: Exchanges on Truth, Fiction and Psychotherapy*. London: Vintage.

Cooke, M. (1994) *Language and Reason: Study of Habermas' Pragmatics*. Cambridge, MA: MIT Press.

Christakis, N., Fowler, J. (2009) *Connected: The Amazing Power of Social Networks and How They Shape our Live*. London: Harper Press.

Craig, E. (1990) *Knowledge and the State of Nature*. Oxford: Oxford University Press.

Cronqvist, H., Siegel, S., Yu, F. (2015) Value versus growth investing: why do different investors have different styles. *Journal of Financial Economics*, 117 (2), 333–349.

Davis, E. (2017) *Post-Truth: Why We Have Reached Peak-Bullshit and What We Can Do About it*. London: Little, Brown.

Durkheim, E., Simpson, G. (1951) *Suicide: A Study in Sociology*. Translated by J.A. Spaulding & G. Simpson. London: Routledge

Elliott, L., Atkinson, D. (1998) *The Age of Insecurity*. London: Verso.

English, F. (1972) Rackets and Real Feelings: part II. *Transactional Analysis Journal*, 2 (3), 23–35.

Fraser, N., Honneth, A. (2003) *Redistribution or Recognition?: A Political-Philosophical Exchange*. London: Verso.

Fricker, M. (2007) *Epistemic Injustice: Power and the Ethics of Knowing*. Oxford: Oxford University Press.

Furedi, F. (2004) *Therapy Culture: Cultivating Vulnerability in an Uncertain Age*. London: Routledge.

Goffman, E. (1959) *The Presentation of Self in Everyday Life*. London: Penguin.

Habermas, J. (1976) *Legitimation Crisis*. Translated from German by T. McCarthy. Cambridge: Polity Press.

Habermas, J. (1987) *The Theory of Communicative Action, Vol. 2: Lifeworld and System: A Critique of Functionalist Reasons*. Translated from German by T. McCarthy. Boston: Beacon Press.

Hall, S., Winlow, S., Ancrum, C. (2008) *Criminal Identities and Consumer Culture: Crime, Exclusion and the New Culture of Narcissism*. Cullompton: Willan.

Haylett, C. (2003) 'Culture, Class and Urban Policy: Reconsidering Equality', *Antipode*, 35 (1), 55–73.

Harris, C.C. (1987) *Redundancy and Recession in South Wales*. Oxford: Basil Blackwell.

Hobsbawm, E (1994) *Age of Extremes: The Short Twentieth Century 1914–1991*. London: Michael Joseph.

Honneth, A. (1995) *The Struggle for Recognition: The Moral Grammar of Social Conflicts*. Translated from German by J. Anderson. Cambridge: Polity.

Honneth, A. (2012) *The I in We: Studies in the Theory of Recognition*. Translated from German by J. Ganahl. Cambridge: Polity.

Hutton, W. (1996) *The State We're In: Why Britain is in Crisis and How to Overcome It*. London: Vintage.

James, O. (2007) *Affluenza: How to be Successful and Stay Sane*. London: Vermillion.

Kakutani, M. (2018) *The Death of Truth*. London: William Collins.

Karelis, C. (2007) *The Persistence of Poverty: Why the Economics of the Well-off Can't Help the Poor*. New Haven: Yale University Press.

Karpman, S.B. (1968) Fairy Tales and Script Drama Analysis. *Transactional Analysis Bulletin*, 7 (26), 39–43.

Kohut, H. (1977) *The Restoration of the Self*. Madison: International Universities Press.

Kohut, H. (1984) *How Does Analysis Cure?* Edited by P. Goldberg & P. Stepansky. Chicago: University of Chicago Press.

Laclau, E., Mouffe, C. (1985) *Hegemony and Socialist Strategy: Towards a Radical Democratic Politics*. London: Verso.

MacDonald, R., Shildrick T., Webster, C., Simpson, D. (2005) Growing Up in Poor Neighbourhoods: The Significance of Class and Place in the Extended Transitions of 'Socially Excluded' Young Adults. *Sociology*, 39 (5), 873–891.

Mair, P. (2013) *Ruling the Void: The Hollowing Out of Western Democracy*. London: Verso.

Malmendier, U., Nagel, S. (2011) Depression Babies: do macroeconomic experiences affect risk taking. *The Quarterly Journal of Economics*, 126 (1), 373–416.

Milgram, S. (2010) *The Individual in a Social World*. 3rd edn. London: Pinter and Martin Ltd.

Mouffe, C. (2005) *On the Political*. Abingdon: Routledge.

Napper, R. (2010) 'The individual in context: how do I fit in around here?', in R.G. Erskine, Ed., *Life scripts: A Transactional Analysis of Unconscious Relational Patterns*. London: Karnac, 179–202.

Noelle-Neumann, E. (1991) The Theory of Public Opinion: The Concept of the Spiral of Silence. *Annals of the International Communication Association.*, 14 (1), 256–287.

Pickett, K., Wilkinson, R. (2010) *The Spirit Level: Why Equality is Better for Everyone*. London: Penguin.

Plato (1987) *The Republic*. 2nd edn. Translated and introduction, D. Lee. London: Penguin.

Prilleltensky, I., Nelson, G. (2002) *Doing Psychology Critically: Making a Difference in Diverse Settings*. Basingstoke: Palgrave Macmillan.

Richards, B. (2018) *What Holds Us Together: Popular Culture and Social Cohesion*. Abingdon: Routledge.

Scott, J.C. (1990) *Domination and the Arts of Resistance: Hidden Transcripts*. New Haven: Yale University Press.

Seabrook, J. (2013) *Pauperland: Poverty and the Poor in Britain*. London: Hurst and Co.

Searle, J. (1969) *Speech Acts: An Essay in the Philosophy of Language.* Cambridge: Cambridge University Press.

Sibley, D. (1995) *Geographies of Exclusion: Societies and Difference in the West.* London: Routledge.

Smail, D. (1993) *The Origin of Unhappiness: A New Understanding of Personal Distress.* London: Constable.

Verhaeghe, P. (2012) *What about me? The Struggle for Identity in a Market-Based Society.* Translated from Dutch by J Hedly-Prôle. Melbourne: Scribe.

Williams, B. (2002) *Truth and Truthfulness: an Essay in Genealogy.* Princeton: Princeton University Press.

Willis, P.E. (1978) *Learning to Labour: How Working Class Kids get Working Class Jobs.* Farnham: Ashgate.

Winnicott, D.W. (1960) 'Ego Distortion in Terms of True and False Self' in D.W. Winnicott (1965) *The Maturational Processes and the Facilitating Environment.* London: Karnac.

Winnicott, D.W. (1971) *Playing and Reality.* London: Routledge.

Young, J. (1999) *The Exclusive Society: Social Exclusion, Crime and Difference in Late Modernity.* Los Angeles: Sage.

3

THE PARENT EGO-STATE
REDISCOVERED

So far, I have argued in favour of a significant rethinking of the relationship between self and world where the 'I' emerges out of, but never fully separates from, the 'we' that precedes and surrounds it. This self-and-world replaces a more familiar picture of a pre-formed self, coming into contact with a world which gets 'inside' it during the course of living. Within transactional analysis our favoured way of explaining how the world comes to be part of us is to talk of Parent ego-states. These distinct, episodic variations within the psyche are thought to come originally from someone else and remain less fully 'us' than the other ego-states. Whilst the theory of the Parent ego-state is often taken to be the best starting point for understanding the relationship between self and world, many of our current ideas about it seem to inhibit rather than enhance our understanding. Without judicious reform of our settled presumptions, we may head off once again in the wrong direction in our endeavours to understand what contribution the world makes to who we are. What follows is a progressive rethinking of Parent ego-state theory which incorporates new observational hunches and critical engagements. The chapter arrives at conclusions which are ultimately as much a rediscovery as a revision.

Ego-state theory

I cannot reasonably proceed with a revision of the Parent ego-state without first offering a discussion of ego-states more generally, what I take them to be and why I think they are still useful concepts. This is not as easy as it sounds for in spite of its apparent simplicity, ego-state theory is a muddle. A muddle from which useful ideas can be plucked, fascinating debates can be had and in which fresh ideas can be planted without immediately withering, but a muddle none the less. The sole foothold of near-complete agreement amongst differing theoretical tribes remains the descriptive definition that Berne repeated (with minor variations) across the course of his published writings. Each definition reiterates that we simultaneously experience and show distinct patterns of thinking, feeling and behaving and that these patterns are largely consistent across time (Berne, 1961; Stewart & Joines, 2012): this much is uncontentious. A further assumption, not overtly stated but undeniably implied, is that because all ego-states have these common features, they are either essentially or functionally alike in some significant way: this is a far more unsteady proposition than it might first appear.

It seems clear from Berne's writings that he regarded ego-states as distinct from each other, internally coherent and defined by a consistency between internal experience and outward display or behaviour. This provides the primary means by which ego-states are identified; it also intimates at their usefulness as explanatory concepts. If our outsides and insides match then it appears client and therapist have tangible markers for tracking important interior shifts in the course of interaction. These shifts are regarded as significant; they go on to form the basis for a range of psychological and behavioural explanations. These ideas about ego-states are readily graspable and intuitively correct, an initial impression which surely accounts for the enduring direct appeal of transactional analysis.

Since these starting points show promise, it's understandable that we have used ego-state theory in a range of explanatory and clinical accounts, but upon further reflection complications become apparent. What Berne has offered here is nothing more than bare description rather than an explanatory theory. Observing that people seem to have ego-states doesn't tell us *why* they have them or why we should be interested in them. Positing the existence of ego-states does not itself vouch for their capacity to explain important facets of human experience. Without this further leap they are nothing more than observational curios.

What might have proved a fatal objection to the theory rather curiously turned into an advantage. Unencumbered by greater specificity, ego-state theory became extended in multiple and sometimes incompatible directions simultaneously. Rather than one theory of ego-states we ended up with many, each one the product of a determination to tie the concept in to whatever needed explaining at the time. Within Berne's writings alone, ego-states are used to map out the structure of the personality, they are treated as repositories of particular attributes, they are explanations for functional clusters of behaviours and they are incorporated into an account of psychological development (see Heathcote, 2010; Trautmann & Erskine, 1981; Oller-Vallejo, 1997). The ego-state model was even extended away from individual psychology to belief structures in groups and culture (Berne, 1963; Drego, 1983). In the realm of clinical application, ego-states are cited in explanations of internal conflict, internally inhibited contact with reality and developmental deficits (Clarkson, 1992; Erskine et al., 1988). Berne was a restless, creative thinker who seemed temperamentally more interested in leaping ahead to the next fresh idea than in turning backwards to tie his loose ends together. His legacy has enabled subsequent transactional analysts to use the concept of ego-states in a huge range of ways whilst also claiming a legitimating Bernean line of inheritance.

From a distance there may appear no strict incompatibility between these different applications; upon closer inspection the seamless interlinking necessary to proclaim a satisfactory theoretical synthesis isn't achieved. The closer you look, the more the loose ends multiply. The different strands of ego-state theory are roughly bound together by no more than what Wittgenstein called 'family resemblances', meaning a cluster of ideas that somewhat overlap in varying ways but without a central, defining principle or feature which they all include (Wittgenstein, 1953). This has left transactional analysts in a peculiar limbo where surrendering the gains offered by ego-state theory is unacceptable yet limited progress has been made towards final unification.

When you can't find an answer sometimes you have to change the question. Nobody has attempted to ask what ego-states are from the starting point of self-and-world before. Moreover, the suggestion that Parent, Adult and Child ego-states may share descriptive features but have no wider essence or functions in common has not been seriously entertained. Bring context back into the picture, look at ego-states 'horizontally', loosen (at least initially) our need to bind everything together at the centre and our starting assumptions open up new possibilities. Rather than adding to the effort to draw together the scattered fragments of theory into unity, I intend to start by considering the Parent ego-state in isolation, include awareness of context and revisit what it is we think we are talking about. The need to cling to the hope of a unified, psychological theory is perhaps less pressing than is sometimes assumed.

Whilst I do not advocate abandoning further rigorous disputation of ego-state theory, I suspect such a process is always going to fall short of full reconciliation, honourable partial victories notwithstanding (Rath, 1993; Oller-Vallejo, 1997; Stewart, 2001; Cornell, 2015). No recent developments provide the necessary starting point. I do not see much promise in appealing to neuroscience as a way of sifting between alternatives (Gildebrand, 2002; Cornell, 2002). Quite apart from the numerous philosophical objections that could be raised to mapping psychological phenomena onto brain states (Bennett & Hacker, 2003) we can't look to neuroscience for answers until we better understand what we are asking it to explain. Recent attempts to understand ego-states developmentally (Hargaden & Sills, 2002; Erskine, 2015) prioritise early experience and by extension the Child ego-state, a move I suggest obscures some features of our mature inseparability from the world. I cannot guarantee that the following argument will persuade those who are already convinced that these old ideas provide the best beginnings for further integration, but if my argument succeeds then at least I may have stimulated the search for fresh justifications.

The parent ego-state redefined

In order to see the Parent ego-state clearly, I need to unbolt and pull apart some cherished assumptions about it before reconstructing the theory from the ground up. I will abstain from filing down its unique features to force it into essential consistency with the other ego-states. This redefinition will shed fresh light on the relationship between the Parent and the Adult in the mature ego-state structure. It may be that our different views on ego-states are less about the confusions inherent in the theory itself and more about the different wider notions of psychological structure, human functioning and distress we adhere to. Like a Rorschach test, we discover in ego-states only what our wider picture about people leads us to find there. As it stands, the theory simply can't stretch to accommodate my own assumptions about self-and-world. The arguments offered here for my view will only make full sense if the wider arguments of this book about the best ways to understand certain kinds of psychological difficulties are accepted.

My disassembly begins with a trio of provocative challenges. The problem with our existing accounts of the Parent ego-state is that they don't recognise it isn't always derived from parents, it is increasingly less 'parental', and it isn't really introjected. It isn't always derived from parents because it is clear to me that a range of relationships and influences across the lifespan become integral parts of our thinking including siblings and extended family, friends, school, community, religious institutions, the media and the wider society, what Moiso calls the social Parent (Moiso, 1979). Where once flesh and blood relationships were all, the increasing penetration of our lives by communication technology means that the next generation are children of worlds far beyond the family home. Whilst the family continues to provide the most formative relationships, simple observation alone can show us that we continue adopting ways of seeing, talking and acting from subsequent relationships across the years. Around the enduring core of influences from those that raised us we remain open and porous across life, both borrowers and dependents of the views and experiences of others.

We never quite stop being 'parented' even when we are past the ages of dependence. The psychic organ exteropsyche (Berne, 1966) – literally 'outside mind', quite different from just parent – is not a receptacle in which we store our family dramas before sealing it shut against later influences. It needs to be thought of figuratively as an ever-open space, a constantly shifting constellation of outside influences of varying prominance and strength, sometimes complimentary, sometimes discordant. This entails a rather different definition of maturation's peak than mere separation from others. It acknowledges that autonomy is always balanced with ongoing dependence and co-operation. It also challenges the view that the Parent is always a replay of past experience (see Summers & Tudor, 2000). Thinking and feeling in ways which are not-quite ours are unavoidable, prevalent aspects of our ongoing experience.

In the West, the Parent is decreasingly 'parental'. The intervening decades since Berne first outlined his theory have witnessed a wealth of changes in the structures of family life and attitudes to parenting. The rise of non-traditional family structures including lone-parents, blended and LGBT families have arisen from a general questioning of inherited norms governing domestic life (White & Klein, 2008). People are increasingly producing novel and varied answers to the question 'what is a family?' resulting in a significant rethinking of the values and ideas guiding child-raising. Early transactional analysis broadly reiterated the then-prevalent picture of families as units of nurture and socialisation (see Chambers, 2012) aimed at preparing children for future roles as good students, workers, spouses and citizens. Parents were required to offer clear instruction in the ethos and workings of the world and to perform the discipline necessary to reign in wilful and selfish impulses.

These dramatic social changes sometimes result in rather different clinical presentations. Far from hammering their children into a socially respectable shape, we are now seeing parents whose main concern is to support their children in contentedly determining their own path through life. Younger clients often describe their parents as being like good friends. Parenting has becoming more facilitative and sensitive to particularity, trying to anticipate and support the child's own wants. Public awakening to previously hidden abuses that befell children followed subsequently by greater intervention of the state into family life has encouraged children to understand themselves as bearers of rights, entitled to protection, respect and consideration. This has resulted in a subtle realignment of power in family relationships with parents increasingly frightened of failing their children in ways which predestine them to future unhappiness (Jamieson, 1988).

These shifts are happening over a gradual transition period: their impact is uneven, enhanced or impeded by other, intersecting social factors. Strict and prohibitive parents who produce the forbidding Parental introjects of Berne's imagining continue to exist, but such a family ethos is no longer reinforced by the wider community. The child of strict parents will now leave the family home and find teachers, welfare professionals and parents of friends who model a more permissive attitude. I now most often encounter an impasse between Parent values and Child wants (Goulding & Goulding, 1978), played out in within individuals from ethnic minority communities. Here an emphatic, dogmatic imposition of traditional values by first generation immigrant parents on their children bespeaks the need to protect a cherished way of life from engulfment in the majority culture. Occupying an overlap between cultural majority and cultural minority worldviews, such clients continue to display a commanding Parent voice, though this is a Parent painfully aware of its own probable demise. It is dogmatic control resulting from a sense of cultural decline rather than cultural pre-eminence. The Parent as a crisply distinct, rigid and unchanging presence lodged within the psyche, the solemn mouthpiece of shared values, permissions and prohibitions may perhaps never have been a context-invariant feature of the psychological landscape after all.

It may be more unsettling still to let go of our assumption that the Parent is introjected, so central is this notion to our working explanations about the relationship between mind and world. Whilst Berne used 'introjected', 'internalised' and 'copied' somewhat interchangeably, his intent seems best captured by the first term. Introjection refers to the psychic act of taking inside ourselves aspects or the whole of another person (see Laplanche & Pontalis, 1973). In contrast to the lived memory of the Child, we have never actually 'been' our Parent ego-state we have only been in a significant relationship with the persons from whom they are derived. The theory of introjection tries to account for how they can come to be a central yet separate part of our psyche. It is this co-mingling of intimate proximity and unassimilated otherness which the term introjection captures so well.

Renouncing the theory of introjection, whatever its seeming charm and convenience, is a necessary step to clarifying our thinking about the Parent. The problem with the notion of introjection is that it rests on a bad metaphor; minds are not like physical objects. They can't be understood spatially, they don't have 'insides' any more than they have colours, shapes or textures. Nor are thoughts well understood as objects stored in the 'space' of the mind: if you ask someone to point to where their thoughts are they may gesture towards the head but even the most invasive brain surgery won't find them. If the notion of storing our own thoughts doesn't make sense then we can hardly expect to find thoughts from other people in the same non-existent place.

These failings of understanding are easy to forgive. As Lackoff and Johnson show, we are so accustomed to using spatial metaphors as a way to describe our minds because we cannot easily get away from the sense that our selves are inseparable from our physical bodies. Whilst our minds are abstractions, our bodies are distinct, concrete objects with insides and outsides located at particular points in space and time. Understanding mental abstractions using spatial metaphors of inside and outside is so commonplace that it is almost an unavoidable, necessary fiction (Lackoff & Johnson, 1980, 1999).

If spatial metaphors are to be laid aside, then something must take their place. The psychoanalyst Roy Schafer has carefully unpicked these metaphors, arguing convincingly that we should think about mental processes as particular kinds of 'psychological actions' rather than spatial objects (Schafer, 1976, 1983). Rather than saying we are taking something inside, what we are actually meaning when we use the term introjection is that we are thinking in a recognisably coherent and distinct manner, something we do often enough that it feels like a consistent part of our self. At the same time, we are acknowledging that this pattern of thinking is recognisably similar to those of people with whom we have had important, formative relationships. We are also noting that we are persistently disposed to think in this borrowed pattern even when the people from who they are copied are not physically present to prompt us to think this way. Finally, when we use the term introjection, we are describing ways of thinking which are hardy and seem to endure in spite of the persistent influx of new experiences. Unpacked in this way, we have accomplished everything the metaphor of introjection tries to do without the accompanying implausibility.

In transactional analysis, when we talk of someone introjecting or cathecting their Parent ego-state, we are really saying that a person's thinking is commonly and recurrently more like someone else's than their own. Without this distinction between thoughts that are like other people's and those that are more like what we usually take to be ourselves, the concept of the Parent would be redundant.

As with introjection generally, we are also saying that this distinct pattern of thinking, feeling and acting persists unaltered across time and is more ingrained than fleeting thought. We are also acknowledging that this pattern feels very important to our way of being in the world. It seems we can refer to distinction, permanence, prevalence and importance in our psychic life whilst dropping metaphors of inside and outside all together.

This extends the argument I made in Chapter 1 about how we usually define identity and autonomy via separateness. Clinical opinion has been split on the matter of if or when introjection supports or impedes optimal development (Perls, 1969) but once maturity has been achieved, autonomy is usually thought of in terms of separating ourselves from the viewpoints of others. Identity and autonomy are presumed to rely upon the necessary borders of our selfhood remaining unbreached. Here again, introjection speaks to our fear of losing ourselves in thinking more like others. Small wonder we are so keen to kick the Parent out or tame it and integrate it into our sovereign Adult.

The metaphor of introjection certainly bundles a great many ideas economically into one. Perhaps we lose a little 'poetry' if we retire it from our clinical vocabulary. I hope the reader will forgive me if I continue to make illicit use of the occasional spatial metaphor across the remainder of this book for these same reasons. None the less, the advantages of relinquishing the theory of introjection are that it takes us away from fruitless speculations about what it means to have another person 'inside' us and returns us to the pressing issues of why we seem to think in distinct and sometimes incompatible ways across the course of our lives and what value we assign to each of them. If we untangle ourselves from unhelpful preoccupation with which thought belongs to whom we can return more fruitfully to the real issue of why we continue to think like that and whether there are better ways of being and acting.

The question of why people sometimes talk and think distinctly like other people still requires further attention. Berne sometimes hinted that the Parent represents a kind of necessary scaffolding of outside viewpoints that young child uses and then gets rid of once it has the mature Adult resources to work things out for itself (Cornell et al., 2016). This functional argument is plausible, for as children we do take things on trust that we later supplant with confirmatory experience. Whilst this account crosses over with my own there are lingering ambiguities about exactly how a belief transitions from being a Parent one to an Adult one. Moreover, if our model insists that the Parent is a universal feature of a mature psychological structure, then we end up with the potentially grim allegation that no-one ever achieves full psychological maturity. My response to these concerns will be developed as the chapter progresses.

Richard Erskine has returned to the Parent ego-state afresh (see Erskine, 2002; Moursund & Erskine, 2004; see also Fowlie, 2005) and argued that it needs to be understood as a defensive construct. The Parent remains in place whilst the need to keep certain feelings at bay and maintain psychological equilibrium endures. Offering a quite different solution to the question of how the

Parent ego-state gets introjected, Erskine effectively argues that it was never 'outside' us to begin with, being no more than a necessary projected fantasy welling up within the psyche. For Erskine, the Parent is always just another aspect of us. The surface splitting of the self into separate ego-states gives way in therapy to reveal the underlying defensive rationale. Healing this secret hurt is thought to smooth the path to healthy integration.

Erskine's account solves some problems at the expense of exacerbating others. At best it is an account of *some* Parent ego-states resulting from a difficult early history. Since not everyone has the kind of parenting experiences which call forth defences, it can't be a universal picture of psychological structure. More importantly, if the Parent is a defensive creation of our own making then there is no genuine encounter with a separate parental other, their identity or perspectives. Erskine circles back to underlying subjective need at the expense of acknowledging reality. He thereby reduces the Parent to an idealist projection of our unacknowledged needs with functional aspects downplayed. The Parent is only ever the hermetically sealed mind refighting the battles of the past with itself.

So far, I have widened the list of contributors to the exteropsyche and hinted that certain social conditions are likely to produce particular subtypes of Parent. Once we give up the idea that the Parent is always our parent or always parental, we relegate a specific portrait of family drama to the background and acknowledge the expansive range of influences which make up our worldview. The Parent becomes legion, a subtle symphony of different voices and experiences which comes together at points into a climate of opinion, as likely to inform or permit as to prohibit. I have disagreed with the idea that introjection adequately explains why we have a parent or what functions it might perform, but as yet the work of erecting a substitute is incomplete.

If we follow the argumentative line of Chapter 1 and substitute the metaphor of introjection *of* the world with that of emergence *from* the world then new possibilities present themselves. Of course, as a spatial metaphor, emergence can be subject to exactly the same critique as introjection. I therefore need to spell out clearly what the metaphor is intended to convey for emergence must be explained by reference to the specific social practices, opportunities and constraints that are part of inheriting, sharing and using beliefs from the common world around us. I will suggest that our Parent and Adult ego-states correspond to different degrees of emergence from the world. For this theory of emergence to gain traction, an account of socialisation is first required.

Initiation, socialisation and the parent

We need a model of socialisation; we have a model of development in relationship. The increasing focus in contemporary clinical theory upon an intrapsychic relationship between the Parent and other ego-states (e.g. Hargaden & Sills, 2002) at the expense of the 'active Parent' (Goulding & Goulding, 1978) which

70

participates in the world of others is neither accidental nor innocent of negative consequences. It reflects a confident, psychodynamically informed near-consensus in some quarters that the primary business of transactional analysis is a subjective affair, the relationship of self-to-self, the formation of identity, an integration of separate parts, the achievement of acceptance, insight and whole-ness (Schmuckler, 1991; Moursund & Erskine, 2004; Hargaden & Sills, 2002). Although relationship may be stressed, issues of environmental competence are downplayed as a secondary matter whilst relationships to others are pared down to intimacy and the meeting of developmental needs.

This theory of individual development, useful for approaching vertical prob-lems, maps the formation of the self. It leaves untouched the place of learning, the development of outsight and the acknowledgement of co-operative, not just intimate, relationships across the lifespan: these require a separate explanation of equal worth. Our acquired capacity to participate successfully in the place and time that we arrive in is assumed to be a simple combination of achieved self-hood, innate cognitive attributes and the uncomplicated handing over of 'information' from parent to child (Steiner, 1974). Environmental competence is assumed to flow naturally from knowing who we are and what we need. Over-come our internal conflicts, bring together our fragmented parts and everything else falls into place.

A theory of socialisation presumes that we become more fully ourselves by first becoming more like others. We need to borrow, learn, imitate, collaborate and share as an ongoing process from infancy throughout adulthood. Since we cannot begin such a task unaided, those charged with raising us act as both carers and initiators. Winnicott's statement that 'there is no such thing as a baby', only a symbiosis of parent-and-baby, captures this idea somewhat although Winni-cott's aim was to show how a child acquires a sense of security and identity whereas a theory of socialisation is more interested in the fostering of compet-ence (Winnicott, 1964, p. 88).

Since participating in the world starts at once and never ceases, we may be thought of as outward focused before we are inward focused: being emerges out of doing. As the notion of self-and-world intimates, we never stand fully apart or alone. Much of what we think is shared with others. The question then becomes what does this process of learning from others to become the selves, the people, the citizens we need to become look like when it goes well and how does it sometimes go wrong? Responding to this question requires us to widen our attention to include not merely the development of people but of collectives, to establish how we achieve the awareness needed for productive co-operation. At least some of the difficulties we routinely think of as inside us, as ours alone, can be re-understood as a consequence of limited opportunities for optimal socialisa-tion. Failures of socialisation result in deficits in self-and-world.

The suggestion that we become ourselves through participating in the world finds its roots in the distinguished contributions of John Dewey, George Herbert Mead, Jean Piaget and particularly Lev Vygotsky. In their different ways each thinker extended Darwin's notion of adaptation. If you wish to understand what people are, you look first of all at *where* they are and what they are required to accomplish to get by (see Dewey, 1922; Mead, 2015; Piaget, 1959; Vygotsky, 1962, 1978). You can't understand who a person could be until you know their corner of the world. It is crucial that we see learning from others as a formative and collaborative development of the capacity to think and make use of the common language and beliefs rather than the mere handing down of information. We might then see the apex of socialisation as the increasing Adult independence from Parental support, but not full departure from shared and inherited beliefs.

The Parent ego-state needs to be understood in terms of 'tools', not 'rules'. The worldviews, knowledge and experience of our parents are things we can reach out and make use of in our interactions with the world. The child is always an active, learning participant rather than a passive receiver of instruction. Behavioural antecedents of the Parent ego can be witnessed in the tendency of children to repeat previous interactions with adults during play. In the repeat, the child often acts out the adult's part of the interaction as well as their own (Corsaro, 2005). Early versions of the Parent can also be seen in the ways that children come to instruct and comment on their actions in the same way their parent once did. Far from representing the early signs of an inhibition of impulse, the child is expanding their sense of self through play, manipulation of physical objects and, increasingly after nine months, words (Music, 2017). Repetition and copying of actions and words are evidence of the child borrowing its parent's tools and using them with increased sophistication, mastering sense through application, practice and variation. Here is the emergence of what Kohlberg (citing Piaget) and Gopnik refer to as the child-as-philosopher, expanding the repertoire of their thinking through successfully applying what has been shared with them (Kohlberg, 1987; Gopnik, 2009).

If the growth of learning is conceptualised as the gaining and mastery of tools then we understand that our parent figures bequeath us essential building blocks of our capability. We are inducted into a world already made and in motion at the time of our arrival by those who came ahead of us. The child strives to learn and the world, through the parent figure, meets them halfway by fitting new tools to their untutored actions. Rather than viewing the Parent ego-state through the metaphor of introjection, of 'taking in', it might be more use to think of the Parent as a residue of us 'reaching out' into the common space of the world. We are not passive or unwilling receptivity but coping, experimenting, borrowing and trying out our parents' volunteered competence. Our reaching out is met by being invited in. We are starting down the crucial pathway of turning the world from an inherited 'yours' into a shared 'ours'.

This is view of cognitive development is most commonly associated with Lev Vygotsky. He proposes what we might call a symbiotic theory of learning (Harré, 2010) whereby a sensitive and capable parent figure provides the interpersonal preconditions for cognitive growth. The constant interaction with an adult already skilled in the use of language and conceptual thought and an infant yet to acquire these things creates opportunities for growth through initiation (Vygotsky, 1962). Adults create what Vygotsky referred to as a 'zone of proximal development' (Vygotsky, 1978, p. 86), judiciously stepping in to help children complete tasks that lie just outside their current competence. Balancing between simply doing something for the child and abandoning them to flounder, the zone of proximal development refers to an action which is just one step beyond what the child can already do. Vygotsky identified that adults or older children anticipate and understand what the child might be trying to accomplish if they knew a little more and step in to supplement the action. The parent's behaviour has the intentional structure of 'this is what I think you would be doing if you knew how'.

This partnership between parent figures and child provides a scaffolding for the latter's burgeoning competence. The parent progressively withdraws support over time as the child acquires the ability to act and think without assistance. This concept of scaffolding has already been hinted at within transactional analysis by Tony White's two ego-state model. White suggests that the Adult 'grows inside' the Parent as transmitted information becomes subject to reappraisal in the light of new experience (White, 1988). What Vygotsky adds to this picture is that what is acquired and revised is not merely information but an inherited capacity for intelligible thought and action of which information is only a part. Whilst these scaffolding interactions are initially wordless, the child

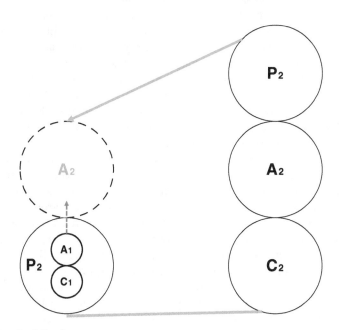

Figure 3.1 Socialisation.

increasingly comes to use language as a tool for communication and action. Whilst Daniel Stern suggests that the awareness that others have minds begins in the period between seven and 15 months (Stern, 1985), the capacity to understand other people's intentions is expanded and refined as the child matures by the progressive acquisition of linguistic concepts.

Against the temptation to see interactions between self and world primarily in terms of isolated egocentricity as Piaget and Freud had done, Vygotsky suggests that we need to understand that the child's interest is initially turned outwards in doing with others. It strives for competence with others, the self congealing in its wake like a kind of byproduct vapour trail. Children first participate in speech with others, then they talk outwardly to themselves before finally outward speech turns into inner or private speech. The external interactions between self and world become replayed 'within' the action of thought. What is now 'ours' – flexible, articulate habits of mind – was once 'theirs'. Once the child can use language to comment on and direct its actions as its parent figures once did then it can make a key transition to be both subject and object of its actions. Vygotsky teaches us that the competence acquired during socialisation is the means to becoming who we need to be. It isn't a break on an already knowing nature.

This sense that social interaction precedes and produces identity also encompasses the formation and expression of emotion. In the earliest hours, days and weeks of development our care givers are already responding to and mirroring our early needs. This process of nurture and socialisation enacts a peculiar alchemy over time, transforming the raw, somatic tugs of *affect* into complex, evaluative and socially intelligible expressions of *feeling* and *emotion* (see Kennedy-Moore & Watson, 1999). A full and complete ability to understand, experience and act on emotions is not accomplished until later development because, as Harré and Gillett note, mature emotions are social acts which incorporate both sophisticated conceptual judgement and embodied expression (Harré & Gillett, 1994). They run upwards from our viscera to the peak of our thought. This progressive addition of learned responding drawn from local expressive idioms incorporates pre-social bodily stirrings into complex evaluations which produce our self-and-world (see Wittgenstein, 1980).

The idea of a Child ego-state that is pre-socially endowed with a sufficient emotional repertoire therefore needs to be reconsidered. Some types of emotion and some aspects of emotional expression can only be understood as both taught and emerging out of particular cultural contexts (Harré & Parrott, 1996; Harré, 1986). Whilst the new born infant needs no tutoring to scream if it is in discomfort or return its mother's smile, these crude, native dispositions are progressive transformed through initiation into cognitively complex, embodied and socially literate cluster of thoughts, feelings and actions (see Harré, 1998). Those aspects of emotional experience and expression that we acquire are no less important than the innate responses they incorporate. There is little that is 'Child-like' about our mature emotions. This theory has important consequences for our therapeutic work with early disturbances and developmental deficits for we are doing more than just putting words to unmet needs, we are also helping clients learn possible ways of feeling and thinking. Our aim must not just be to connect people with themselves but to connect them meaningfully with others against the background of a shared world.

This framework for socialisation illuminates one of the pathways by which we develop from infancy into adulthood. Our journey does not end there. Achieving physical, emotional and cognitive maturity are necessary but not sufficient conditions for the social and political awareness needed to fully understand and participate in the world. There are subtler wisdoms and reflective, critical capacities we can, but do not necessarily, acquire in mastering our place in the social. There is more to seeing how things are than simply acquiring the basic 'cognitive machinery' necessary to process information. There is more to socialisation than a rigid parroting what we have been taught. If this were all we became then socialisation would be a production line for dull, conformist machines. Since individuality and originality are clearly compatible with social competence, we need to think of effective socialisation as leading someone to equal participation in the world. At the apex of socialisation, we stand alongside our forebearers, not merely inheritors of a fixed world but worthy custodians and capable transformers of it.

George Herbert Mead, who echoed Vygotsky is his insistence that learning moves from outside to in, argued that socialisation results in an individual coming to posit a 'generalised other' – a projected amalgamation of the community's viewpoint. The formation of this generalised other allows the individual to see themselves from the common perspective (Mead, 2015). Identity oscillates between the 'me', comprising the socialised view of myself which I take others to hold, and 'I', the unfolding, subjective, autonomous position from which I respond. This might be understood in terms of oscillating between an original, creative Adult position and the vantage point of a posited cultural Parent (Drego, 1983). Mead argues that after an initial, passive shaping by the world we go on to discover an autonomous 'I' within socialisation culminating in the novel possibility of mutual influence. If Mead is correct then the end point of optimal socialisation is a transition into full outsight, an equal and informed participation in the common life where the intelligibility of the order of things is firmly grasped. At the end of socialisation the world becomes 'our' world too. At this point, we can go on to assume a parental role to others, handing on the resourcefulness of knowledge and traditions which we have audited, sanctioned or reshaped in the light of our own present experience. We gain far more from socialisation than we learn by our own isolated experience and we can then use that authority to guide and tend the development of others.

In Chapter 2 I argued that only contexts which met certain conditions could support this kind of optimal socialisation into adequate social and political identities. This is a conclusion largely alien to theories of human development which tend to map out how things typically go right individually rather than focusing in on how things go wrong collectively. A good enough world can be understood along similar lines to Vygotskian zone of proximal development, the only difference being that since we cannot absorb the whole world's capabilities into ourselves, we can never entirely relinquish our dependence. The provision of enough resourcefulness, responsiveness, truthfulness and integrity extends our minds and capabilities, raising us up to be more than ourselves alone.

Where the world is not yet good enough, salvation lies only in the social and political imagining of a world better than this and acting to turn that vision into reality. Mead acknowledged that socialisation can provide the resources to challenge and disobey what was once presumed. His reformist vision suggested we can look beyond our current understanding to an alternative, imagined community of reason, a better version of our collective selves to whom we might appeal in times of strife (Mead, 2015). It is this capacity to imaginatively transform the world we live in by seeing it both for what it is and what it might yet be, this balance of respectful realism and informed yet hopeful reformism that I understand to be the necessary peak of social development and the main aim of contextual transactional analysis.

Clinical vignette

Sometimes you meet clients who act like children because they have never been given the opportunity to grow up: Ricky gives me that impression. A frustrated mass of tics and fidgets, as we talk his foot taps the floor, he fiddles with the rings on his fingers, he drinks water even though isn't thirsty and then repeatedly rolls the empty cup between his hands. Ricky tells me he drinks two or three energy drinks per day. He takes cocaine with his mates when he goes clubbing. He's so used to feeling pumped and loaded that he has forgotten how flat and dull he would feel otherwise. Ricky tells me that he needs to grow up and take responsibility for his life. He sounds like he means it, but gives no indication that he knows how to do this.

If I had already marked down Ricky's self-criticism as the intrusion of a Parental voice, the unexpected appearance of his actual mother in session one day confirms it. Sitting stiffly on the edge of her seat during the meeting, dressed in her work uniform, bag clasped firmly between her hands, Ricky's mother explains that she is worried he will be a layabout like his dad (from whom she is long-term separated). She works two jobs and has a long-term partner she speaks about without fondness who does not get on with Ricky. Her voice is firm and her answers to the point, intimating both a weary resentment at her lot in life mixed with a pointed refusal to openly complain. She talks to Ricky as though he is a naughty child and he responds by becoming one, sullenly dipping his chin into his chest and fidgeting even more than usual.

When his mother is not there Ricky is bright and perceptive about the common predicament he shares with his friends. He knows the cocaine masks unhappiness but he doesn't know what to do apart from keep turning up to his part-time warehouse job and pursue one-night stands. In my world the undirected affect which emerges as restlessness would have been described by the community as boredom. Where I come from bored children are a sign that parents have failed to provide appropriate stimulation. Something would be done, but in Ricky's world no change ever comes. As such, his relentless motor discharge has no name apart from naughty. If I introduce the word boredom it won't be heard in the way I intend it for Ricky and his mother simply don't have the same sense of being able to pursue your wants I take as given. Their world is not resourceful or responsive in the same way. In their world the word boredom would smack of childishness and selfishness. Life is hard and things are as they are and so Ricky spins his empty cup in circles, going nowhere.

The role of the Adult

So far it may seem I have taken away more than I have added. It may appear less easy to carve out the distinct features of the Parent ego-state. The dividing line between the 'I' and 'we' has lost its clear borders. Our socialised minds are always learning, reaching out, copying, using the perspective and knowledges of others but there is yet more to say about how autonomy is compatible with this picture. It may seem that I stand guilty of expanding the Parent ego-state to include all social constituent factors rather than the specific psychological product of formative relationships. Not only might the concept of the Parent ego-state simply swallow up every aspect of our psyche which involves an outside influence but it might as a result lose any specific explanatory weight. In order to address this objection, a new and meaningful distinction between Parent and Adult ego-states must be introduced to help us better understand their distinctive aspects and the nature of their relationship.

Definitions of the Adult ego-state are also a tangled mass of assumptions hidden behind a thin veneer of consistency. The most pressing initial reconsideration is that the Adult quite obviously does not fit within the standard definition of ego-states as coherent and distinct constellations of thoughts, feelings and behaviours. Such a description leaves no room for the flexibility, novelty and openness which are the Adult's defining features. By definition, the Adult doesn't stand still; we can't limit it to the hardened summation of yesterday's patterns because it needs to cope with the new of today. I don't deny that people possess a certain continuity of character, but our Adult ego-states are definitionally unfinished, something which also rules against using Clarkson's description of ego-states as chunks of time (Clarkson, 1992).

Since the Parent and Child have been somewhat easier to define, the Adult faces a further risk of shrinking into irrelevance and redundancy. If all outside influences are clustered in the Parent (exteropsyche) and anything from the Past is retained in the Child (archaeopsyche), then the Adult is reduced to a fleeting speck of original and present-focused thinking (Mohr, 2016). It would be dwarfed by the ego-states on either side of it. If this view were taken seriously then the Adult could only be defined in the negative, a tiny residue which the other Ego-states fail to include.

Berne may have intuited that the Adult suffers from this problem and he came up with a novel solution, albeit one with complex, knotted repercussions. He seems to have understood that if the Adult could not be defined by either content or description then it would have to be identified by its particular function. As such, Berne granted the Adult a role within the psyche as the exclusive seat of reality testing and computation. The Adult ego-state remains defined in our literature by what it can do rather than its content. Berne thereby solved the problem of definition, but only at the expense of placing the Adult in a separate order of creation. A unifying theory of ego-states was placed out of reach.

The idea that the Adult meaningfully aligns thought to reality has remained constant in the theory and I intend to make this assumption my starting point. Raising Adult capacity out of the confusing murk of Child and Parent contamination was at the heart of the classical model. It has also regrettably led to the lingering prejudice that the Adult ego-state is no more than a desiccated calculator, a prejudice which often dovetails with the assumption that reality testing isn't a terribly important part of therapeutic change (Trautmann & Erskine, 1981; Stewart & Joines, 2012). Against this view, I endorse Keith Tudor's welcome corrective that the Adult can possess an abundance of useful attributes besides computation and that a capacity for creative, original perspectives might be a more accurate and generous attribution (Tudor, 2003). There is no reason to think that understanding the world cannot involve both heart and mind, accuracy and ingenuity.

It remains to say what we mean by reality testing and whether our current suppositions about it withstand scrutiny. Berne seems to have presumed that there were two complimentary preconditions for being in contact with reality. The first is captured in his notion of 'awareness', understood as the bare, unmediated use of our sensory apparatus to see, smell, touch, hear and taste what is around us (Berne, 1964), This position comes close to what philosophers call 'naïve realism' (Putnam, 1994; Searle, 1998). We might call this a naturalist theory of reality testing which is to say that having a functioning brain and nervous system is all we really need to be aware of how things are around us. The second precondition is that reality testing depends upon decontamination of the Adult ego-state. The Parent and Child ego-states must move aside so that we can see things as they actually are, not as we remember them being or as we have been told they are by others. Reality testing for Berne is exactly this combination of natural endowment and freedom from internal interference.

Berne may have compared the Adult to a computer, but he never acknowledged that computers are only as good as their programming by people. His definition of awareness further exhibits his suspicion of the social and his belief that autonomy only comes when we cast off outside influence. He was correspondingly required to place unassailable faith in our innate capability at the expense of justly recognising what we learn from others. This places transactional analysis, along with its fellow humanistic brethren, squarely as a descendant of the American Romanticism of Ralph Waldo Emerson where a person seeks an original relationship with nature away from the muffling effects of tradition (Emerson, 1990). In order to see things as they are, we must stand apart from what we have been told and treat the evidence of our senses as unimpeachable.

The belief that human beings are prone to seeing what they want and need to see is also part of transactional analysis' psychodynamic heritage (Berne, 1966). It seems to me fairly self-evident that people can and do deceive themselves as matters of necessity whether we subscribe to the wider psychodynamic picture or not. Yet whilst our willingness to see things as they are is an important pre-condition for being able to do so, simply giving up the habit of self-deception doesn't in itself guarantee that we understand things. Sincerity is not enough to guarantee accuracy. When we believe that we see a green apple on the table, being sure that we are not deceiving ourselves is not in itself enough to guarantee that our belief is true. Reality testing only occurs when nobody could deny there actually is an apple on the table. Neither insightful honesty nor natural endowment automatically guarantees that we reach the best account of things possible.

I don't intend to argue that the contact between an ongoing stream of external stimuli and the firing of our nervous system have no part to play in forming our picture of the world, I simply wish to dislodge the unhelpful suggestion that basic sensory experience can underwrite our whole spectrum of original, creative, conceptually intricate thinking. Reality testing isn't just about perceiving colours and shapes. Our given capacity to pick out the distinction between red and green cannot explain complex existential and ethical mediations on how we should live. Awareness of sensory stimuli is simply not a ladder we can climb to this higher order thinking. There is something missing here which needs to be accounted for if we intend to fully grasp what reality testing might mean.

I propose to draw a meaningful distinction between this basic sensory ability to respond differentially to things that we share with animals, and the distinctively human capacity for reason and conceptual thinking that is developed and enhanced through the use of shared concepts. We are not just limited to understanding the sensory dimensions of that apple on the table, for the use of concepts in reasoning allows us to know it in ways the senses alone can't grasp (for example, artistically, scientifically, etc.). Wilfrid Sellars and John McDowell refer to these human conceptual capabilities in terms of occupying 'the space of reasons'. Accessing the space of reasons is enabled by our innate human rationality and the accompanying, linguistically enabled ability to explain and justify our use of particular concepts by using other concepts (Sellars et al., 1997; McDowell, 1996). As occupants of the space of reasons, we can penetrate the layers of reality more completely than bare perception alone allows.

The space of reasons is where we reach understanding about how ideas and concepts fit together. It is the complex product of social activity formed and maintained by other concept-using people engaged in the process of living intelligibly. Whilst our innate capacity to reason opens the door, our teachers and forebearers guide us in through words, teach us how and why they have been used as they have and lead us to understand how things fit together. A dog will yelp in pain if struck but will never be able to understand that what happened to it could be called 'wrong'. The concept of 'wrongness' can only be understood by a rational occupant of the space of reasons. The fact that I can feel pain and fear as any animal does are not enough to account for my distinctively human concepts of love, truth, justice, oppression, beauty, acceptability or identity which mingle with my basic biological endowments. These are ways of seeing and being that I can only develop from my ongoing conceptually enabled inter-actions with other reasonable people. The concepts and words we share with others, far from imposing themselves between us and the world as Berne thought, allow us to know it more deeply. Any definition of Adult reality testing must therefore include this socially-supported, conceptual understanding. Intan-gibles such as love, justice and oppression are no less part of reality than rocks and stones.

If our developed capacity to reason provides part of the bridge to the world, then access to reliable information provides another. A good portion of what we know about the world comes from what we have learnt from others, much of it useful and true. Our Parent ego-state is therefore not less in contact with reality purely by virtue of comprising inherited beliefs. After all, the people upon whom our Parent ego-states are modelled will all have their own equally sovereign, capable Adult ego-states. Unless we have specific grounds to condemn all others as incompetent or dishonest we surely cannot automatically deny their Adults the cognitive authority we hope to claim for ourselves. Social co-operation works on the basis that other people sometimes know some things better than us but are willing to pool and share their knowledge for mutual benefit.

It is neither possible nor always necessary for us to confirm by direct experi-ence things we have been taught and take on trust. Philosophers are now taking greater account of such 'testimony-based beliefs' as a valid form of knowledge in their own right even without direct, confirmatory experience (Coady, 1992; Lackey, 2008). Pathways to knowledge don't end with our eyes and ears, they fan out across conversations, books, newspapers, the media and the internet telling us of things outside the circumference of immediate experience. Our viewpoint is partially assembled from the words, ideas and stories of others. If the social world is 'good enough' then sufficient levels of resourcefulness, responsiveness, truthfulness and integrity ensure that reliable testimonial know-ledge is generated and circulated appropriately.

Social epistemology argues that a great deal of knowledge is held by collec-tives rather than located inside the skull (see Goldman & Whitcomb, 2011). Net-works of trust are fostered amongst people working to produce different kinds of knowledge so that what is discovered is pooled for the greater good (Gureckis & Goldstone, 2006). We rely on others to know how to heal our bodies and fix our cars, to provide us with advice on legal matters, conduct scientific research and manage our shared institutions, We also share stories of love, struggle, triumph and pain so that a collectively woven tapestry of experience might help us to understand ourselves better. We further enhance the sharing, storing, processing and transmission of information by creating objects such as books, computers and phones (Latour, 1993) to supplement and increase our ability to retain, access and process information. Against the generous credit we assign our Adults as inherently and sufficiently aware, we need to embrace the view that our capabilities are propped up and supplemented by a range of co-contributors.

Our ongoing dependence on others to provide us with knowledge leaves us in a predicament that I will call *cognitive vulnerability:* this refers to the fact that in order to develop the socially sophisticated outsight necessary to understand the world, we must take many shared beliefs on trust. Cognitive vulnerability is the price we pay for *cognitive opportunity* – the possibility of knowing more than our meagre individual experience grants us. If cognition is distributed in this way (Clark & Chalmers, 1998) then self-and-world has a more expansive world-view than it would have alone: the price is some uncertainty about how to distinguish between what I am sure of and what I must grasp on blind faith. The precariousness of trust threatens awareness from the outside in the same way that self-deception does from the inside. We cannot plausibly opt out of shared knowledge but the enlarged awareness it enables may be cracked apart by lies and inaccuracies that we are blind to.

Acknowledging the sheer scale of the Adult's cognitive vulnerability can induce a vertiginous sliding into the opposite conclusion – that we can no longer trust anything we believe. It may seem as though our knowing Adult can no longer emerge from under the shadow cast by a voluminous Parent of borrowed and inherited knowledge. I'm not proposing that we catastrophise unnecessarily. There is always enough native ability and social co-operation for us not to stumble around blindly. It's more that the kind of social and political outsight this book is concerned with is particularly vulnerable. A resourceful worldview stitches together a wealth of experiences, stories and knowledge into an intricate whole, but it binds together so many inherited strands that it is singularly dependent upon the conditions of the good enough world being in place. With effort, luck, the compass of reason and direct experience plus a few good souls in whom we have established trust, we can often keep our grip on things. Things may be bad, but they are rarely completely hopeless.

Neurology, reason and honesty are preconditions; they take us closer to how things are, but they cannot alone guarantee that we see the world as it is. The Adult's native capabilities are not enough to get a grip on things during those times when the world fails to co-operate with our efforts to understand it. Consider a scenario where a person believes their partner is loving and faithful but we have independent evidence (not available to the person themselves) that the partner is having an affair and plans to terminate the relationship. Such a person lives in a world where their description of things is that they are loved and cherished. That such a belief is false is unrelated to cognitive impairment or script. The person is not in contact with reality because someone has induced them to live under a false description of things. If we observe this person we are unlikely to conclude that they are cathecting anything other than their Adult, but if an Adult ego-state is definitionally in contact with reality then our theory cannot currently explain what is happening here. It would suggest that an Adult ego-state being in contact with reality isn't just a psychological phenomenon, it is an emergent, contextual state of affairs of which our individual, psychological endowments are only a part.

Clinical vignette

Ricky goes round in circles of self-criticism. He can't see a way out. In thinking about how differently Ricky and I understand the notion of boredom, I acknow-ledge that our encounter is taking place across a divide of culture, social class and life experience. I take seriously that his community has their way of doing things and mine has its own but I worry that Ricky's world lacks the resourcefulness necessary for him to live fully. I wonder how it would feel to initiate him respect-fully into the resourcefulness of my world, one where the twitching of his body denotes wasted promise rather than a failing of character.

Ricky views my efforts to offer a counter-point to his Parent condemnations with understandable suspicion. He simultaneously understands and does not under-stand that he is bored, as though he gets the idea in two dimensions rather than three. He cannot quite reconcile it with his sense of how things are. At least his mother's view that his difficulties are the result of immaturity are compatible with his worldview and offer a path to a known future, however unhappy. He swings between interest in and rejection of what I am offering. Over time we revisit a string of early memories to see if boredom plays a part. He begins to understand that at home and at school nobody ever had the time to see him for what he could be, merely for what they needed him to be – inobtrusive and unambitious. He begins to understand himself as capable as he flips between new, unsustainable bursts of optimism and bouts of clinging to old certainties. In the middle, a new curiosity about how things can be different begins to stick.

Conclusion

I have ended not quite rediscovering the Parent ego-state as the chapter title promised for what I have engaged in may perhaps be more accurately described as making a case for a redefinition. Perhaps one reason ego-state theory has failed to converge is because we think we have all been trying to explain the same phenomena when all the time our disagreements have followed inevitably from different starting definitions. The argument made here therefore has taken the form 'this is what I think we should mean when we say Parent and Adult ego-states'. It's a redefinition that I hope will be vindicated by its usefulness and persuasiveness rather than its capacity to bind prior theories together.

Our usual certainties have been scrambled. We do not quite know where our worldviews begin and shared beliefs end. Whilst never without guile and reason, we can never be completely sure which shared beliefs drag us into error and which expand our knowing. Our given biological and rational endowments are necessary but not sufficient to guarantee awareness. We cannot retreat to our usual observational markers to tell the ego-states apart for there is nothing there to tell us if we are more or less in contact with reality.

Our reliance on notions of inside and outside, of yours and mine to clarify the identity and function of our Parent and Adult ego-states has been less successful than we might have hoped. My solution is to suggest we move instead to questions of what I will call *authority*. Thinking and acting with authority refers to an ability to use, explain, manipulate and justify ideas, either shared or original, to navigate the world as competently as those whose beliefs we share. It doesn't mean we have to be supremely separate or original, merely that we have reached a place where nothing is concealed and where nobody stands above us.

Defining awareness and identity as founded on separation is therefore neither possible nor necessary. If Adult awareness emerges from the shared fabric of the social then being an Adult cannot be attributed solely to our innate capabilities: it isn't just in the head, it's part of the world. Authority always stands on the shoulders of others, an emergent by-product, a gift of good enough circumstances. Once they are 'our' ideas as well, we have the authority to revise them in the light of new experiences. I suggest that authority might usefully replace the concept of awareness in Berne's definition of autonomy.

Parent beliefs are defined precisely by the absence of authority. It's not that Parent beliefs are necessarily wrong, it's that they turn us into ventriloquist's dummies, the mouth pieces for ideas we can use competently but subordinately: we have no opportunity to test or revise them. Authority is a matter of degrees, particularly where what we are trying to accomplish entails uncommon knowledge. As such, distinguishing our Parent and Adult ego-states may not always be easy. Since nobody knows everything, authority doesn't presume anything as grand as ultimate contact with reality it just means we are no less fallible than anyone else. There was once a time when everyone falsely thought the world was flat; it would be remarkably ungenerous of us to conclude that nobody who once thought that had a functioning Adult. No one can guarantee that tomorrow new ways of seeing the world won't break through. Authority is simply the best that can be managed today.

Binding the various ideas proposed across this book so far, I therefore propose the following new definition of what it means to be in our Adult ego-state *Our Adult ego-state is the emergent product of a confluence between our innate capacity to think, a resourceful frame of reference, a personal disposition to be accurate and sincere, and shared cognitive resources which underwrite the authority to reach the best view of the world currently possible.* Against this, a new definition for the Parent ego-state must be correspondingly carved out. *Our Parent ego-state is the emergent product of the successful functioning of our innate capacity to think and where efforts to be accurate and sincere may also be present, but under social conditions where, due to deficits in our current frame of reference and the conditions necessary for a good enough world, we cannot hold beliefs in full authority.*

These definitions complete the move away from conceiving of ego-states in terms of inside and out, reality testing or self-deception, and show how the concept of authority can take their place. We are always selves without borders but this is no impediment to us emerging distinctively from the background of shared beliefs in instances of authority under the right conditions. Parent ego-states mire us in a 'your truth' position, capable but always subordinate. Adult ego-states represent the achievement of an 'our truth' positions where we take our place amongst others as a capable equal.

The previously secure assumption that ego-states should always be linked to observable changes in behaviour or shifts in the texture of experience, the only constant in a theoretical landscape of disagreement, does not it seems prove sufficient to bind the varying uses of the theory together (though I happily acknowledge that these tell-tale markers will often be present). If my new definitions hold, then the Parent ego-state can only be identified from a position where we come to realise that there is a better way of seeing things.

The Parent ego-state is identified either from the outside or in hindsight. The sporadic achievement of authority allows us to glimpse that we were once living subordinately under the shadow of someone else's description of the world all along but unable to perceive the restrictions. It was only ever 'your truth' never 'our truth' as we thought. The social realities underpinning cognitive vulnerability means that the Parent ego-state is a permanent part of our psychological landscape. Its scope can be reduced but omniscience will always be out of reach. Autonomy and authority are not achieved once and kept forever, they are hard fought accomplishments fraught with peril. This is the price and privilege of our shared existence as we navigate the flux of the ever-changing world.

References

Bennett, M.R., Hacker. P.M.S. (2003) *Philosophical Foundations of Neuroscience.* Malden, MA: Blackwell.

Berne, E. (1961) *Transactional Analysis in Psychotherapy.* London: Souvenir Press.

Berne, E. (1963) *The Structure and Dynamics of Organisations and Groups.* New York: Grove Press.

Berne, E. (1964) *Games People Play.* London: Penguin.

Berne, E. (1966) *Principles of Group Treatment.* New York: Grove Press.

Chambers, D. (2012) *A Sociology of Family Life: Change and Diversity in Intimate Relationships.* Cambridge: Polity.

Clark, A., Chalmers, D.J. (1998) The Extended Mind. *Analysis,* 58, 7–19.

Clarkson, P. (1992) *Transactional Analysis Psychotherapy: An Integrative Approach.* London: Routledge.

Coady, C.A.J. (1992) *Testimony: A Philosophical Study.* Oxford: Oxford University Press.

Cornell, W.F. (2002) Babies, brains and bodies: somatic foundations of the Child Ego-state. In C. Sills, H. Hargaden, Eds, *Ego-states.* London: Worth Publishing, 28–54.

Cornell, W.F. (2015) Ego-states in the Social Realm: Reflections on the Theories of Pio Scilligo and Eric Berne. *Transactional Analysis Journal*, 45 (3), 191–199.

Cornell, W.F., de Graaf, A., Newton, T., Thunnissen, M., Eds (2016) *Into TA: A Comprehensive Textbook on Transactional Analysis.* London: Karnac.

Corsaro, W.A. (2005) The Sociology of Childhood. 2nd edn. Thousand Oaks, CA: Pine Forge.

Dewey, J. (1922) *Human Nature and Conduct: An Introduction to Social Psychology.* Reprint 2007. New York: Cosimo.

Drego, P. (1983) The Cultural Parent. *Transactional Analysis Journal*, 13 (4), 224–227.

Emerson, R.W. (1990) *Ralf Waldo Emerson: A Critical Edition of His Major Works.* Edited by R. Poirier. Oxford: Oxford University Press.

Erskine, R.G., Clarkson, P., Goulding, R.L., Groder, M.G., Moiso, C. (1988) Ego-state theory: Definitions, descriptions, and points of view. *Transactional Analysis Journal*, 18 (1), 6–14.

Erskine, R.G. (2002) Resolving Intrapsychic Conflict: Psychotherapy of Parent Ego-states. in C. Sills, H. Hargaden, Eds, *Ego-states.* London: Worth Publishing, 1–27.

Erskine, R.G. (2015) *Relational Patterns, Therapeutic Presence: Concepts and Practice of Integrative Therapy.* London: Karnac.

Fowlie, H. (2005) Confusion and Introjection: A model for Understanding the Defensive Structures of the Parent and Child Ego-states. *Transactional Analysis Journal*, 35 (2), 192–204.

Gildebrand, K. (2002) 'An Introduction to the Brain and the Early Development of the Child Ego-state', in Sills, C., Sills, H., Hargaden, Eds, *Ego-states.* London: Worth Publishing.

Goldman, A.L., Whitcomb, D., Eds (2011) *Social Epistemology: Essential Readings.* Oxford: Oxford University Press.

Gopnik, A. (2009) *The Philosopher Baby: what Children's Minds tell us about Truth, Love & the Meaning of Life.* London: The Bodley Head.

Goulding, R.L., Goulding, M. (1978) *The Power is in the Patient: A TA/Gestalt Approach to Psychotherapy.* San Francisco: TA Press.

Gureckis, T.M., Goldstone, R.L. (2006) Thinking in Groups. *Pragmatics and Cognition*, 14 (2), 293–311.

Hargaden, H., Sills, C. (2002) *Transactional Analysis: A Relational Perspective.* Hove: Routledge.

Harré, R., Gillett, G. (1994) *The Discursive Mind.* Thousand Oaks, CA: Sage.

Harré, R. (Ed.) (1986) *The Social Construction of Emotion.* Oxford: Basil Blackwell.

Harré, R. (1998) *The Singular Self.* London: Sage.

Harré, R., Parrott, W.G., Eds., (1996) *The Emotions: Social, Cultural and Biological Dimensions.* London: Sage.

Harré, R. (2010) 'Social sources of mental content and order', in L. Van Langenhove, Ed., *People and Societies: Rom Harré and Designing the Social Sciences.* London: Routledge, 121–150.

Heathcote, A. (2010) Eric Berne's development of ego-state theory: Where did it all begin and who influenced him? *Transactional Analysis Journal*, 40 (3), 254–260.

Jamieson, L. (1988) *Intimacy: Personal Relationships in Modern Societies.* Cambridge: Polity.

Kennedy-Moore, E., Watson, J.C. (1999) *Expressing Emotion: Myths, Realities and Therapeutic Strategies.* New York: Guildford Press.

Kohlberg, L. (1987) *Child Psychology and Childhood Education: A Cognitive: Developmental View.* New York: Longman.

Lackey, J. (2008) *Learning from Words: Testimony as a Source of Knowledge.* Oxford: Oxford University Press.

Lackoff, G., Johnson, M. (1980) *Metaphors We Live By.* Chicago: University of Chicago Press.

Lackoff, G., Johnson, M. (1999) *Philosophy in the Flesh: The Embodied Mind and its Challenges to Western Thought.* New York: Basic Books.

Laplanche, J., Pontalis, J.B. (1973) *The Language of Psychoanalysis.* Translated from French by D. Nicholson-Smith. New York: Norton.

Latour, B. (1993) *We Have Never Been Modern.* Translated from French by C. Porter. Cambridge, MA: Harvard University Press.

McDowell, J. (1996) *Mind and World.* Cambridge, MA: Harvard University Press.

Mead, G.H. (2015) *Mind, Self and Society.* Edited by C.W. Morris. Chicago: University of Chicago Press.

Mohr, G. (2016) *Ego and Mindfulness: New Transactional Analysis.* Berlin: Pro Business.

Moiso, C. (1979) The social parent and the adaptation impasse. In C. Moiso, Ed., *TA in Europe.* Rome, Italy: EATA Books, 168–172.

Moursund, J.P., Erskine, R.G. (2004) *Integrative Psychotherapy: The Arts and Science of Relationship .* Pacific Grove, CA: Thomson: Brooks/Cole.

Music, G. (2017) *Nurturing Natures: Attachment and Children's Emotional, Socio-cultural and Brain Development.* 2nd edn. Abingdon: Routledge.

Oller-Vallejo, J. (1997) Integrative Analysis of Ego-state Models. *Transactional Analysis Journal*, 27 (4) 290–294.

Perls, F.S. (1969) *Ego, Hunger and Aggression: A Revision of Freud's Theory and Method.* Gouldsboro, ME: Gestalt Press.

Piaget, J. (1959) *The Language and Thought of the Child.* 3rd edn. Translated from French by M. Gabain, R. Gabain. London: Routledge.

Putnam, H. (1994) Sense, Nonsense, and the Senses: An Inquiry into the Powers of the Human Mind. *The Journal of Philosophy*, 91 (9), 445–517.

Rath, I. (1993) Developing a Coherent Map of Transactional Analysis Theories. *Transactional Analysis Journal*, 23 (4), 201- 215.

Schafer. R. (1976) *A New Language for Psychoanalysis.* New Haven: Yale University Press.

Schafer, R. (1983) *The Analytic Attitude.* New York: Basic Books.

Schmuckler, D. (1991) Transference and transactions: Perspectives from developmental theory, object relations, and transformational processes. *Transactional Analysis Journal*, 21 (3), 127–135.

Searle, J.R. (1998) *Mind, Language and Society: Philosophy in the Real World.* New York: Basic Books.

Sellars, W., Rorty, R., Brandom, R. (1997) *Empiricism and the Philosophy of Mind.* Cambridge, MA: Harvard University Press.

Steiner, C. (1974) *Scripts People Live: Transactional Analysis of Life Scripts.* New York: Grove Press.

Stern, D.N. (1985) *The Interpersonal World of the Infant.* New York: Basic Books.

Stewart, I. (2001) Ego-states and the Theory of Theory: The Strange Case of the Little Professor. *Transactional Analysis Journal*, 31 (2), 133–147.

Stewart, I., Joines, V. (2012) *TA Today*. 2nd edn. Melton Mowbray: Lifespace Publishing.

Summers, G., Tudor, K. (2000) Co-creative Transactional Analysis. *Transactional Analysis Journal*, 30 (1), 23–40.

Trautmann, R.L., Erskine, R.G. (1981) Ego-state Analysis: A Comparative View. *Transactional Analysis Journal*, 11 (2), 178–185.

Tudor, K. (2003) 'The neo-psyche: the integrating Adult ego-state' in C. Sills, H. Hargaden, Eds, *Ego-states*. London: Worth.

Vygotsky, L. (1962) *Thought and Language*. Translated from Russian by E. Hanfmann, G. Vakar. Cambridge, MA: MIT Press.

Vygotsky, L (1978) *Mind and Society: Development of Higher Psychological Processes*. Translated from Russian by M. Cole. Cambridge, MA: Harvard University Press.

White, J.M., Klein, D.M. (2008) *Family Theories*. 3rd ed. Los Angeles: Sage.

White, T. (1988) The Two Ego-state Model. *Western Pacific Association of Transactional Analysis Bulletin*, 1, 45–55.

Winnicott, D.W. (1964) *The Child, The Family and the Outside World*. London: Penguin.

Wittgenstein, L. (1953) *Philosophical Investigations*. 2nd Edn. Translated from German by G.E.M. Anscombe. Oxford: Blackwell.

Wittgenstein, L. (1980) *Remarks on the Philosophy of Psychology, Vol. 1*. Edited by G.E.M. Anscombe & G.H. Wright. Translated from German by G.E.M. Anscombe. Chicago: University of Chicago Press.

Part II

THEORETICAL CONTEXTS

4

COMPETITOR THEORIES AND
A PRAGMATIC ALTERNATIVE

The account I am assembling of self-and-world and a distinct type of psycho-logical distress (horizontal problems) associated with it shows the social penet-rating far deeper into the self than previous accounts allow for. For my conclusions to be not merely entertained but embraced, then some of transac-tional analysis' most steadfast and cherished ideas about people and their prob-lems will have to be called into question. Possible objections to such a move will have to be anticipated, taken seriously and respectfully answered. There is no unnecessary threat intended here. I believe the better parts of our familiar ideas will survive the cull and emerge stronger for the challenge.

These potential objections fall into two distinct positions, groupings of roughly compatible ideas which I believe will be readily recognisable to anyone who has undergone therapy training as a transactional analyst even if they have not been identified in this way before. People subscribing to the first of these positions may reject my ideas about inseparability from and dependence on the social as unnecessary and unduly pessimistic. They will believe clients are already endowed with the all that is necessary to successfully grow, change and solve their problems irrespective of their context. These objections are related to a particular psychological conception of what it means to be human. I shall refer to this position as 'the myth of internal sufficiency'.

The second position is rooted less in psychology and more in a certain philo-sophical and political ethos that I take to be typical, if unofficially so, of many people who train and work as therapists. People who occupy this second position may find themselves shifting uncomfortably at my mentions of truthfulness and reality testing and at my intimations that a therapist can make reasonable judge-ments about problems in social contexts not their own. They may be similarly resistant to my favourable mentioning of social co-operation, perhaps fearing an underhand way of shuffling people back into a conformist respecting of majority views irrespective of the personal consequences. I call this position 'liberal scepticism'.

The clustering of ideas that I am tracing here has not been previously named in this way. They cannot be illustrated by naming example texts. These positions are rather something abstracted and generalised from a host of individual sources. They won't feature exactly the same combination of elements each time they appear. I am tracing a loose cluster of ideas that often seem to appear together without being inextricably linked, a pervasive mood or ethos if you will. I make no claims that these positions accurately represent the various pivotal thinkers cited in their support, merely that they are commonly thought to do so by many in the profession. It is not a necessary precondition for a useful discussion that the considered phenomena are distinct and unchanging. I think I need do no more than say that these position are things I think people will recognise when I draw their attention to them. Objecting to my characterisation on one or two details will not necessarily refute my wider charge of a more general drift of thought whose course I would like to shift. My wider aim here is ultimately to show, point by point, an ethos which I think better suits the contextual thinking I am introducing and which might usefully supplant these two positions in a more general sense.

The myth of internal sufficiency

The myth of internal sufficiency encompasses two broad assumptions, the first of which is that there is some aspect of us which is either innate and pregiven and to which therapy seeks to bring out. In most versions of the myth this aspect pre-dates and escapes any socialising influence. It was pristine before the world sullied it and it properly resists full assimilation . Whatever the course of life there is always something that is uniquely, separately us.

The second assumption is that this innate, pre-social aspect of 'us', be it a precious grain of subjectivity, innate motivation, capacity to reason or unvanquishable spirit, if properly focused upon during therapy, is *sufficient* to inaugurate therapeutic change. The myth of internal sufficiency presumes a second myth which I call the myth of therapeutic facilitation. This is the belief that therapy is in the business of recognising, validating and encouraging the emergence of this separate, asocial 'already there' in the client without unnecessarily adding anything else to it. Therapy which embraces both these myths will strive for maximum sensitivity to what is already present in the client's experience, conscious or otherwise, and minimise the possibility of their own intrusion.

In stronger variants, the myth of internal sufficiency and the myth of facilitation place strong prohibitions in the way of approaches to psychological healing which are more directive or educative, which entail the client learning something from the world and which see experience as something made through new action and not necessarily discovered in the quiet, long-undisturbed corners of the self. It encourages reflexivity and internal exploration but not criticality and experimentation.

Outside of transactional analysis, the myth of internal sufficiency has had many manifestations. It can be found in the humanistic insistence that there is an organismic valuing process or a form of contact with unmediated experience which, if appropriately accessed, can act as a final court of appeal for what a person might think or do (see Perls, Hefferline & Goodman, 1951; Rogers, 1951; Tudor & Worrall, 2006). It is present in the psychodynamic assumption that insight into and acceptance of unconscious experience is the key to greater integration and awareness, or in the Freudian insistence we contain foundational drives towards love or life which strive for fulfilment (Mitchell & Black, 1995). It stands behind the idea, offered by very different thinkers, that there is such a thing as a 'true' or real self (Horney, 1937; Laing, 1959; Winnicott, 1960) which can be retrieved from the rubble of compromising socialisation.

The myth of internal sufficiency encourage us to focus on the person in isolation, to dig deeper, to squeeze the necessary meaning from what is in front of us, to peel back the surface and find the authentic thought, the hidden motive, the held back emotion and the long-thwarted potential: if not the organism then the unconscious, if not the unconscious then the body, a wellspring of unsullied, personal potential to tap and let loose. Focus closely and see every motion, every sigh as a trail of breadcrumbs which will lead us to back to the most genuine, rich and true about the person. Whilst the myth of internal sufficiency fits more easily with dynamic and humanistic therapies, CBT has its own weaker version of the myth, presuming that our capacity to reason, to reach the right answer to a problem if asked the right questions is enough for change (Ellis, 1994). Subtly steering us down a particular path, the myth of internal sufficiency almost always turns the conversation back to the experience of the self rather than outwards to an accounting for the world.

Transactional analysis has subscribed to the myth of internal sufficiency in three different ways which continue to be cited by contemporary practitioners. These are the notion of an innate Adult ability to reality test, the concept of physis and the free or natural Child. Each is eminently contestable and none are essential for the viability of the wider theory. I have already argued in Chapter 3 that our Adult capacity for reason and awareness is not enough in isolation to outweigh our cognitive vulnerability so I will not repeat my arguments here. I will simply re-iterate that where therapy aims to help people achieve better understanding and practices of living, this may actually require better socialisation rather than desocialisation.

The concept of physis, described as a naturally occurring tendency to grow which exists in all living things, appears too often in Berne's writings to be entirely ignored and not enough to persuade me that he was fully convinced of its viability, centrality or usefulness (Berne, 1968, 1972). His acknowledgement that he treats it as merely a speculative construct (see Berne, 1968, p. 99) has not prevented it from generating respectful subsequent mention (Barrow, 2014; Clarkson, 1992; Mellor, 2017; Piccinino, 2018), usually on the grounds that it might encourage us to take an optimistic view of human nature and of our client's change capacities.

I suspect Berne was compelled to find grounds for hope inside individuals because he was so broadly pessimistic about collectives. When you portray a standard maturational path as the relentless suffocation and deformation of your innate potential then it becomes entirely necessary to posit and champion an internal principle which might lead the fight back. Without the hope of physis riding to the rescue, the story goes, nothing would change and we would all be resigned to painful unthinking acquiescence.

The problem is that it isn't clear exactly what the growth associated with physis refers to, how we might usefully recognise it, and what its limits are. It's a theory that floats hazily above anything that might count as verification and therefore has little explanatory use. The bigger objection is that if we follow Berne in saying that our inherent growth capacity is stymied by something as flimsy and everyday as routinely unsympathetic parenting then physis can't really be described as a robust resource to draw upon (see Totton, 2010). Whilst many will concede that optimal growth only triumphs under certain conditions, if all we are really claiming is that people seem to be happier, healthier and able to make different choices in benign circumstances then it seems to me we are only making a fairly obvious observation which doesn't requires the existence of an esoteric underlying principle to explain it.

The concept of the free or natural Child, an early part of us which knows what it wants and acts free of external interference, draws upon the streak of Rousseauist Romanticism which runs through transactional analysis (Dalal, 2016). Although negative aspects of the free Child are noted (Stewart & Joines, 2012), most often the theory is a prelapsarian fantasy with our Child as an abandoned Eden, a pure, lost self to which we must return to become well. The free Child has fallen from favour somewhat in clinical transactional analysis alongside the functional model from which it is derived, but an inheritor theory prospers in the idea proposed by integrative and relational theorists that the rediscovery of early, unmet needs long lost to our awareness usefully returns us to a condition of self-awareness and full feeling. Here the idea that at some level we just know what we need is paramount. For both versions, the primal and presocial are always the most important, vital and true.

In packing the Child with useful attributes, Berne and his fellow humanists followed Freud in the radical democratisation of creativity (see Rieff, 1959). Now everyone supposedly has inside them untapped reservoirs of imagination that therapy can unleash. However charming this view is it conflates two very different notions of creativity. We should not confuse the uninhibited making of mud pies with the visionary aesthetic transformation of our sense of things which is the mark of real artistry (Bloom, 1973). We should not mistake the mere departure from norms with an intelligible, knowing and original reshaping of them. Children have not yet gained the ability to be creative in this latter sense and yet this is the kind of creativity that therapy usually requires. Instinctive rebellion has its appeal and occasional uses, but an original vision is what we really strive for.

The suggestion that we are born OK before being polluted by inevitable associations and innately endowed with the capacity to know our own wants inevitably burdens our early history and innate attributes with a responsibility they cannot bear alone. That children can distinguish between experiences they prefer and don't prefer, that they know without instruction to be satisfied when they are fed and tended, does not mean they are endowed with the cognitive sophistication necessary to make the kinds of responsible, complex, socially informed judgements necessary to determine how to live as an adult.

That we have more free, true or authentic selves was imported into, rather than found in, the consulting room. It is a consequence of viewing our clients through the lens of unquestioned, deep-rooted assumptions about the nature, values and entitlement of selfhood which represent the common inheritance of post-enlightenment Western societies. Modernity's challenge to religious authority with the simultaneous liquifying of the social fabric have left us free of higher constraint and with no one to answer to but ourselves (see Taylor, 1991). The self has moved into the place once occupied by God. There has become no more secure foundation or higher purpose than authenticity. Regarding people as capable and worthwhile by definition seems to me to represent an act of faith and generosity which none the less fails certain empirical tests. It is simply a currently persuasive story we tell ourselves, not an instance of revelation about how we really are. Its hold over us will vanish if we find better ways of talking about people.

I am not claiming that all ideas orbiting the myth of internal sufficiency are always without value. I take it that many clients do have something within their existing capacities, dispositions, knowledge and experience which might be usefully brought out in the service of relieving their distress. I am thrilled when clients seem to leap ahead, grasp the possibilities of change, become something that was previously beyond them but on a case-by-case basis I see no reason to presume that everyone is capable of this. Approaching our clients with expectation rather than hopeful realism risks overburdening them. Insisting upon the existence of physis, that people can change irrespective of circumstance and life experiences, that they are innately wise but have forgotten what they once knew risks setting struggling people up to fall short of our extravagant ideals for them.

Adopting a non-intrusive therapeutic stance out of faith in resources that people may not have cuts off the impetus to pursue outsight, gain new experience and learn something they don't know. It can also obscure the recognition that a change of circumstances rather than personal growth is what is really needed. The myth of internal sufficiency gets in the way of acknowledging our dependence and cognitive vulnerability, that we need the world to be good enough as a precondition of individual flourishing. We risk underestimating how much needs to be added to the client's resources, experience and worldview because our theory leads us to overestimate how much is already there (see Smail, 1996).

You cannot become the self you could be until you have been given a chance to know that certain ways of being and knowing are possible. If you think that what you already once were, your misplaced authenticity, is more important than what you have yet to become then you will look backwards and inwards rather

95

than outwards and forwards. We risk underestimating how much socialised, lived familiarity with certain ways of being is a precondition of us being able to see those things in ourselves. The danger of presuming that there is always another layer of the self to discover and tap into where the answers lies is that therapy swims around in ever decreasing circles, but never looks to widen the circumference of experience to embrace what has not yet been encountered and learned. We overpraise the seed and spend too little time thinking of the soil.

A therapy which embraces the myth of internal sufficiency sees the person's full potential as rather like an already-complete, beautiful portrait painting, locked up in a dingy basement. It takes therapy to be a process of undoing those locks, venturing into forgotten places, making it possible to recover the painting and bring it into the light. The contextual view adopted here regards potential as more like a room containing an easel, blank paper, brushes and paint. It would acknowledge that no painting was possible unless you possessed these materials but that the painting of who we are is incomplete in advance of experience. It sees potential not as a given but as a process, premised upon learning how to use the tools the world has given you as a precursor to knowing what you wanted to do with them. It would presume that learning to use the common conceptual resources provided by others was essential for becoming the selves necessary to thrive in the world as it is. It would take it that full growth and learning were unlikely to take place outside conditions of resourcefulness, responsiveness, truthfulness and integrity. Full credit for our achievements would belong properly to the self-and-world.

Finally, I cannot help but note that many people who espouse variations on the myth of internal sufficiency, who eulogise the return to pure, pre-social and separate states of being as the best path to therapeutic change, seem themselves to have greatly benefitted from reading a lot of books written by other people. •Having committed themselves to a vision of therapy as desirably non-intrusive because they need to conceive of a part of us unsullied by the world as our prized attribute, they are required by definition to dismiss the usefulness and necessity of learning in therapy even as they are themselves good, living examples of its transformative power.

In the final analysis, the myth of internal sufficiency is always shadowed by a fear of external intrusion, a fear which must presume our vulnerability even as we assert that we are strong. This apprehension has political resonance as well as psychological meaning. It is to the question of the political we must now turn.

Liberal scepticism

In as much as therapy professionals collectively can be said to have a common political ethos, then liberal scepticism is it. The term brings together two philosophical ideas which are taken to be complimentary though, as we will see, I think this is far from certain. Liberalism is a term laden with accrued meanings and associations but I am using it here in its most basic, standard sense to mean a political stance in favour of freedoms of expression, speech, association, action and (increasingly) individual and cultural identity which can be enjoyed to the extent that they do not curtail the liberty of others (Christman, 2018). Scepticism refers to a persistent strand of Western philosophy which treats certain dogmatic claims to knowledge with suspicion. Liberal scepticism fuses these two ideas by suggesting we can be *for* human liberty and dignity by being *against* certain kinds of ideas about truth and knowledge which are taken to stand in their way.

Liberal scepticism and the myth of internal sufficiency may not seem like natural bedfellows. I want to suggest they dovetail around the affirmation of what Isiah Berlin called negative liberty (Berlin, 1969). This can be understood as freedom made possible by things getting out of the way, the absence of constraint and convention (see Taylor, 1989). Many therapeutic ideas implicitly endorse this notion of negative liberty. Rid yourself of the need to see things as others do, overturn convention and claim the freedom to think and be as you were meant to be. Knock things down as a precursor to building yourself up.

In order to clear a space for this freedom, the liberal sceptic takes aim at a fairly standard list of targets. Colin Feltham has described the therapy profession's collective political mindset as 'a privileged leftwing, anti-positivist, pluralistic, romantic and re-enchantment stance heavily linked to continental philosophy and critical theory' (Feltham, 2014, p. 378). Truth, objectivity, science, capitalism, traditional identity categories and western cultural pre-eminence find themselves put to the sword in the service of a supposedly greater good.

All of these things are taken by the liberal sceptic to suffocate minority perspectives, both collective and individual. The further presumption is that happy consequences will automatically follow as a result of these things being criticised and cut down to size. Liberal scepticism certainly achieves some indirect good by making people more thoughtful and hesitant, but these gains come at a price. Trying to keep the baby from being thrown out with the bathwater, I contend that some of what is under fire here remains indispensable to personal and collective efficacy and social change.

There are three core ideas that I take to be essential to an understanding of liberal scepticism. The first is that there is no such thing as truth or objectivity merely a plurality of equivalent perspectives. The second is that the seemingly greater prestige, influence or prevalence of certain viewpoints results from inequities in power rather than due to their innate superiority. The third assumption, which proceeds inevitably from the first two, is that pluralism of both perspective and identity are virtuous and desirable by definition. Ideas which stand against these positions are therefore not merely disagreed with but condemned.

The liberal sceptic will often draw upon postmodern ideas in support of their arguments, though increasingly these ideas are now so prevalent that they are being used by people with minimal direct familiarity with the works first responsible for articulating them. I am unconvinced that the thinkers associated postmodernism (itself a maddeningly imprecise term) would consider their ideas well represented by liberal scepticism though I doubt this argument alone will persuade anyone to change course. However much of a departure from its philosophical antecedents liberal scepticism may represent, it has been a remarkably successful departure. It enjoys a momentum which has detached from its starting points. Each constituting strands of liberal scepticism therefore needs to be addressed on their own merits.

To paraphrase Mark Twain, reports of the death of truth, objectivity and science have been greatly exaggerated. Postmodern ideas have generally been ignored or ridiculed in science and strenuously contested within philosophy itself (see Haack, 2007; Nagel, 1997; Rosenberg, 2012; Scheffler, 1982). A more serious charge is that no major thinker linked with postmodernism has denied that our understandings of the world can be better or worse. Jean-Francois Lyotard, whose work on the postmodern is perhaps the best-known articulation of the movement, does not deny that science is often successful at testing predictions and describing specific phenomenon (Lyotard, 1984). The objection is to these achievements being used to catapult science to the status of a master narrative, the discipline that discloses the ultimate truth about the world. Science, it is claimed, can tell us how things work but it leaves questions of meaning and value untouched. Its province has been restricted but not demolished.

These are interesting though modest philosophical claims, but the liberal sceptic will tend to misinterpret them as having dramatic consequences for how we conduct our daily lives. They take it that once science and truth have been dethroned, if we have no solid bedrock of certainty beneath our feet, no 'god's eye view' from which to survey things from above, then it follows that what we think or say is never more than just perspective. At a stroke, radical egalitarianism seems to have been established. Unfortunately, nothing so grand has been argued. As Hilary Putnam clearly states, 'It is not the notion of truth that has let us down, but rather a particular conception of how that notion is to be philosophically founded (and improved)' (Putnam, 1994, p. 265).

Whatever the outcome of philosophical conversations about how truth might be understood, Putnam reminds us that the ordinary business of sifting better from worse accounts of the world continues uninterrupted. Postmodernism doesn't take it that a client's belief that they will jump out of a nine-storey window and fly is as likely to pass the test of experience as the concerned clinician who insists that they will fall. When liberal sceptics require open-heart surgery, they presumably want the scalpel to be wielded by a trained and experienced surgeon because they correctly believe the surgeon will have knowledge likely to lead to a better outcome. In Charles Pierce's words – 'let us not pretend to doubt in philosophy what we do not doubt in our hearts' (Peirce, 1868, p. 140).

Postmodern ideas don't have the kind of leverage over our daily lives that the liberal sceptic hopes to find in them because philosophy simply 'leaves everything as it is' (Wittgenstein, 1953, p. 49; see also Rorty, 1984, 1989, 1999). These ideas are best thought of as a conversation amongst professional philosophers, not an order to uproot our functioning worldview. The mistake here may be an honest one for as Baggini notes, in doggedly straining to get their ideas about truth right, philosophers may have unwittingly generated the impression there were grounds to be suspicious about it (Baggini, 2017). There was no intention for non-philosophers to misuse these arguments to doubt the possibility of getting to grips with the world. The routine business of sifting better beliefs from worse, however imperfect, necessarily continues. The liberal sceptic celebrates a revolution which has never happened.

There is an important reason that the liberal sceptic necessarily clings to these unsuccessful arguments. Having taken themselves to have pulled truth up by the roots they can then bring into play their second concern, that it is power rather than truth which is really at stake in our conversations and disputations about how things are. Whilst the liberal sceptic often uses the word power either in a general sociological sense to mean a greater opportunity to pursue freely chosen ends (Bauman & May, 2001) or to designate coercive interactions between people with unequal means, the figure most often cited in support is Michel Foucault (see Foucault, 1984). Whilst a case can be made that his complex ideas are sometimes misrepresented by liberal scepticism, the one aspect of Foucault's arguments which is strongly taken up is that power is shadowy and ubiquitous: it hides everywhere, including the most inconspicuous places. Foucault is less interested in the obvious power of physical force, money or governments or even the soft power of social prestige. His main concern is the subterranean ways that language and discourse produce and form us into ourselves outside of aware-ness. It's easy to understand how such ideas have caught the attention of a profession whose primary currency is words.

If power gets everywhere then even the deepest certainties about who we are and what we believe are subject to suspicion. Han makes a similar argument when he claims that power is stronger when invisible, when it creeps inside to persuade us that something else's will is really our own (Han, 2019). For the liberal sceptic references to truth are just the hidden whisperings of power, always tugging us at the end of invisible strings, making us into the fools of history. This should be a despairing realisation, yet the liberal sceptic curiously embraces these conclusions as grounds for hope. If power is everywhere then it can be evoked at any given moment to overthrow and delegitimise beliefs which stand in their way. Claiming to see through the top layer of the world to the secret organising principles underneath, the liberal sceptic emits the rallying cry of resistance, greeting every unwanted assertion by dismissing it as really some-thing else in disguise. Since nothing can fully escape suspicion then any claim to authority over another's perspective is instantly razed to the ground. Knock truth off its pedestal and all opinion rises to equal prominence.

Whatever its seductive appeal, invoking power in this way creates as many problems as it solves. Whilst sensitivity to questions of power can bring to our attention the ways in which even seemingly innocent interactions can be shaped by forces outside of immediate awareness, Richard Rorty argues that Foucault tends to gothicise the concept of power, making it so pervasive that we can never fully know we have escaped (Rorty, 1998). Aiming at liberation, the liberal sceptic condemns us to live in a state of permanent suspicion, mute and endlessly penitent, unable to escape the dread that we are power's unwitting accomplice. Power assumes the position vacated by original sin, a first pollution from which we can never be fully cleansed no matter how hard we try.

At the level of clinical practice this often results in a relentless scouring of our counter-transference in the vain hope of breaking free from positional bias. In disagreements, all knowledge-claims are simply turned into struggle, a cynical 'well-you-would-say-that-wouldn't-you?' which pre-emptively destroys the prospect of agreement, progress or learning as too tainted to contemplate. In trying to show that power is everywhere, Foucault's adherents may have inadvertently led to an assumed equivalence or levelling down between arguments (Sahlins, 2002).

Liberal scepticism doesn't just risk collapsing distinctions between degrees of power, it also fails to distinguish between power and coercion or violence. Power is treated as a yah boo word, used to generate an immediate recoil. It's always written about as something to be reduced or confronted, never used in the right spirit (for example, see Loewenthal, 2015). This sometimes leads to a peculiar moral panic where practitioners are chastised for insensitivity to power imbalances in the therapy room whilst the more obvious concern should be that therapists simply aren't powerful enough to counterbalance the vast array of external forces bearing down on our client's lives. Scared and repulsed by power in any form, liberal scepticism sometimes risks prohibiting the little good therapists may sometimes do by sharing what power they have.

If the liberal sceptic has turned away from acknowledging these flaws in their position then it often seems to be because they feel assured that their efforts will result in good outcomes. It appears they imagine that these are arguments favouring their own chosen ends. The liberal sceptic ultimately lifts their own moral vision of pluralism, alternative ways of knowing and equivalence of perspective above the fray into a certainty that they deny other ideas. It is as though they somehow believe that the corrosive acid of postmodern scepticism can be selectively poured over only the things they don't like such as capitalism, patriarchy, cultural imperialism and truth claims and yet the value and integrity of the minority viewpoints and identities they savour will somehow miraculously be spared (see Latour, 2004). They alone claim to have spotted the subtle operations of power without specifying how if power is everywhere their own verdict on things escapes the finger of suspicion (see Habermas, 1985). Sometimes it can appear that what is being claimed is simply a relativism of convenience.

Aiming at liberation, liberal scepticism collapses into incoherence and political impotence. If everything falls under suspicion, if all becomes simply perspective then what means do oppressed and marginalised groups have to make strong moral and political claims for change? There is no point in disinterring hidden injuries in the disenfranchised if in doing so you destroy the only means of pleading with the wider community for a better, fairer world. Oppressed groups don't need an escape into multiple realities, they need a more just common world. As Terry Eagleton has argued, a welcoming stance of this-is-my-viewpoint-and-this-is-yours only really works for those who don't really need much to change (Eagleton, 1996; see also MacKinnon, 2000). It would be very naïve to assume that winning a moral argument automatically translates into social improvement but without the force of the stronger claim there is no hope at all. There is a reason that totalitarian societies do the most to destroy the very possibility of truth claims. They understand well that this is amongst the best ways to ensure that nothing changes.

There are good intentions mixed in with this theoretical muddle. As Barbara Held has argued, therapists often feel they *should* endorse something like liberal scepticism because they are trained to prize the perspective of each client as unique and to provide space for quieted voices to be heard (Held, 1995). Here liberal scepticism crosses over with the myth of internal sufficiency for the latter has faith that something important is set free in the act of overturning constraints. There is an almost inevitable slippage in liberal scepticism from 'there's no such thing as truth' to 'you have to take *my* truth seriously'– an unworkable, contradictory starting point. The aim must be to show the liberal sceptic that their cherished goals of freedom and dignity are in no way incompatible with some of the things they seek to overturn.

Perhaps liberal scepticism has succeeded so well because people hear its more objectionable claims as close to more reasonable ones. Suggesting that truth is possible doesn't imply that it is self-evident or easily reached. The world does not want for confusion, ignorance and self-serving dogmatism. Whilst we may reach consensus in science, it's hard to argue convincingly that ethics can achieve much more than cultural pluralism (see MacIntyre, 1988). Amidst such uncertainty, arriving at the best available viewpoint can feel like such an onerous, sensitive task that it's very tempting to give up and endorse subjectivism. Imbalances in power do exist and can often be shown to sometimes account for the way things work out. Whether one subscribes to postmodern philosophy or not, contemporary existence seems to be characterised by flux and value pluralism. Humility in the face of complexity and difference can seem the only acceptable alternatives to nihilism.

Acknowledging these complexities should be enough to find common ground with liberal scepticism and yet I detect a further underlying concern within the position, an overwhelming dread of imposing a viewpoint on others (see Brennan, 2006). This fear of violating the requirements of pluralism emerges from a confluence between the myth of internal sufficiency and a looming post-colonial guilt around the sins of the recent and not-so-recent past which haunts contemporary Western thinking (see Bruckner, 2010). The liberal sceptic is often increasingly preoccupied not merely with imposition on individuals but on cultures and identity categories, a sensitivity which unmistakably echoes recognisable contemporary political developments.

We find ourselves in a time of reckoning. As Cornel West argues, the rise of postmodern thought cannot be separated from the painful and necessary requirements by Western nations to come to terms with their own national decline and their historic maltreatment of people both within and outside their own borders (West, 1989). The therapy world seems to be engaged its own parallel process of reflection and regret about its historic insensitivity to the specific needs of marginal identities. The moral sting of these past failures raises the apprehension that if we have been so very wrong before then every effort must be made to ensure that we are never wrong again. Dreading the future verdict of history, everything must be questioned, caution becomes synonymous with capitulation and nothing of the old order must be left standing. Perhaps best summarised by the radical feminist Audre Lorde's pronouncement that 'The Master's tools will never dismantle the master's house' (Lorde, 1984, p. 110) the liberal sceptic will often believe that only a total separation from the old order is enough. Here is the underlying moral imperative driving the remorseless sniffing out of power in every corner.

The greater willingness to challenge, question and dissolve old certainties and inequalities has often resulted in a benign culture of thoughtfulness and respect and a decline in unnecessary hatred and exclusion. It also sometimes unwittingly tips over into moral and political paralysis over what to do for the best, inadvertent nihilism and too often a kind of regrettable faux-Socratic vanity where the more you find to doubt and blame in yourself the wiser and more virtuous you must be. Restricting its accusations to an approved list of villains, liberal scepticism is often blind to injuries other than those inflicted by the hands of the obviously powerful (Dalal, 2000). It prods us into a questioning but holds back from offering better answers about what we might say and do to make a better world.

If liberal scepticism were as enthusiastic about freedom as it takes itself to be, it would acknowledge that the positive freedom *to* be and do which springs from resourcefulness, responsiveness and truthfulness is as crucial as negative freedom *from* constraint, tradition and universalism. Intent only on hacking down rather than creating, the liberal sceptic is compelled to fall back on the myth of internal sufficiency, that we need no more than to be ourselves unconfined. In doing so they cross over from the acceptable view that we have no transcendent foundation from which to compare the relative merits of viewpoints to the unwarranted conclusion that we are certain all cultures or individual perspectives are equal valid. The liberal sceptic ironically ends up with the kind of universal grand narrative they claim to denounce.

Informed respect for differences across identities and cultures engenders a spirit of humility, curiosity and tolerance to which therapy should usefully aspire, but granting respect pre-emptively to all cultures runs dangerously close to denying any meaningful distinction between oppressive and non-oppressive social formations. Claiming that all social forms deserve respect as they currently are must imply that a given social group would always have been exactly as they are irrespective of circumstance. Yet if the term oppression is to mean anything at all, it must designate a successful thwarting of people's collective self-understanding, actions and cultural formation. The whole point about oppression is to eliminate it, not mistakenly celebrate it as the fullest expression of the general will (see Michaels, 2006).

Are we really willing to say that cultures formed under conditions where people are denied access to information, terrorised out of authentic political participation and fear the secret police knocking at the door for expressing the wrong opinion are worth equivalent respect to open, free and politically responsive societies? As therapists our calling is surely to respect people for what they could have been had the world not been against them and do the best we can to provide the means for them to become those selves and communities.

Fear of cultural intrusion needs to be tempered with the opposite concern that we won't intrude enough to be useful for people who need to escape their current sense of how things are rather than accommodate themselves to it. Not all intervention is haunted by the ghost of colonialism. A therapist committed to liberal scepticism who sat opposite a client and assumed that the cultural divide in their perspectives could not and should not ever be bridged would be denying that they could ever distinguish between more or less useful things to say to that person. This is a pitiful scenario, a therapist not enabled by liberal scepticism but paralysed by indecision and pre-emptive guilt about what they might do wrong. We might usefully remind ourselves here that digging away the ground of better arguments beneath your feet is not the pathway to progress, it just leaves you stuck in a big hole. I struggle to see how someone who had fully embraced such a position could practice with any efficacy or integrity.

The biblical story of Babel, a once common people driven apart by difference was once thought to be a tragedy; now it has been recast as the pride of our age. All identity differences are now defined in terms of Western explorers discovering lost tribes in the Amazonian rain forest, stark and pure difference without common ground (Wolin, 2016). Yet most cultures and identities we encounter in our practice are mongrel and none are purebloods. All are formed across time through multiple interactions with neighbouring cultures. All cultures represent responses to circumstances, nothing remains identical in the face of change. The identity categories we hold definitive may themselves one day melt into the air and reform in ways we cannot yet imagine. In this regard, if nothing else, the liberal sceptic often isn't postmodern enough. Liberal scepticism leaves us in a state of confusion, tearing down some of the things like truth which we might need and tiptoeing reverentially around social formations we might usefully approach in a critical spirit.

Pragmatic solutions

We need to achieve by other means what the myth of internal sufficiency and liberal scepticism aim at, to respect their aspirations and avoid their pitfalls. We want neither to underestimate nor overestimate what people are already capable of, but we must balance our faith in individuals with an appropriate hope in collectives. In order to understand and sometimes transform the world we need to steer between the complacency and passivity of dogmatism and the resignation of cynicism. We need a picture of socially-situated personhood which is neither infallible nor powerless. Sometimes we may underestimate how far power reaches into our viewpoint, but we must recall that power in the right hands is a precondition for change.

There is no picture of a self which is not also a picture of how it responds to the world. Any new ethos must embrace truthfulness, the irreducible interest we have in differentiating between better and worse ways of seeing things. Truthfulness underwrites the authority our Adult requires to climb out from under Parental subordination. At the same time, we will never be omniscient so the Parent will always be with us. Our ethos should acknowledge, however begrudgingly, the social nature of knowledge and the fallibility and opportunity that accompanies this.

The picture of selfhood I am outlining derives very approximately from the general lessons of pragmatist philosophy (see Brandom, 2002; Bernstein, 2010; Colapietro, 1989; Dewey, 1922; James & Gunn, 2000; Peirce, 1958; Putnam, 1995; Unger, 2007). As with most approaches to philosophy, it is characterised by a common body of ideas which its architects spend their time mostly disagreeing about. At its most general level, pragmatism is best summarised as a theory of knowledge which branched out into conceptions of education and democracy (Misak, 2000). It replaces a notion of truth as being in touch with reality, of the deciphering of God's handwriting and substitutes it for an earthbound, somewhat Darwinian picture of situated individuals sifting and refining their beliefs in the light of new experience. There are no infallible foundations, just what seems to be the best way to think given our abilities and histories. Self-and-world is cognitively vulnerable but honest experience is the grit in the pearl of reform; it keeps it engaged, persuasive and improving. We recognise that tomorrow's experience may overturn today's conclusion, but this does not exempt us from doing our best to get things right now.

The myth of internal sufficiency and liberal scepticism mistrust this sense of selves as situated. The former relegates the world to a background role by insisting on individual exceptionalism; the latter is suspicious of broad commonalities as often coercive and the enemy of pluralism. Socialised and situated always, I take that we have no choice but to simply start from where we start from enmeshed in place, relationships and culture. We begin with what is shared and inherited from others and either accept or develop the authority to move beyond them. This requires engagement. There is no delete button to eradicate the social or any aspect of ourselves which render it unnecessary.

As a pragmatist interested in the resolution of horizontal problems, I'm not convinced about returning to a 'true' or 'authentic' self and more interested in how we can think with more authority to better meet today's world. There is less harm in minimising questions about correctness of viewpoint when we are working with vertical problems since we are helping people to understand and accept themselves. The resolution of horizontal problems requires workable outsight. Our minds have to have successfully got a grip on how things are. Only a more accurate, persuasive, coherent, justifiable story about the world can settle our minds, sharpen our purposes, formulate better social organisations and enhance solidarity. This pragmatic stance does not aim to crush legitimate viewpoint diversity (Rescher, 1993). There will often be more than one right way to live but this categorically isn't the same as anything goes. As Jeffrey Stout puts it – 'Let a thousand flowers bloom, but keep killing weeds' (Stout, 1988, p. 98).

Pragmatism understands that truth can't be grounded on the solidity of our starting points and so must look forward to the persuasiveness of our conclusions. True belief is simply the opinion that everyone would come to agree on at the end of inquiry reached under idealised conditions (see Talisse & Aikin, 2008). Truth is the final destination, not the starting point. Put somewhat crudely, a traditional realist argues that when we believe that jumping out of a window will result in us falling to the ground this is because our mind is corresponding with reality. A pragmatist suggests instead that what's true is simply what no honest person could fail to agree with; the world constrains us to think this way. Truth is the endpoint when the argument has been won, when every reasonable doubt has been answered.

We betray our clients and ourselves if we always take starting beliefs and cultures as the finished article. In instances where our viewpoints diverge from our clients, I wish to steer between the twin perils of dogmatically insisting on my viewpoint and assuming all perspectives are equally fine: sometimes there is a better answer waiting. I may have compelling reasons to think the client wrong but otherwise the moment calls us to recognise that the best way of seeing things has not been reached. There is more to learn, more to say, more to discover, more thinking to be done, our labours in the service of outsight not yet ended. Our beliefs may not converge on a single answer, but hopefully our plural viewpoints will be individually strengthened and more comprehensible to each other. Truth might usefully be thought of in therapy as the mind coming to rest when it can no longer deny the power of its own conclusions, a clarifying stillness that Habermas calls 'the unforced force of the better argument' (Habermas, 2003, p. 140).

Asserting that there is no such thing as truth strives for revolutionary zeal but risks disregard for the consequences. A life where people had no interest in distinguishing between better and worse beliefs would be a life without consequences. Uncritically celebrating every viewpoint simply downgrades all thought to mere opinion. This cannot be a sufficient foundation for our social and political identities. Questions are not idle and freedom is nothing unless it is the freedom to move to a better belief in the light of experience. All 6,000 known languages have an equivalent of the verb 'to know' which indicates that all known cultures are interested in distinguishing between better and worse beliefs (see Nagel, 2014). Without these starting premises the rationale for engaging in a therapy of horizontal problems collapses. We would consign clients to be prisoners of their current limitations when the need is to move beyond them.

This can all sound very spirited and optimistic, but pragmatism also acknowledges that fallibility, error and limitation are inevitable without seeing them as either prohibitive or permanent. Our ethos must be one of humble experimentation, trying out new ways of thinking and being to see how they work and being willing to turn back if they don't. Answering sceptics who charge that until we have answered every last initial doubt that might be raised we cannot claim to know anything, a pragmatist replies that we should have as much reason to doubt our beliefs as to maintain them (Putnam, 1995). 'Have you got a better idea?' is the more plausible starting position than 'can you be certain?'. As a situated and engaged self-and-world, it's not possible to radically call everything into question at once, to hover in mid-air believing nothing though specific doubts for specific reasons are welcome spurs to reform (see Margolis, 2012).

Pragmatism supports an ethos of responsible, careful, progressive reform rather than the liberating toppling of idols celebrated by postmodernists. The liberal sceptic will see their job as done once tradition and universalism are vanquished and pluralism reigns. A pragmatist knows that at this point the real work begins. We have earned our freedom from yesterdays' truths and, if so, what are we going to do with it? We can only live with more authority, however temporary. Our Adult selves can usefully assume the mantle of responsible inquirer, the keeper and custodian of ideas. The person who has taken the questions of their life seriously, who has answered the test of experience and has the stillness of belief which comes from having reached the best answer will take the best place in the world that occasion and ability allows.

Conclusion

Postmodernism intuitively appeals because it mirrors what I have called chaos, the swirling, fragmented, melding cacophony of voices and identities without a centre of late modernity. It isn't just that therapists are meeting an increasingly diverse range of clients, it's that those clients are themselves multiples. Our perspectives subdivide, sprawl, surge and reform in a rapid, kaleidoscopic world.

I take it that pragmatism better answers the challenge of these conditions than either the myth of internal sufficiency or liberal scepticism. Since the world is in a state of flux, increasingly complex and hard to manage, we must make greater efforts towards achieving authority in the face of cognitive vulnerability. It's more complicated to live in this churning void than postmodernism will concede. We need to develop better habits of mind, to question our ideas without recklessly burning down the whole house of belief, to remake our own calm centre ground at a time when it is no longer given. Physis and the free Child can't stand in place of old certainties. The responsibility for coming to terms with the world, for getting things right are unavoidable even when fallibilism is acknowledged.

A pragmatic therapy ethos is also better placed to acknowledge the irreducibly social aspect of who we are and what we believe. Getting rid of overarching narratives or the possibility of truth leads inevitably to a stunting of the political imagination. The possibility of robust consensus between people, solid ideas that unify and persuade represent out best starting points joining with others and reforming our world. The question remains will we hear the call of the moment. We may fail, but neutrality about social and political questions is not an option.

Pragmatism leaves us not merely with a different notion of selfhood, but with a different picture of the relationship between freedom and the social. Freedom isn't a return to a pre-social us as the myth of internal sufficiency proclaims nor a shattering of truth, commonality and convention into 1,000 splinters as liberal scepticism believes. It is the opportunity to reach a better viewpoint and to have the means to pursue it with integrity. It is rooted in and enabled by the shared resources of the social and the 'our truth' position we achieve through their mastery. It accepts that an affirmative social and political identity demands ultimately that we be *for* things as well as *against* them, that we take a stand and try to make things work.

References

Barrow, G. (2014) Natality: An Alternative Existential Possibility. *Transactional Analysis Journal*, 44 (4), 311–319.

Baggini, J. (2017) *A Short History of Truth: Consolations for a Post-Truth World.* London: Quercus.

Bauman, Z., May, T. (2001) *Thinking Sociologically.* 2nd edn. Oxford: Blackwell.

Berlin, I. (1969) Two Conceptions of Liberty. In *Four Essays On Liberty*, Oxford: Oxford University Press, 118–172.

Berne, E. (1968) *A Layman's Guide to Psychiatry and Psychoanalysis.* Harmondsworth: Penguin.

Berne, E. (1972) *What Do You Say After You Say Hello.* London: Corgis.

Bernstein, R.J. (2010) *The Pragmatic Turn.* Malden, MA: Polity Press.

Bloom, H. (1973) *The Anxiety of Influence: a Theory of Poetry.* Oxford: Oxford University Press.

Brandom, R.B. (2002) When Philosophy Paints its Blue on Grey: Irony and the Pragmatist Enlightenment. *Boundary 2*, 29 (2), 1–28.

Brennan, T. (2006) *Wars of Position: The Cultural Politics of Left and Right.* New York: Columbia University Press.

Bruckner, P. (2010) *The Tyranny of Guilt: An Essay on Western Masochism.* Translated from French by S. Rendall. Princeton: Princeton University Press.

Colapietro, V.M. (1989) *Pierce's Approach to the Self: A Semiotic Perspective on Human Subjectivity.* Albany: State University of New York.

Christman, J. (2018) *Social and Political Philosophy: A Contemporary Introduction.* 2nd edn. New York: Routledge.

Clarkson, P. (1992) *Transactional Analysis Psychotherapy: An Integrated Approach.* London: Routledge.

Dewey, J. (1922) *Human Nature and Conduct: An Introduction to Social Psychology.* Reprint 2007. New York: Cosimo.

Dalal, F. (2000) Ethnic Tradition: A Source of Emotional Well-Being or a Cause of Emotional Pain? *European Journal of Psychotherapy, Counselling & Health*, 3 (1), 43–60.

Dalal, F. (2016) The Individual and the Group: The Twin Tyrannies of Internalism and Individualism. *Transactional Analysis Journal*, 46 (2), 88–100.

Eagleton, T. (1996) *The Illusions of Postmodernism*. Oxford: Blackwell.

Ellis, A. (1994) *Reason and Emotion in Psychotherapy*. 2nd edn. New York: Birch Lane.

Feltham, C. (2014) If Merely More Words then What's the Point? A Critical Response. *European Journal of Counselling and Psychotherapy*, 16 (4), 376–387.

Foucault, M. (1984) Truth and Power. In P. Rabinow, Ed., *The Foucault Reader*. New York: Pantheon Books, 51–75.

Haack, S. (2007) *Defending Science: Between Scientism and Cynicism*. Amherst: Prometheus Books.

Habermas, J. (1985) *The Philosophical Discourse of Modernity*. Translated from German by F. Lawrence. Cambridge: Polity.

Habermas, J. (2003) *Truth and Justification*. Translated from German by B. Fultner. Cambridge: Polity.

Han, B. (2019) *What is Power?* Translated from German by D. Steuer. Cambridge: Polity.

Held, B. (1995) *Back to Reality: A Critique of Postmodern Theory in Psychotherapy*. New York: Norton & Co.

Horney, K. (1937) *The Neurotic Personality of Our Time*. New York: Norton and Co.

James, W., Gunn, G. (2000) *Pragmatism and Other Writings*. New York: Penguin.

Laing. R.D. (1959) *The Divided Self: An Existential Study in Sanity and Madness*. London: Penguin.

Latour, B. (2004) Why Has Critique Run of Steam? From Matters of Fact to Matters of Concern. *Critical Inquiry*, 30, 225–248.

Loewenthal, D. (2015) 'Introduction' in D. Loewenthal, Ed., *Critical Psychotherapy, Psychoanalysis and Counselling: Implications for Practice*. Basingstoke: Palgrave MacMillan, 3–28.

Lorde, A. (1984) The Master's Tools Will Never Dismantle the Master's House. In *Sister Outsider: Essays and Speeches*. Berkeley, CA: Crossing Press, 110–114.

Lyotard, J.F. (1984) *The Postmodern Condition: A Report on Knowledge*. Translated from French by G. Bennington, B. Massumi. Manchester: Manchester University Press.

MacIntyre, A. (1988) *Whose Justice? Which Rationality?* London: Duckworth.

MacKinnon, C. (2000) Points against Postmodernism. *Chicago-Kent Law Review*, 75 (3), 687–712.

Margolis, J. (2012) *Pragmatism Ascendant: A Yard of Narrative, A Touch of Prophecy*. Stanford, CA: Stanford University Press.

Mellor, K. (2017) Life the Hidden Template, Life Energy the Driving Force, Grounding the Action. *Transactional Analysis Journal*, 47 (1), 54–67.

Michaels, W.B. (2006) *The Trouble with Diversity: How we Learned to Love Identity and Ignore Inequality*. New York: Metropolitan Books.

Misak, C. (2000) *Truth, Politics, Morality: Pragmatism and Deliberation*. London: Routledge.

Mitchell, S.A., Black, M.J. (1995) *Freud and Beyond: A History of Modern Psychoanalytic Thought*. New York: Basic Books.

Nagel, J. (2014) *Knowledge: A Very Short Introduction*. Oxford: Oxford University Press.

Nagel, T. (1997) *The Last Word.* New York: Oxford University Press.

Peirce, C.S. (1868) Some consequences of four incapacities claimed for man. *Journal of Speculative Philosophy*, *2*, 140–157.

Peirce, C.S. (1958) *Charles S. Peirce: Selected Writings.* Edited by P. Wiener. New York: Dover.

Perls, F., Hefferline, R.F., Goodman, P. (1951) *Gestalt Therapy: Excitement and Growth in the Human Personality.* London: Souvenir Press.

Piccinino, G. (2018) Reflections on Physis, Happiness, and Human Motivation. *Transactional Analysis Journal*, 48 (3), 272–285.

Putnam, H. (1994) *Words and Life.* Edited by J. Conant. Cambridge, MA: Harvard University Press.

Putnam, H. (1995) *Pragmatism: An Open Question.* Oxford: Blackwell.

Rescher, N. (1993) *Pluralism: Against the Demand For Consensus.* Oxford: Clarendon Press.

Rieff, P. (1959) *Freud: The Mind of the Moralist.* London: Victor Gonzales.

Rogers, C.R. (1951) *Client-Centred Therapy.* London: Constable.

Rorty, R. (1984) Deconstruction and Circumvention. *Critical Inquiry*, 11 (1), 1–23.

Rorty, R. (1989) *Contingency, Irony, and Solidarity.* Cambridge: Cambridge University Press.

Rorty, R. (1998) *Achieving Our Country: Leftist Thought in Twentieth Century America.* Cambridge, MA: Harvard University Press.

Rorty, R. (1999) Phoney Science Wars. *The Atlantic*, 284 (5), 120–122.

Rosenberg, A. (2012) *Philosophy of Science*, 3rd edn. New York: Routledge.

Sahlins, M. (2002) *Waiting for Foucault, Still.* Chicago: Prickly Paradigm Press.

Scheffler, I (1982) *Science and Subjectivity.* 2nd edn. Indianapolis: Hackett.

Smail, D. (1996) *How to Survive Without Psychotherapy.* London: Constable.

Stewart, I., Joines, V. (2012) *TA Today.* 2nd edn. Melton Mowbray: Lifespace Publishing.

Stout, J. (1988) *Ethics after Babel; the Languages of Morals and their Discontents.* Cambridge: James Clark and Co.

Talisse, R.B., Aikin, S.F. (2008) *Pragmatism: a Guide for the Perplexed.* London: Continuum.

Taylor, C. (1989) *Sources of the Self: The Making of the Modern Identity.* Cambridge, MA: Harvard University Press.

Taylor, C. (1991) *The Ethics of Authenticity.* Cambridge, MA: Harvard University Press.

Totton, N. (2010) *The Problem with Humanistic Therapies.* London: Karnac.

Tudor, K., Worrall, M. (2006) *Person-Centred Therapy: A Clinical Philosophy.* London: Routledge.

Unger, R.M. (2007) *The Self Awakened; Pragmatism Unbound.* Cambridge, MA: Harvard University Press.

West, C. (1989) *The American Evasion of Philosophy: A Genealogy of Pragmatism.* Madison: University of Wisconsin Press.

Winnicott, D.W. (1960) Ego Distortion in Terms of True and False Self. In *The Maturational Process and the Facilitating Environment.* London: Karnac, 140–152.

Wittgenstein, L. (1953) *Philosophical Investigations.* Translated from German by G.E.M Anscombe. Oxford: Blackwell.

Wolin, S.S. (2016) *Fugitive Democracy and Other Essays.* Edited by N. Xenos. Princeton: Princeton University Press.

5

LANGUAGE, PRAGMATISM
AND DIALOGUE

Why do we need to talk about language?

In the course of the first session Emma says she is struggling with depression. This is an innocent enough comment, but it raises questions about how I come to understand what Emma means by this word. Although I generally take myself to comprehend what depression means, my understanding doesn't cover every divergent use and rule out every ambiguity. I know from experience that people use the word depression in slightly different ways yet overlapping ways. I also know that sometimes it's a word people use as what I have called a partial explanation, when they are struggling and can't really say why. Once I have heard enough of Emma's words in therapy to catch the general drift of her meaning a better word may suggest itself to me or to her. How is it that Emma's words and my hearing of them sometimes coincide precisely and sometimes drift slightly apart and is this latter state of affairs something to be corrected or better understood? Our first two meetings feel like a series of false starts, a sputtering dance of comprehension. I don't quite know what she means and she doesn't quite know how to explain herself fully. It feels as though neither of us has quite reached the right words.

It would be a curious omission to write a book about context and not talk about language. It's our principle means of communicating and co-ordinating our actions with others, the building blocks of the social. It provides the conduit by which we can learn from their experiences. It is the primary vehicle for our socialisation into the shared conceptual world and the means of our original expression within it. Materially, language is only marks on paper and sounds on the air: it is far less substantial than the physical things which exert a brute influence on us, yet we have no way to peel our minds and worldviews out of the words we use. Intangible though it may be, language constrains and enables us. It is, in Heidegger's evocative phrase, 'the house of being' (Heidegger & Krell, 1993, p. 214), the only home we have known. Being self-and-world is being self-and-language by extension.

The aim of this chapter is to show that language does not merely express thought, it also *enables* it. Once we have achieved proficiency it is 'our language' not just 'your language', inseparable from our competence. Initiation into a language opens up possible ways of being we would not otherwise have known. Being a competent user of common words is a necessary precondition for what I called the authority of our Adult ego-states in Chapter 3. We know what we are doing because we can account for it using words. An adequate account of how we acquire, use and form ourselves through language therefore holds a comparable place in contextual transactional analysis that the workings of the mind occupy in more purely psychological frameworks. We attend to it here because it binds together and underwrites most of the conceptual innovations introduced in this book.

That our identity emerges from initiation into a shared language does not entail that we always have the words to fully understand ourselves or others. As therapists we know that the bridge of language is usually incomplete, not always true under foot and that error and misunderstanding are commonplace. It is also the only bridge we have so repair, persistence and improvement are our only options. Understanding how language works just a little better give us theoretical permission to adopt the learning-focused approach necessary for the resolution of horizontal difficulties. Since we may still not be sure whether to greet variations in language use as a problem to be corrected or a difference to be respected, some theoretical clarification may legitimise and sharpen our sense of when or how to intervene.

Given that our profession depends upon the use of words, it is surprising that we have not thought about language more often (exceptions are Edelson, 1975; Fiumara, 1992; Russell, 1987). Perhaps language seems either so obvious or so irrelevant a subject that digging into how things work appears superfluous. In addition to postmodern concerns about the slipperiness of words (Derrida, 1978), there may be a belief that language is simply a vehicle to express states of mind formed apart from it. Related to the myth of internal sufficiency, this view guides us to believe that our job is to sensitively excavate and recover the subjective sense of things the client already has rather than help them to a new one. We must steer a path between the twin danger of underestimating the robustness of language and overestimating our client's established narratives as sufficient, if temporarily hidden and unavailable.

As therapists we need an alternative account which acknowledges that linguistic understanding usually goes right, sometimes goes wrong in varying degrees, but always provides opportunities for understanding ourselves and the world in ways which would otherwise not be possible. Understanding why this ongoing dance of divergence and convergence in our linguistic understanding of others happens may grant us permission to use these moments more productively. My argument draws upon contemporary pragmatist theories of language though it falls well short of a comprehensive account of these ideas. The aim is just to borrow enough to get a useful argument moving.

The main reason for talking about language is that some have not had the opportunity in the course of their lives to learn to say what they need to. Every language user can competently name things, ask questions, give orders, tell jokes and create rhymes. Beyond this there exists an advanced critical and reflective use of language which pushes understanding to the point where the underlying social order can come into view (Habermas, 1971). It is this kind of advanced language use which underwrites the formation of an adequate social and political identity. When people have not had the opportunity to live their lives in the light of this kind of linguistic awareness, self-and-world is correspondingly restricted. The communities some are socialised into may be said to suffer from a deficit in linguistic resourcefulness and integrity (as introduced in Chapter 2). If people don't collectively develop an enriched, penetrating language to disclose the world more fully then it will be missing from the sense of the world they are socialised into. Fortunately, language is learnable: new ways of speaking and thinking, new ways of telling stories can always be gained. When fortune permits, the therapist may be able to hear in the spaces between the client's words the ungrasped possibilities that lie just outside the person's understanding and guide them step by step to a transformed expressive range.

Language and relationship

Discussing language inevitably borders on talking about relationships for language is the achievement of collectives rather than individuals, maintained by ongoing communicative action. There may be a concern that our time would be better spent talking about relationship and leaving language to one side for as therapists we often take ourselves to aim at kinds of understanding that surface words cannot convey. Particularly where there is an emphasis upon the presumed primacy of early experience (Erskine, 2015) there is a subtle call to get out of our chattering minds and into our wordless hearts. Seeking an understanding that is more than words, a purer communion is laid out in a path to more genuine recognition and healing (Agassi, 1999).

Suggesting that there are experiences beyond words can seem evocative and intuitively plausible, as though pure, raw empathy could deepen understanding in a way that clunking words alone cannot reach. The position taken here is that to fully grasp what people are experiencing or feeling is inseparable from linguistically-enabled understanding of what people mean and why they mean it (see Zahavi, 2014). Peering behind someone's words, detaching the empathic, embodied human impulse to connection from our linguistically-enabled sense of ourselves seems blind to their full meaning. I'm not seeking to prioritise language alone. The most I am advocating for is *language-led* understanding rather than a *language-exclusive* one. I want to make sure the body and heart are brought along with the words as an inseparable unity.

Talking about language also needs to be carefully distinguished from talking about communication. Berne's theory of transactions usefully alerted us to the fact that our spoken words are often only the visible tip of what is communicated and may sometimes conceal what is really thought. The theory observes that communication takes place between psychologically complex individuals pursuing certain kinds of relational outcomes with the psychological and social dimensions of the transaction often quite distinct (Berne, 1961). The theory of transactions reminds us that what is said cannot be meaningfully separated from who is saying it, to whom, and under what conditions. It also reminds us that what is communicated openly may be less important than what is covertly intended. Sensitivity to the vagaries of communication – and the psychology of communicators – will remain essential. My focus on language isn't intended to imply that we can always take the words the client actually uses at face value. Sometimes people won't always give the most accurate statement of their preferences, worldview and state of mind. My interest is in the way that words always guide, shape and structure thought for we may not yet have learnt to think in ways we need to. Contra Berne, what matters isn't necessarily what's hidden but what the person has never yet had the chance to think.

The rules of language use

Before I introduce my chosen theory of language, I need to name and rule out alternative accounts. One rival idea which can sound initially plausible states that words simply express the thoughts we already have in our heads (Brandom, 2000a; Hacking, 1975). This view of language has previously found respectable endorsement in the writings of John Locke and David Hume and may once have been considered the consensus view (Margolis, 1995). Here language doesn't create or enable anything that isn't already there, it's just a vehicle for thought to be released communicatively into the world. In the wake of philosophy after Wittgenstein, this priority of thought and language has often been reversed (Lycan, 2008; McGinn, 2015; Wittgenstein, 1953). The popular current view which this book endorses is that we don't draw upon language to express what we already think, we learn to think by participating meaningfully in linguistic interactions with other people. To paraphrase Wilfrid Sellars, talking is thinking out loud and thinking is just private speech (Sellars, 2007). Language is in at the ground floor of the mind. There is no basement of thought beneath it.

Wittgenstein's second blow to accepted wisdom was to suggest that language shouldn't be thought of as a matching of words to things in the world – sometimes known as the referential view of language (Hacking, 1975). This can also seem like common sense until you come to realise that we can use words to talk about things which don't actually exist and which can't be physically pointed at. Instead of a process of matching words to things, Wittgenstein came to understand language use as learning to follow rules. To speak or write a language is simply knowing how words are *used*.

Wittgenstein didn't mean by this that using language was like following an instruction book; language rules aren't usually so formal. It's more like following a trail of intelligible precedent laid down by others. Previous speakers have used words in this particular way and we must follow their lead. Language rules

113

don't invent themselves; they are not set by formal committees, they congeal out of the day to day course of life. This means words we use are not created once and then fixed in stone, their meaning is confirmed and renewed by ongoing practice. Words therefore have a history rather than a fixed essence. To speak a language is to know, however approximately and unreflectively, how those who have come before us have used these words. We are required to master these precedents in the present task of understanding. I have referred to this acquired competence in this book as moving into an 'our truth' position.

We follow the rules of language by a kind of unconscious 'know-it's-right-when-I-see-it' competence. This know-how cannot always be readily account for by simple reflection but we are unconsciously proficient at it. Think of how quickly our mind snaps out of its easy groove in the middle of a conversational flow when someone appears to use a word incorrectly or we have the sense that we aren't fully grasping what they are saying. The confusion only stands out in this way because saying we understand someone is really just a way of saying we are able to follow their use of language rules. When we understand our clients, it is not because they have magically attached their pre-verbal states of mind to a word and sailed it in through our ears, but because we are both drawing upon the same rules of use. Language use is therefore an acquired competence at participating in an established, complex fabric of social practices.

Language rules will vary in terms of their history and complexity, which is another way of saying that some words are simpler than others. We might think of following a rule as being like crossing a field. Sometimes those who have come before us have crossed in exactly the same way many times over leaving a single, clear track cut into the verbal landscape. Under these circumstances the correct use of a word is easy to grasp. An example of this kind of path might be the word dog. Almost every competent speaker of English would be able to tell immediately if someone is using the word 'dog' correctly. The person would also be able to demonstrate their competence at using the word by explaining what they meant. Simple rules accompany simple meanings. They make the achievement of equal competence a fairly effortless endeavour.

Not all words and sentences are so simply. Some are polysemous (have multiple meanings), are rarely used or belong to specialist technical or academic linguistic subsets. Crossing these kinds of fields may entail multiple paths with points of convergence, sometimes intersecting, at other times diverging. The rules for use here are less clear cut. When Emma and I were discussing her 'depression' it wasn't always clear if we were following the same pathway, the route was muddier, the use less certain. If someone says they are depressed in routine conversation we would understand sufficiently what they meant to allow the word to pass unquestioned and hope that subsequent words clarified the matter. In a clinical scenario, where higher standards of comprehension are essential, we might feel that a follow up question was required. We want to discern in exactly what way the person was using the word.

Complex words fan out along extended lines of association, doing more than just picking objects out. Their rules are thick with meaning and resonance, hard to understand in isolation from the everything else we think and know, from the landscape of human practice from which they emerge. Mastery requires living immersion. We are not equally familiar with all convergent pathways associated with a word. Some uses will be less familiar or absent all together for us in they are not present in the corner of the world we inhabit. If you haven't learnt how to say it, if you don't talk this way routinely to make sense of your life, your ability to think it will not be fluent. When we ask in therapy what someone means what we are really asking is 'what history of use are you participating in when you say that word', what conversations have you been part of, how has that word been used by people you have interacted with so far? Our words and stories betray the opportunities and limitations of our particular, contextual histories and experiences.

Language is not a collection of static 'things' we can pluck out of the air, it is a living practice, it is us co-operating, co-ordinating and sharing. It's held together by reasoning individuals trying to make themselves understood and accepting responsibility for making this happen – what Habermas calls orientation to mutual understanding (Habermas, 1988). I am trying to make you understand me and you are trying to understand me and make yourself understood in return. Even engaging in internal monologues presumes this requirement to make sense for private speech is exactly talking to ourselves. If all this talk of rules sounds slightly austere, then consider a world where everything goes, where every vague or inaccurate use of a word was simply accepted as valid – language rules would liquify and collective sense would become impossible: we simply can't imagine language under these conditions (see Price, 2011). Language is not just glued together by nothing more than passive habit (see Harris, 1988) drifting this way and that over time, blindly following what has come before without higher deliberation and purpose. We are irreducibly responsible for getting our thoughts and words right and in doing so keep 'our' rules of use bound together.

Language and development

Language development starts out functional and ends up original. We exist before language, but are not fully the selves we recognise until we have acquired it. Margolis describes this as a distinction between our given, biological 'first natures' and our acquired cultural 'second natures' (Margolis, 2001), the latter inaugurating self-and-world. Developmentally Tomasello has suggested that language use builds upon the awareness acquired during the first nine months that other people have minds like ours (Tomasello, 2003). At this point during our 'first nature' period, intentions begin to play a part in interactions. He argues that language acquisition is inseparable from the developing capacity to share and direct attentional focus with others. As our communicative competence and reflective capacity increase through maturity, we can begin to use language in a wider variety of ways, but relational, communicative aspects of language remain irreducible. Without a world of others we would have no need of words; once we have them we cannot imagine ourselves without them. Words exceed their communicative starting points and become expressive and constitutive (Taylor, 2016).

Against the notion that language use starts with individual words and builds up to greater and greater unities through combination, the pragmatic view presupposes language *holism*. This takes the sentence or proposition as the basic unit of sense. To speak one sentence we must always know how to speak others. Clearly young children don't miraculously acquire a complete vocabulary in one go, but they always know how to fit words together and make single words work in multiple ways. Knowing our way around a language, understanding its rules and using it to say what we mean presupposes that we understand how words fit with other words.

This seems initially counter-intuitive for we picture an infant pointing at things and learning one word at a time. Tomasello suggests that we think of these single words as 'holophrases' where the single word carries the whole intention of the sentence the infant is trying to convey. Young children use their limited vocabularies in a whole range of ways. For a young child the word 'mama' is a multipurpose tool. It can be used to say 'There is mama', 'I want mama' 'mama get me that' etc. (Tomasello, 2008). As I argued in Chapter 3, the caregiver interprets the intention and child is then initiated into more appropriate expression. These first words will unpack and subdivide into separate sentences. We might think of this process of refinement and replacement as continuing, albeit with smaller gains, throughout life. Our languaged sense of things is an ever expanding and changing whole which refines, gains and sometimes loses ways of saying things across the course of life.

The further we move away from using language to simply pick out objects, the more complex the rules of use become. The simple assertion 'that's wrong' may be a mere two syllables but it is incomprehensible outside of a whole sense of things. It would be a meaningless slogan if cut adrift from a capacity to give reasons for what you are saying. Understanding the notion of wrongness entails being able to expand further and further out to the neighbouring terms. In Brandom's words, 'we must have many concepts to have any' (Brandom, 1994, p. 89). This picture of our languaged minds as always holistic rather than assembled in bits offers an important corrective to therapeutic strategies which try to focus in on isolated thoughts or words. There is always a complex whole sense surrounding the individual word which we cannot cheat in attempting to reason our clients into better worldviews.

There is both gain and loss here. Entering into language is a precondition for Adult authority, for knowing what we are doing. It enables competence, co-operative and constructive relationships with others of otherwise unimaginable sophistication. At the same time the greater reach of our worded minds is accompanied by greater uncertainty. Knowing more of things we are stirred by new, conceptually enabled dissatisfactions. The preverbal child can suffer from hunger and pain, but it knows little of the disquiet which the worded soul can endure. There is no reversing out of language. We can only push forward to greater language-led understanding rather than seek a way back into wordlessness. Only better understanding will do.

This better understanding emerges through re-engaging with the wider languaged world. Learning from others in dialogue never ceases. The greatest riches of meaning lie between us waiting to be explored and discovered. Even after maturity our minds continually draw upon what Habermas calls the lifeworld (Habermas, 1987) which refers to the surrounding ecosystem of talk and meaning, the unregulated spheres of interaction which encompass the family, the workplace and the wider culture. It is a permanently available backdrop of implicit and intuitive assumptions against which our specific acts of thinking and speaking take place. The lifeworld enables cognitive opportunity and sometimes cognitive vulnerability: its resourcefulness and integrity generally support Adult articulacy, but if the world of talk becomes depleted through deficits in responsiveness and truthfulness then it becomes harder to understand the whole of what is happening. Our general stories no longer get a grip on things. Under such conditions, confusion and Parental perspectives which we have no choice but to depend on may proliferate.

The dialogical situation

Relationship is coming to be with others; dialogue is coming to learn from and communicate with others. In dialogue our understandings are bridged, but they retain their separate authority (Holquist, 1990). Dialogue puts comprehension to the test. We come away either with our understanding strengthened or changed. As we draw upon the background lifeworld in dialogue it become molten, subject to the reconfirmation or challenge of the moment. The rules of language are a mix of fixity and occasional flux, the taken-for-granted and the up-for-grabs. Contextual transactional analysis aims at a language-led dialogic encounter, sensitivity to the flow of convergence and divergence between client and therapist understanding. Properly understood, these present opportunities for either deepening or transformation of present understanding. My aim here is to present a nuts-and-bolts account of what exactly is happening during these moments of convergence and divergence to show how they might represent doorways to beneficial learning.

Robert Brandom argues that all language presupposes a particular kind of interactive doing between people, a basic 'rule of conduct' if you will from which no language use can depart. He refers to this as the game of 'giving and asking for reasons' (Brandom, 1994, p. 496). What he means is that in using language, a speaker is in principle capable of making explicit to others what they take a word to mean upon request. Since speaking a word presupposes knowing how to use it, a competent language user will give 'appropriate' reasons which the receiver can match to the rules of use. This is one aspect of Adult authority over language, the ability to really mean what one says.

Brandom believes that the giving and asking for reasons distinguishes word use by merely sentient creatures like parrots from that of 'sapient', second-natured human language users. You can train a parrot to squawk the word 'car' when it sees a car but this ability to successfully match sound to object does not indicate that the Parrot understands what it is saying. No matter how many words a parrot learns to match with different objects in this way, they will never be able to genuinely explain what they mean by giving reasons for it upon request to another language user. From the outside they accurately match sound and object but do not understand what they are saying. They are the mouthpieces but not the authors of what they say; there is no authority here.

By contrast, when a human being uses a word, Brandom believes that this act can be understood as undertaking a kind of *commitment*, that in principle you will say what you believe to be so by using a particular word. To use the meta-phor introduced above, this is a bit like saying you can explain the rules of word usage. If you asked a person what they meant by car, they might show they knew how to use the word by talking about it being a mechanical vehicle, usually having four wheels etc. They would show that they know how words fit together. Even in interior speech, the basic situation of taking reasonable responsibility for our meaning, or imagining another person who seeks to understand us by holding us to account for the appropriateness of our word use, never leaves us.

To commitment Brandom adds a second feature to his basic rule, that of *entitlement*. This corresponds to things a person would have been entitled to mean by using a particular word in the eyes of the person listening, but didn't. Imagine a person exclaiming that it's snowing today. They may be taken by the listener to the speaker having *committed* to snow being a form of precipitation, it being frozen water, it being cold etc. They know that they are saying all these things when they use the word snow. The listener understands that in addition the speaker would also be *entitled* to commit to snow's being white even though they had not done so. The listener therefore legitimately adds something to the speakers meaning that the person did not know they could commit to. An entitle-ment is something another person knows the speaker *could* have meant. As therapists looking for opportunities to expand our client's sense of their worlds, it's crucial that we are able to notice those instances where someone was entitled to have meant something but didn't. This has potentially radical implications for our practice for rather than trying to deepen a client's narrative by delving further into their intentions, we can sometimes expand it outwards by introduc-ing new possibilities already legitimated by what has been said.

The legalistic tone of commitment and entitlement is intentional, for Brandom thinks of language as people using the rules to holding each other to account. The speaker is metaphorically responsible for honouring their commitments and the listener is responsible for keeping track of what they take a person to be committed and entitled to. The seemingly innocuous, smooth running of everyday understanding is revealed as a rather busy process of evaluating and tracking which Brandom describes by the term 'score-keeping'. In score-keeping, a listener ensures that all commitments undertaken by the other person are entitled (permitted), that commitments don't contradict each other whilst also noting the things that could have been meant (entitlements). Language is the product of this ongoing effort to make sense. A client who said 'I'm so happy because I'm depressed' would not at first glance be entitled to their commitment to both happy and depressed by a competent score-keeper because the commitments and entitlements associated with the words happy and depressed are incompatible. Unless used in a highly creative way, the phrase simply wouldn't match up with our broader background sense of how these words worked and an interruption to clarify the misunderstanding would be necessary.

Verbal sense builds progressively. The gradual unfolding of words in an exchange are evaluated in this way against the holistic background of other available words. Understanding the words which have been spoken is like the tip of an iceberg, the surface protrusion depending upon a broad spread of background meanings which are implicated in what has been said but not stated. The words just said (committed to) will themselves be entitlements for what has yet to be said, meaning interlocking plausibly, picking out a particular path of sense. Words always entail committing to one thing at the expense of others, opening up possibilities for expression and meaning whilst closing down others.

This notion of listening as a process of evaluation and monitoring may sit uncomfortably with a professional psychotherapy ethos of non-judgemental receptivity as will the idea that understanding someone is premised on tracking their rule-following. Yet Brandon is reminding us we cannot refuse score-keeping in favour of an unmediated form of reception. There is no capacity to think, speak, listen or understand, however seemingly original, which is not dependent upon knowing and using linguistic rules. I can only understand you if our second-natured minds occupy the same world of words and concepts. We could no more reach across into an entirely alien subjectivity than we can spontaneously grasp the utterances of a foreign language.

Therapists and clients are therefore managing minor disagreements and small confusions in understanding against a backdrop of unchallenged shared sense on an ongoing basis. Brandom compares linguistic understanding to a dance (Brandom, 2000b) where the effortless flow of concurrence sometimes judders into discord, sometime consolidating, sometimes resolving into a new pattern of understanding. Assuming we are truthful dialoguers, nobody leaves the dance unchanged: minor convergences require either effort to restore sense or contestation to resolve disagreement. A scorekeeper is constantly navigating between their own sense of what counts as commitment and entitlement and the divergent senses they receive from the other, a usually robust process which keeps mutual understanding on the rails. If we see two language users as engaged in a dance of understanding then the invitation is to pay close attention to how the usual smooth flow of uncomplicated agreement sometimes gives way to a sense that the person's meaning is spinning away from ours, the times when we might want to contest, disagree, pull the dance into what we take to be the right direction or sometimes allow ourselves to be pulled into learning, exploration and change.

Clearly 'dancing' with others becomes more challenging the further away someone is from our understanding. A productive dance is only possible when divergent senses of things take place against this background of common agreement. Concerns that our score-keeping capacity cannot reach across cultural divides should be taken seriously but not elevated to the status of foreboding impediment. It isn't clear that there are ways of seeing things that are so radically separate that there are no bridges between them (see Davidson, 1984). If we truly did not understand someone then we would know it in the same way that we would recognise we did not understand someone speaking in a foreign language. We must simply take such instances as a call to learn more rather than a sign to give up.

Score-keeping each other's commitments and entitlements shows the perils and the opportunities in dialogue. Divergences in word use risk misunderstanding, but they are also fertile grounds for learning and expansion of sense, sometimes mutual, sometimes one way. Consider the case of a five-year old child stating that 'my dog is called George'. An adult score keeper who better understood how the word dog was used would know that George was a mammal because they would understand there are no circumstances in which George could be a dog and not also be a mammal. It's simply part of the rules of use the child has yet to learn: it would be no imposition to assume this. A productive gap opens up between what the child committed to and what was understood, between what was meant and what could have been legitimately meant.

Consider the implications for recognising that the listener has legitimately understood something on the basis of the child's *words* not their *intentions*. The score keeper has spied an opportunity for understanding that the child does not yet know exists. If the knowledge that George is also a mammal is shared then an expanded range of possibilities for thought and expression are made available. These are intentionally simple examples miles away from the abundance and complexity of a therapeutic hour, but they show in miniature how verbal interaction expands the circumference of what it is possible to think and say. Perhaps we might usefully conceive of therapeutic dialogue as a dance through many such interludes with client and therapist both attentive to places where the story might have taken a different road but didn't, where confusion might have been clarified, where something might have been learnt or where something might be added to strengthen what the speaker has already committed to.

Therapy turns on many words rather than isolated ones, some of them complex and sometimes neither party in a dialogue can score-keep the full range of commitments and entitlements associated with it. Nobody has the whole of the lifeworld immediately at their fingertips. Sometimes neither therapist nor client grasps all the commitments one might make in speaking. Joint limitation gets circulated and reinforced without being noted. We might discuss capitalism with someone and experience a sense of uncomplicated agreement between ourselves and yet from a more knowledgeable vantage point it might be obvious that neither of us fully understands how the term can or should be used. We knew enough to say something about capitalism, but not everything that might have mattered. Here we need the opportunity to reach beyond the horizon of our current understanding by learning new commitments. Therapy of horizontal problems can't be the blind leading the blind, something new has to enter the frame.

Knowing what one has said and what could be said is therefore a matter of degrees. They are subject to our varying levels of knowledge and experience. All of us are competent to get by but we may still fall short of supreme fluency. Here is the theoretical justification for contextual transactional analysis' main contention, that we change by turning our attention outwards, learning, enhancing our competence, interacting more fully with world and words and by doing so we expand our sense of how things could be seen. Our job as therapists is to create possibilities for clients to dance in dialogues where what they say and who they are can be deepened and expanded. In order to sometimes lead in these dances, we must acknowledge a greater obligation to know what we are saying.

I hope my argument is not taken to suggest that we encourage our clients to consult dictionaries and attend lectures, I'm simply inviting us to notice that attending therapy is often a sign that a person has exhausted their current ways of understanding and something new may be required. I am also simply drawing attention to the way that contestation and learning are already present in routine linguistic understanding, they aren't special tricks we have to add. The kind of language we use to discuss how we might live, mostly rises out of the thick web of living tradition (Brandom, 2002), rarely the findings of the lab or the jargon of the text book. A deepened sense of our common language use must be a starting point we lean on to launch something more penetrating and original. Judicious, occasional borrowings from specialist or unfamiliar knowledge should shake up and refresh our common linguistic know-how but rarely replace it.

The dance of learning never stops. If we shed our familiar complacency about understanding others and turn our ear to what usually gets overlooked we may find ourselves noticing the subtle ways in which one person seems to know something the other doesn't from their use of words. Can we listen for those moments where we notice that we need to know more to keep up with what the client is committing to or where we notice that we might say something differently? Do we recognise those moments when we seem to hear something in the client's words that they don't intend, things they might say if a new sense of things was made available to them? These moments provide the clearest markers we can have that opportunities for learning, sharing and enhanced understanding are nearby. Simple error and misunderstanding, knowing lies and willing distortions will remain commonplaces aspects of our relationships. Yet since language must presume co-operation, orientation to mutual understanding and responsibility for what we have committed to then there is a basic floor of intelligibility below which it cannot crash. Let us have faith that for all its frailty and disappointments, language is OK, enough to support our efforts to know and to learn.

Clinical vignette

Four meetings in and Emma describes the night that her partner knocked her unconscious in front of their two children. The relationship had been abusive for some years, and Emma had put up with this because she felt it was important to keep the family together. Night after night she had kept the peace by appeasement. She conceded the grains of truth in his various insults about her appearance, attitude and housekeeping in the vain hope that he would stop. Over time her understanding moved further and further under his description of her as useless and worthless, a terrible mother and ungrateful girlfriend. Sometimes this calmed the situation; sometimes it resulted in his finding new reasons to hit her. Her partner would follow his outbursts with tears of contrition, gifts, hand-written apologies, endless promises that this would be the last time. Emma neither loved him nor thought very much about whether she believed him, but his pleas strengthened her resolve to keep on trying. Her most vivid descriptions centre on her children who reportedly clung to her when her partner was around. They say they don't want daddy to come home when he isn't there.

Emma commits to a story of events which is largely descriptive. She speaks only of facts not judgements. I get no sense from how she speaks that she is inviting sympathy or solidarity. She does not link the violence with her unhappiness. I cannot dance in the same way as Emma here and notice my understanding converging. I receive her sense but wonder if there is more to understand. The outrage at this narrative belongs to my sense of what she is entitled to mean, my narrative about her life which emerges one step outside her words. Our understandings remain marooned, travelling mostly in parallel. It is not part of her current description of things that her partner's actions have anything to do with why she and I are speaking. Emma works as a health visitor and understands that when these things happen to other women they are called domestic violence but these words are a bland platitude, a piece of professional jargon. They find no place in her own story.

A petite and well-dressed woman, Emma was raised by immigrant parents who placed great premium on family. Her parents were supportive and Emma doesn't remember ever being *told* how to live. There is no distinct Parental presence announced by the tell-tale signs of an ego-state shift but over time a way of talking about things which displayed unexamined presumptions emerged. Listening to her words I intuit that Emma was *shown* but not told how to live via inevitable immersion in her parent's worldview. Dedication to family was presumed, something you worked at and when things weren't happy you just worked harder. What happens to those other women has nothing to do with her. What she learnt in her work and how she thought at home never crossed over.

The way Emma told her story to me echoed those of so many women I have worked with who had never learnt to describe themselves and their lives in the language of right and wrong because there was no background picture of things in which right and wrong might make sense. Life is hard, People have their own problems. This is just what men do. Nobody is coming to help. Get on with it. The exhaustion of coping without end eventually turns from a weariness of the body into a shrunken worldview.

From my position in the dance, I hear that although Emma commits to describing her children as 'upset', 'crying', 'scared', I am hearing moral entitlements that she could say but doesn't. If Emma took one step beyond what she means into what could be meant then she might say that what was happening to her children was 'wrong'. To say this word and commit to it fully would bring with it a whole host of meanings which would transform her story. Sharing this understanding, Emma pauses seemingly ambivalent about agreement. She agrees that the violence is wrong but she understands that she cannot describe something a certain way without acknowledging the wider consequences of her description. This is confusion not ambivalence. If what her partner is doing is wrong then her sense that her children need a loving relationship with their father no longer works in quite the same way.

Across the course of the remaining sessions we revisit Emma's narrative word by word, scene by scene. I invite her to consider expanding what she believed herself to mean in the light of what she *could* have meant. Emma does not make every jump that I take to be there and at these moments we work to restore our mutual understanding. New ways of speaking appear which replace old confusions. Over time Emma's own view of family begins to emerge from the detailed reconsideration of shared and settled beliefs. Seeing her partner's treatment as abusive feels too big a jump, a gap in our understandings that I cannot fully bridge, but she becomes clear that it is he who is failing the family and that no family is worth the name which fails the children in its care. Here is learning for me about how Emma's commitments around responsibility are more expansive than I could initially comprehend. The word depression fades out of her account and she commits to a new description of herself as someone who cares about family and has felt very defeated by events. Emma describe this process as like laying out all the piece of a jigsaw and putting them back together again in a new way, as fair a description of the construction of outsight as I have heard.

Language and freedom

All this talk of rules, commitment and entitlement show us how to usefully follow in other people's footsteps: it says little about how we can strike out on our own path. Fortunately, there is no conflict here. Shared language use is consistent with individual expression rather than being opposed to it. So far, I have only hinted at how 'their' language, what we inherit and borrow from a shared history of use, can become 'ours'. I have talked about how authority is synonymous with the ability to make full use of words and beliefs, to turn them into 'ours' but this still sounds like rule following rather than rule bending. Without this further move in the argument we will be left with a picture of arid conformity, encouraging our clients to shuffling along in others' footsteps but deprived of the capacity to transform things.

The solution comes from rejecting a view of freedom as synonymous with a complete departure from history, rules and common norms, a purging ourselves of any trace of other people, jumping outside the shared world to stand unsupported and proud. Berne seems to have ultimately endorsed this view of freedom in his later work where he argued that dropping our script led to both liberation and 'despair', hanging in the void with nothing but endless responsibility for our own self-creation (Berne, 1972; Heiller & Sills, 2010). Here he implicitly endorses the existential view of freedom most frequently associated with Jean-Paul Sartre (see Sartre, 1956). In this view, freedom cannot be reconciled with the social, the collective or the historical, it can only stand in opposition to it.

The view taken here is that what we learn from and share with others is the necessary enabler of self-expression. Consider how it would sound if someone claimed to us that the only way to create an original piece of music was to refuse to use notes and to see the basics of rhythm and melody as hopelessly compromising. The protestations of the avant-guard notwithstanding, we would probably see such complaints as peculiarly extreme and defeatist. The creation of original work from common materials is easy enough to grasp. Similarly imagine a novelist claiming that their originality had been stifled by being forced to use the same 26 letters of the alphabet as everyone else. Freedom demands only that we fashion something new within common grounds. Unprecedented originality on this model would be blankness and silence. Even the most creative and visionary minds must come to terms with the interconnection of freedom and constraint by tradition (Bloom, 1973).

Following his reading of Hegel, Brandom refers to this dependence of linguistic freedom upon the social as 'expressive freedom' (Brandom, 1979). Language fuses constraint and freedom since it is only by learning the rules they can become pliable, a shared phenomenon through which we find our singular voice. Springs' suggests that we see originality, freedom and independence of mind as like jazz musicianship, taking flight from an inherited starting point, weaving and improvising around historic language structure without completely leaving it behind (Springs, 2009). Understood this way, participating in the use of a shared language is a precondition of our freedom and authority.

Competence in language use must therefore precede originality. We make words work mechanically before we can move past orthodox use to make them sing. Learn the rules till you know how to bend them. It would be a tall order to suggest that all clients had to become accomplished poets to recover, but therapy should meaningfully aim at lightning flashes of original outsight which illuminate the landscape of people's lives in new ways. Livening up language, stoking its potential for novel expression is vital in contexts where impoverishment of the lifeworld makes horizontal problems more likely. We can notice cases where the lifeworld of words, knowledge and stories within which people live has thinned out and become depleted leading certain things to become progressively more unthinkable. When certain things are never discussed, when talk becomes narrow, routine and repetitive, when truthfulness is in retreat and the dull convenience of getting by replaces the energising fizz of creative and lively discussion, productive contestation and creative thinking, then expressive freedom retreats. Words not used to their full potential will eventually become banal, losing their full range of meaning without a conscious reaching beyond the familiar circumference of experience.

Contexts make expressive freedom more or less likely. Basil Bernstein's work on restricted speech codes shows that in social contexts where people interact mostly with familiar and similar peoples, language starts to take short-cuts. Lacking challenge, it becomes routine, patterned and predictable because communicative intent can be readily understood through minimal means. Easy conformity and the habitual repetition of social norms produce highly restrictive and conformist collective mindsets. These are not good breeding grounds for Adult authority. By contrast when people spend more time interacting with others who are not like them, their use of language must be 'elaborated', more sensitive to differences, complexities and vagaries and wary of the possibility of misunderstanding (Bernstein, 1964). We have to strain productively to bridge the gap and in doing so expand the authority and capacity of our Adult and the circumference of our expressive freedom. Language is best kept on its toes. We need to invite our clients into responsible improvisation where conversation points at the novel, the contested, the yet-to-be explored so that stale words freshen and come to new life.

Responsible improvisation commits to rebuilding sense, not erasing it. Inviting clients into a torrential spewing of words, the kind found under conditions of chaos (see Chapter 1) might actually erode expressive freedom from the other direction leaving us saying everything and nothing. It would be almost impossible to bend language until it snapped but there is a risk that our client's stories won't come together to form a new and durable centre. Han suggests that the increasing domination of our lifeworld by abundant mass communication leaves us drowning in information but with little in the way to hold on to (Han, 2012). Words speed past us, lacking their usual power and transformative potential. We are hyper-literate but not wise, playful but not disciplined. If our clients do not leave therapy with an account of things which reforms and strengthens their commitments, a more resourceful account with all the depth, reasonableness and authority necessary to understand themselves and their worlds better, then novelty will have worked against rather than for our intent.

It only takes a little originality to make therapy catch fire. Most of our clients simply want to live a little clearer and a little easier, to understand better, how they can weave around and through the traditions of thought and language in which they find themselves. Everyone not encumbered by a cognitive impairment is capable of sophisticated, appropriate and occasionally creative uses of language to accomplish a range of tasks. My goal has been to suggest that the kind of complex, intricate, penetrating vision of the social and political needs a particular kind of social climate to thrive in. These worldviews are hard to produce alone. Emma was perfectly capable of speaking from within her world, but she never took herself to the limits of her linguistic horizon and peered beyond it for she did not fully know how such a thing was possible. It was my adding something to what she knew and the way the dance of our contact expanded her context which provided her with the means to think differently. The resolution of horizontal difficulties requires exactly this opportunity to inch beyond the circumference of the known.

Brandom argues that if pursued collectively and with enough purpose, expressive freedom means we can almost talk ourselves into being different kinds of people. At our most visionary we can look back on the conventions and traditions that provided our starting points and transform them for the better in the light of current knowing. We don't just belong to history, sometimes we can make it even if just in small ways. At the edge of their understanding, clients like Emma are, in their own small way, pioneering. They are people who will return to their families and communities and begin to inch the conversation in a new direction beyond current limits. Under favourable circumstances, with a little luck and a lot of willing, the kind of transformations of self and world we are seeking in therapy might just take root.

References

Agassi, J.B., Ed. (1999) *Martin Buber on Psychology and Psychotherapy: Essays, Letters and Dialogue.* Syracuse: Syracuse University Press.

Berne, E. (1961) *Transactional Analysis in Psychotherapy.* New York: Grove Press.

Berne, E. (1972) *What Do you Say After You Say Hello?* London: Corgi.

Bernstein, B. (1964) Elaborated and Restricted Codes: Their Social Origins and Some Consequences. *American Anthropologist,* 66 (6), 55–69.

Bloom, H. (1973) *The Anxiety of Influence: A Theory of Poetry.* Oxford: Oxford University Press.

Brandom, R. (1979) Freedom and Constraint by Norms. *Philosophical Quarterly,* 16 (3), 187–196.

Brandom, R.B. (1994) *Making it Explicit: Reasoning, Representing & Discursive Commitment.* Cambridge, MA: Harvard University Press.

Brandom, R.B. (2000a) *Articulating Reasons: An Introduction to Inferentialism.* Cambridge, MA: Harvard University Press.

Brandom, R.B. (2000b) Facts, Norms and Normative Facts: A Reply to Habermas. *European Journal of Philosophy,* 8 (3), 356–374.

Brandom, R.B. (2002) *Tales of the Mighty Dead: Historical Essays in the Metaphysics of Intentionality.* Cambridge, MA: Harvard University Press.

Davidson, D. (1984) *Inquiries into Truth & Interpretation.* Oxford: Clarendon Press.

Derrida, J. (1978) *Writing and Difference.* Translated from French by A. Bass. London: Routledge.

Edelson, M. (1975) *Language and Interpretation in Psychoanalysis.* Chicago: University of Chicago Press.

Erskine, R.G. (2015) *Relational Patterns, Therapeutic Presence: Concepts and Practice of Integrative Psychotherapy.* London: Karnap.

Fiumara, G.C. (1992) *The Symbolic Function: Psychoanalysis and the Philosophy of Language.* Oxford: Blackwell.

Habermas, J. (1971) *Knowledge and Human Interests*. Translated from German by J.J. Shapiro. Boston: Beacon Press.

Habermas, J. (1987) *The Theory of Communicative Action: Volume 2, Lifeworld and System: A Critique of Functionalist Reason*. Translated from German by T. McCarthy. Boston: Beacon Press.

Habermas, J. (1988) *On the Pragmatics of Communication*. Edited by M. Cooke. Cambridge, MA: Massachusetts Institute of Technology.

Hacking, I. (1975) *Why Does Language Matter to Philosophy?* Cambridge: Cambridge University Press.

Han, B.C. (2012) *The Transparency Society*. Translated from German by E. Butler. Stanford: Stanford University Press.

Harris, Z. (1988) *Language and Information*. New York: Columbia University Press.

Heidegger, M., Krell, D.F. (1993) *Martin Heidegger: Basic Writings*. Translated by F.A. Capuzzi. San Francisco: Harper.

Heiller, B., Sills, C. (2010) 'Life Scripts: An Existential Perspective' in R.G. Erksine, Ed., *Life Scripts: a Transactional Analysis of Unconscious Relational Patterns*. London: Karnac, 239–268.

Holquist, M. (1990) *Dialogism: Bakhtin and his World*. London: Routledge.

Lycan, W.G. (2008) *Philosophy of Language: A Contemporary Introduction*. 2nd edn. New York: Routledge.

Margolis, J. (1995) *Historied Thought, Constructed World: A Conceptual Primer for the Turn of the Millennium*. Berkeley: University of California Press

Margolis, J. (2001) *Selves and Other Texts: The Case for Cultural Realism*. Pennsylvania: Penn State University Press.

McGinn, C. (2015) *Philosophy of Language: The Classics Explained*. Cambridge, MA: MIT Press.

Price, H. (2011) *Naturalism without Mirrors*. Oxford: Oxford University Press.

Russell, R.L., Ed. (1987) *Language and Psychotherapy: Strategies of Discovery*. New York: Plenun Press.

Sartre, J.P. (1956) 'Existentialism is a Humanism' in W. Kaufman, Ed., *Existentialism: from Dostoevsky to Sartre*. New York: The World Publishing Company, 345–369.

Sellars, W. (2007) 'Language as Thought and as Communication', in K. Sharp, R.B. Brandom, Eds, *In the Space of Reasons: Selected Essays of Wilfrid Sellars*. Cambridge, MA: Harvard University Press, 57–80.

Springs, J.A. (2009) 'Dismantling the Master's House': Freedom as Ethical Practice in Brandom and Foucault. *Journal of Religious Ethics*, 37 (3), 419–448.

Taylor, C. (2016) *The Language Animal: The Full Shape of the Human Linguistic Capacity*. Cambridge, MA: The Belknap Press.

Tomasello, M. (2003) *Constructing a Language: A Usage-Based Theory of Language acquisition*. Cambridge, MA: Harvard University Press.

Tomasello, M. (2008) *Origins of Human Communication*. Cambridge, MA: The MIT Press.

Wittgenstein, L. (1953) *Philosophical Investigations*. Translated from German by G.E.M Anscombe. Oxford: Blackwell.

Zahavi, D. (2014) *Self and Other: Exploring Subjectivity, Empathy and Shame*. Oxford: Oxford University Press.

Part III

THE INDIVIDUAL IN CONTEXT

6

FRAME OF REFERENCE

How we come to know things

The next two chapters try to focus in more detail on the intersection between general contextual conditions and the emergent self-and-world. It's important that we have the means to foreground individual patterns of thought and action, the ebb and flow of authority and how it appears to match the specific contextual configurations of opportunity and constraint. Our frame of reference, the sum total of our experiences and knowledge to date, is always the principle means of making sense of and responding to any given situation. Our intuition about why a person seems to believe some things when they could believe others will be an important prompt for our curiosity, a clue to why they may be struggling and a factor in how we elect to respond.

As transactional analysts, we already have well-formed answers to these questions. We mostly treat deficits or distortions in necessary knowledge as a consequence of our scripts. In principle what we need to know or think is therefore recoverable during the course of therapy once script has been relinquished. I don't think this is the whole story and, when it comes to resolving horizontal problems, I don't think it's the most important part of it. Contextual and other unheralded individual factors can blind people to certain aspects of their present reality in a way which is quite separate from script.

Here I need to deepen my explanation of what I have previously referred to as cognitive vulnerability, our dependence on others to confirm and expand our worldviews, but I will also suggest that irregularities in belief sometimes occur for additional reasons. It would help us as clinicians to distinguish between occasions when insight is what is needed and those where learning about the world may be the more fruitful avenue. What I hope will emerge is clearer thinking about how and why people know things, and the range of circumstances under which they come to change their beliefs. Clinical gains come in helping people to make such changes for the better.

Transactional analysis theory perches atop two quite distinct ideas about how we come to reach our particular view on things. The psychodynamic ideas which inform script theory state that we only know what we permit ourselves to know.

131

Our constellation of consciously available beliefs is shaped by the need to keep some things hidden from ourselves (Erdelyi, 1985; Wollheim, 1991). Less directly cited but no less important, cognitive theories presume that current perceptions are filtered and shaped by previous experience, either to fit new information into our old expectations or to revise those expectations where the assimilation of the new cannot be managed successfully. In the cognitive account, belief is structured according to principles of information processing efficiency, as though our minds prized economy of effort, order, coherence and environmental functionality above all else. The psychodynamic account sees surface irregularity as wilfully and defensively necessary, the cognitive one as the accidental byproduct of otherwise necessary computation.

I don't see that a comprehensive account of human functioning necessarily needs to choose between these ideas. Unless we are determined to squeeze all human experience into one overarching framework, they don't always seem in direct competition. Sometimes one may appear more relevant than another as the particular instance requires. More crucially, I take neither theory to be sufficient to explain everything about how we come to believe things or be mistaken about them. My intention is to keep both ideas as part of a complex picture whilst also supplementing them with the additional notion, established in Chapter 3, that a good deal of what we believe is testimony-based belief. Here problems in knowing are more likely to result from dependence upon others even when they are inaccurate or dishonest. In such cases the problem lies not in the individual self's willingness or ability to see things accurately but in the world withholding what is needed – collective failures of resourcefulness and truthfulness. Therapeutically these difficulties require a different response. If this pluralism seems evasively non-committal rather than inclusive then that's an impression I'm in no rush to discourage. Our worldviews, I suspect, are far less orderly than our attempts to theorise them presume. They may demand therapeutic approaches which are correspondingly pliable and variable.

The limitations of script

The concept of frame of reference has been far less central than the notion of script to our clinical thinking. There may be many reasons for this but I suspect at least part of it is because script centres on the interconnection of knowledge and selfhood. It pares what we think down to a clear story of defensive ignorance thereby linking belief formation to a unitary explanatory apparatus. As script forms, we start out believing what we need to believe to survive and this in turn sets up both a pattern of subsequent experiences and a way of interpreting those experiences which holds script in place. Script theory therefore explains *how* people end up believing certain things it does not merely describe *that* they believe them. The theory always posits an explanatory road not taken, what we might have thought instead had we not headed down our defensive path.

This story would not have succeeded without explanatory heft and clinical utility. Yet script theory has also suffered from a kind of 'concept creep' (see Haslam, 2016), spreading further and further in its explanatory range away from its original psychodynamic sense of a self-limiting and defensive narrative. It now encroaches on broader questions of human development, identity formation and cultural belief patterns. Those who have insisted on enlarging the theory have often done so because they don't believe a theory of how people go wrong can stand apart from a theory of how people go right (English, 1988, 2003, 2010; Cornell, 1988; Summers & Tudor, 2000). Cornell's comprehensive review concludes that there is a need for an additional explanatory concept which outlines human development and identity formation without referring back to defensive psychological structures.

Script theories are useful for understanding the adoption of belief for pathological reasons: they aren't the right tools for this more sizeable job. I follow the cathexis school in arguing that we should regard script only as the subset of our frame of reference which contains discounts (Schiff et al., 1975a). Script beliefs are those parts of our world view which pertain to necessary concealment. Of course, scripts would plunge us into confusion if they didn't also somehow lead to faintly realistic beliefs about what is happening around us, but they are highly personalised narratives which favour need over accuracy where the two come into conflict. They project an overarching narrative about who we are and where we are going onto the world around us but they don't paint a more general picture about how things look. We are the stars – and the victims – of our scripts. Let's not ask of script theory any more than the limited though useful task it can reasonably complete.

Even linking belief with a broader developmental framework continues to presume a tight explanatory link between how we see things and who we are. Perhaps it's worth also remembering that things aren't always about us. The concept of script cannot fully explain horizontal problems for not all ignorance is internally motivated. Contextual transactional analysis is only interested in questions of self-definition and adaptation as part of a wider sense of how we take things to be. The appeal of the concept of frame of reference is that it brings wider questions of the usefulness, relevance, appeal and availability of belief back into the picture. Beliefs are outward facing even where they are internally useful. They appear as part of a collective and varied attempt to live in, enjoy, transform and cope with the world.

Frame of reference defined

My undertaking is now to reformulate the concept of frame of reference so that it better accounts for the limitations, inconsistencies and gaps in necessary knowledge. Frame of reference will become to horizontal problems what script theory is to vertical ones – a descriptive artefact of equal stature.

The term frame of reference has been used both as a description and an explanation. As a description it refers to the total content of our world view; as a theory it accounts for how we come to have that content. The original cathexis theory stressed the adaptive nature of knowledge, seeing the frame of reference as an internally coherent repertoire of possible responses to the world encompassing all three ego-states (Schiff et al., 1975a; Schiff, Schiff & Schiff, 1975b). Here knowledge is always working knowledge, acquired for a purpose and used accordingly. Elaine Childs-Gowell's later account is similarly explanatory, drawing upon Piaget to suggest that the frame of reference either assimilates new experience to old or accommodates it by necessary adjustment (see Childs-Gowell, 2000).

Jean Illsley Clarke and Susan Legender Clarke identified that the original theory did not acknowledge that our frame of reference comprises different kinds of knowledge, some more central to our world view than others, some more open to revision than others (Clarke, 1996; Clarke, 2014). These are primarily descriptive accounts breaking knowledge into types though both authors acknowledge that the frame of reference should be functional. What all these authors agree on is that content and purpose align. Everything we know is thought to have passed the test of experience.

Adaptative suitability is certainly something, but it is not everything. Adopting it as a sole organising principle makes our worldviews somewhat simpler than they actually are. There must be room for dreams, aspirations and imagination. There must be scope for the not-yet-reality vision which emerges from the starting points of the functional to show we might bend and shape the world to our wills. Some pragmatists have argued that beliefs are also conceptual tools for transforming the flux of the world to better fit our hopes (Dewey, 1998; Brandom, 2000; Rorty, 1989). The frame of reference is not just working knowledge, but living knowledge which reflects the co-existence of the ambitious heart and the brute fact. Fluid in its organising principles, a realist responsiveness to circumstance sometimes giving way to dreaming, the frame of reference navigates between what is forced upon us and what is open to our action.

This takes us some way towards a more complete picture but I fear I am in danger of making our minds sound either very efficient or overly dynamic, as though we were well-grooved processing machines or tireless visionaries. Any honest appraisal of an average person's world view will conclude that this is a kindly overestimation. Our minds also contain outdated assumptions, mistakes, errors of judgement and comprehension, tall tales and self-serving lies we have credulously taken in from similarly misguided others, vague impressions and crass generalisations, forgotten facts and inaccurate predictions. Things sometimes hang together as much by the grace of god as they do by machinic efficiency.

We need to make space for a variety of explanations as to how our worldview is composed. We are sometimes fearless truth-seekers but also prone to our vanities, our laziness, our sometime tendency to choose convenience over truth, fantasy over seriousness. The findings of cognitive psychology that we are pre-consciously disposed towards efficient, adaptive pattern finding does not provide the guarantee we are looking for. Instant appraisal is not the same as complex, cumulatively formed and long-fermented judgements. Just because our car engine is in perfect working order doesn't mean we are never going to drive to the wrong place. It confuses the possibility of efficient calculation with the assumption that it is always paramount. We might grant a hearing to similar doubts about collective knowledge. Whilst Richard Dawkins has written about memes, beliefs which are transmitted and replicated along Darwinian lines within a culture, significant deficits in responsiveness, truthfulness and integrity can scupper this process (Dawkins, 2006; Boyd & Richerson, 1985).

This provocative over-correction on my part was a necessary opening move before swinging back some way in the direction of a less regimented psychological orderliness. Drawing upon the philosophy of William James, Stephen Stich has advocated what he calls 'descriptive cognitive pluralism', roughly speaking the idea that people have different habits of mind and that each of these habits may be as good as each other at different times (see Stich, 1990, p. 13; James, 2000). There is no particular reason to think that people always approach thinking about life in the same way. We live our lives according to multiple principles and in varying environments where a pluralism of viewpoints may be possible. Although Stich is talking primarily about differences between people, I see no reason not to assume that an individual may deploy different ways of sorting information at different times.

We may identify a strong core of consistency in a typical frame of reference around which fleeting variation orbits. Stich suggests that this core emerges gradually, that our thoughts move in a general direction, loosely yoking together our different habits of mind, because things sort of hang together and work out for us in the end. I shall refer to this as *cognitive drifting*, the sense that our worldviews have a very general thrust and overall shape but this can't be tied back to a singular explanatory mechanism or intention. The specific shape of a cognitive drift is best discerned in looking back, noticing the overall shape of beliefs and actions across time. The frame of reference is more product than unified process. I have argued that the capacity to make use of norms, rules and shared information are essential prerequisites for co-operation and effective living, but it's also true we can't wholly describe inevitably imperfect people in terms of unblemished ideals. Perhaps we should understand rationality and adaptive capacity as potentially available 'safety nets', things we can – and often do – draw upon when necessary but not always the sole cognitive virtues driving our interactions with the world.

Our frame of reference neither quite refers to a descriptive cataloguing of itemised beliefs nor a singular unifying mechanism: those hoping to open up the frame of reference and find a single, clockwork principle which explains everything will be disappointed. Instead I recommend that we see it as a variable ordering of our collected knowledge and experiential content. It is shaped by a changing assortment of cognitive habits from which a somewhat stable core of beliefs and processes emerge as a byproduct of our largely consistent life paths

135

and environments. Working clinically with a frame of reference requires a dual capacity to hang back and trace the particular outline of the person's cognitive drift, whilst also zooming in to explore the specific cognitive habits which may be most relevant at any given moment. We need to encompass the overall shape and detail of the specific moving parts.

In the ego-state model we already have a way of talking about how we are several patterns of thinking and being rather than the one we sometimes mistakenly take ourselves to be and that these patterns can gradually add up to a somewhat coherent worldview. As the Schiffs noted, our ego-states form co-operative networks so each contributes something to our patterns of thought and action (Schiff et al., 1975a). Parent ego-states, caught between cognitive vulnerability and cognitive opportunity, summarise our habit of leaning from the beliefs of others even without full authority over those beliefs. Sharing out cognitive tasks, trusting and drawing upon other's experiences and knowledge is a cognitive strategy with some clear advantages.

Whilst our cognitive vulnerability means this is sometimes an enforced dependence, we might be said to have an active cognitive habit of 'offloading' some belief formation tasks to others, to pruning back on some responsibilities to maximise the focus on other tasks. So far I have laid primary responsibility for horizontal problems at the feet of the contextual failure to offer people the chance to know and act with authority, but it's important to acknowledge that people may also render themselves more vulnerable to horizontal problems by developing the cognitive habit of leaning too heavily on consensus viewpoints.

The Child ego-state may also make a distinctive contribution to the frame of reference. As our 'old self' returning to the present moment, our Child is living memory – with all the ongoing revision that the term memory presumes. It is the ballast of lived experience weighing against the impetus to meet the present with fresh eyes. At its best the living memory of the Child carries within it a wealth of formative stories and experiences which coalesced in the course of living, at its worst the limitations of script. Perhaps another strand of cognitive pluralism would entail recognising that valued experience and memory should not instantly be outweighed by fresh knowledge. Script-free, the Child ego-state contributes historic, lived experience as a compass into the future: script-bound it may stress that emotional need conquers all.

I am using the concept of the Child ego-state more expansively than may be usual to incorporate not just parts of ourselves formed at times of developmental immaturity but also aspects that have been left behind as obsolete even after maturation has been achieved. I take this to be consistent with Berne's notion of the psychic organ archeopsyche – literally ancient or old mind – which structures our historic experience into the Child ego-state, even if Berne himself didn't authorise this particular use. We leave ways of being behind not just because as human beings we are constantly growing and changing, but also because the world also changes around us bringing with it fresh challenges and freedoms. Being different selves at different times is a reflection of the ongoing flux of circumstance as eras arrive and fade. Our Adult and Child ego-states are therefore doubly distinct, representing not just a time when we were young but also when the world was different. A person entering their senescence will be living in a world changed several times over from the one they were first initiated into in childhood. The psychological value of the Child in such times of change may be akin to the quality of Integrity that I identified as essential for healthy collectives in Chapter 2, a kind of wisdom and sense of connection that won't easily be let go of.

I have already presented a fresh account of the Adult's cognitive virtues in Chapters 3 and 5. Assuming appropriate contextual conditions are met, the Adult is both our ability to perceive how things are and also see how they might plausible be different, it can be both functional and inspirational. The Adult holds the possibility of cutting free of uncritical repetition of the past and unthinking subjugation to common wisdom. These might sound like they should be our supreme cognitive attributes, but clearly rational capacities and the tendency towards giving up our beliefs in the light of new experiences don't always win the day. Adult cognitive capacities are essential to draw upon sometimes, but it's not clear that they should always be dominant.

As an example of how our combined ego-states might result in somewhat loose drifting, consider being part of a crowd arriving at an event and following someone towards the common destination only to discover that the person themselves didn't themselves know where they were going. Evaluated from the stand point of strict efficiency this might look like a lazy, unsatisfactory habit of mind. A kinder view from the perspective of cognitive pluralism might perceive a complex swaying together of our ego-states with their varying cognitive strategies, the remembered Child experiences of following others having worked out before aligning with our Parent need to lean on the knowledge and experience of others in the present with Adult reality testing on hand to ensure that rational appraisal of present reality plays a role. Perhaps we can imagine the impetus to efficiency jostling with the pleasure of ambling lazily, letting others take the lead. This may seem like a motley strategy, different ways of doing things taking the wheel at different times. It's far from obvious that it's efficient, but it works out in the end in a roundabout sort of way. Our frame of reference just adds another episode to its general drift.

We never entirely slip free of a Parent ego-state because cognitive vulnerability is irreducible: that we can never entirely leave behind who we have been before means there is a part of us that is forever Child. Yet this isn't a way of saying that ego-states have a fixed function in the way they contribute to our frame of reference. As anyone who has used any piece of paper to hand for a bookmark before can testify, sometimes what things get used for bears little relation to their intended function. Sometimes it's less about how our ego-states work and more about how our wider psychological structure takes up their contributions. Rather than seeing the frame of reference as the smooth intermeshing of three cogs into an overall motion, a better metaphor might take it to be a varyingly productive conversation between the different parts of ourselves. The Adult might be thought of informally as a kind of 'chair', capable of exercising the casting vote of reason, but one curiously disposed to sometimes letting one of the other ego-states take the lead.

Extending the metaphor, this conversation presumes degrees of agreement, enough common ground for things not to stall, balanced with moments where other options are available: our frames of reference don't always get hung up on details. As the conversation progressed and external demands changed, the varying interests of memory, imagination, offloading, adaptation, continuity, reason and need would rise and fall in prominence. The overall direction of travel which is our sense of our identity resulting from our world view would be nothing more than the consequential trend of thought and action across time. The frame of reference is the tracks we leave behind us in the dirt as we keep on moving. In addition to believing what it's efficient to believe (cognitive), what we need to believe (psychodynamic) and what others lead us to believe (testimonial) we also need to acknowledge that sometimes we believe things just because they sort of fit with how we generally see things.

Taking the frame of reference to be a product of varying processes leads to some subtle alterations in our approach to client work, particularly with regard to what Berne called contamination and his view that confrontation can be used to prise the capable Adult apart from the clouding distortions imposed by other ego-states (Berne, 1966). Berne encouraged judicious pouncing upon inconsistency as the key means to separating out how things really are from internally generated misbelief. These strategies still have their place with either highly disturbed clients who need to be urgently restored to some level of immediate functioning or resourceful, well-integrated individuals who can name the change they want but are ambivalent about deciding to pursue it and are looking to have the balance tipped in favour of change.

I'm less sure that contradiction should be always taken to have this kind of leverage. It isn't my impression that inconsistency is something we can or should be always concerned about. Increasingly I have concluded that client inconsistency is sometimes a sign that I haven't yet appreciated why the belief is held, some deeper value or belief behind the contradiction that hasn't so far revealed itself and isn't ready to budge. I see inconsistency as a call for greater curiosity about how the overall frame of reference hangs together. A general sense of not feeling able to give up a way of believing which had stood a person in good stead even in the face of contradiction may be an indication of cognitive sophistication rather than cognitive failure. A single inconsistency does not shatter a worldview. The overall shape of belief can weather some erosion and sometimes finds grounds for restoration.

This book has advocated for greater Adult authority as the pathway to necessary social and political awareness, but I also acknowledge that sometimes you can't change, improve or replace beliefs without carefully shifting a whole world view. It is counterproductive to press on with attempts to heighten awareness in a certain way when you are working against the grain of competing and disparate cognitive priorities. Carry all ego-states along – even if the Adult often takes the lead. This is a painstaking process which presupposes embracing the full gamut of a person's experience and cognitive dispositions, revisiting each separate strand of belief and adding new ones as required, pausing at each moment to notice how fresh beliefs are received and responded to by the overall frame of reference. This is particularly relevant in the resolution of horizontal problems where the positive and negative aspects of an experientially rich worldview may hang together in a way which may prove hard to disentangle. Integrity of world-view is not surrendered lightly.

Clinical vignette

Paula and Tim came for couples therapy after 8 years of marriage. They had started dating 12 years ago when Paula was a regular in the bar that Tim worked in and connected over a shared love of gig going. They revealed that their early years as a couple were a long haze of late Saturday nights in clubs and Sunday mornings on the sofa watching TV. Questions of marriage and children rolled around for both of them as they entered their thirties. Both appeared ready to put their care-free younger years behind them. Tim set up an events management company and they had two children in quick succession.

It was after the birth of their second child that difficulties sprang up in their relationship. Paula was spending time with other young mums in the town where she and Tim lived all of whom had spouses who earned a lot of money and who had chosen not to work themselves. Having previously been very proud of her independence and successful career in publishing, Paula began to criticise Tim for not earning enough money to afford them the lifestyle she wanted. Paula had always earned more than Tim and he struggled to understand what had happened to the person who always wanted to pay her share of the bill in restaurants. Paula stated that Tim had begun to withdraw and was spending his evenings working in the upstairs office. Rows inflamed by mutual incomprehension were becoming more and more frequent.

During the course of our work, Paula revealed that her father had been an immensely wealthy managing director of an insurance company. The family had money and mixed mostly with similarly wealthy people. As a little girl she had always pictured her future husband having money, taking care of her and them enjoy-ing a good lifestyle. In her teens she had connected her mother's not working with being a subordinate partner in the marriage and had become strongly insistent that women should strive for autonomy and their own money. Paula was surprised to dis-cover in therapy that whilst she had changed her values about herself and relation-ships, she hadn't learnt to dream new dreams about them. Her adolescent and early childhood experiences had sat side by side without ever being brought into dialogue or reconciliation. She didn't want to surrender her Adult belief that independence was right but found that its achievement brought no lasting thrill which could fully replace her childhood wishes. Independence felt like the right thing but was strangely empty. Tim was bearing the brunt of her inability to resolve these tensions.

As a fellow child of the late 1960s, Tim had also grown up in a household where his father worked and his mother didn't. He recalled his parents seeming unhappily married and his father often complaining about the long hours he did as a police man. Tim was happy to quietly let go the expectations surrounding the male role which his father had taken for granted and enjoyed the increasingly assertive attitudes of his female peers though these beliefs tended to enjoy a kind or ironic resurgence when out drinking with his friends.

Tim learned in therapy that as an adolescent he had been happy to slip free of assumptions about the male role but he had not put an alternative model of masculinity in their place. He believed in equality but didn't quite know what it was meant to feel like as a way of living. Tim's Parent ego-state suffered from the fractured pluralism typical of chaos, all choice and no firm centre. Paula's dissatisfaction struck at deep injuries about his not being a man like his dad in his Child, but the world gave Tim no help in guiding him towards what a man might be. He was unsure of his place in the home and with the children, concerned that any act of assertion would make him like his dad yet also determined to have his say. Tim acknowledged that many of his friends were obliquely voicing the same concerns about not quite knowing where their role lay anymore.

Neither Paula nor Tim had worked out individually how to reconcile the competing demands of experience, memory and rationality, where to strike out in original gestures from the shared worldview and where to coincide with it. Our work together helped them to retrace the layering of different experience and beliefs that underlay their conflict. Between them they began to reconstruct a vision of their shared life together from the materials of long-standing hopes, new opportunities and careful rethinking of unexamined experience. Paula realised that it was fine to dream of wealthy white knights but when she returned to reality she wanted someone she could trust, get on with and respect for their sturdiness. For his part, Tim began to distinguish assertiveness from boorishness. Taking his place more fully in the partnership entailed not merely a new understanding that this is what being a man could look like but that permanent unhappiness didn't immediately result from disagreement.

The frame of reference and horizontal problems

So far I have suggested that the frame of reference might work as the residual product of our experience loosely held together by both the overall direction of travel and the uneven co-operation of separate cognitive principles. This doesn't yet say enough about why some beliefs get included and others don't. A matching of knowledge and context is essential for successful living and the resolution of horizontal problems. My undertaking here is to explore in more depth what it means to know something and to have it as part of our frame of reference but also the ways in which significant absences in our frame of reference can be inferred. This makes a fuller case for the inclusion of learning in the therapy process than I have previously advanced.

Everyone's frame of reference has a limit. There is always a horizon of knowledge and experience beyond which we cannot see. Living mortal lives in situated bodies means that nobody can know everything equally. Since cultures and societies tend towards coherence and integrity they also can't be all things to all people. Assuming we are raised under benign circumstances then our limits will be comfortable and unassuming, neither brought to our attention nor problematic. Most people can successfully navigate their way through the world without knowing how to fly a plane, being able to speak Latin or perform advanced calculus because you generally don't need to know this to live successfully. The inevitable convergence of locally shared experience means that the limits of our understanding map approximately on to the limits of those we live amongst.

Social collectives hand down their accumulated knowledge of what the world is like and how best to live to the next generation. Since people are collectively engaged in the ongoing challenge of trying to live successfully in the contexts in which they find themselves, the knowledge that is handed down aims at situational usefulness. It would make little sense to raise children with Japanese as a first language when their community speaks English. Contexts can change and knowledge must be recast and re-forged in the light of new experience but accumulated habits of existence inevitably provide the starting point for fresh thinking directed at today's business.

Under the good enough conditions identified in Chapter 2, communities will be sufficiently resourceful, responsive, truthful and integrated to bequeath living knowledge sufficient to provide the starting points for creative and original responses. When those conditions are not in place, knowledge which might seem necessary for living in that context may not develop. I will use the term *absence* to refer to instances of specific ignorance where a person needs to know something to live successfully or might be reasonably expected to know something based on what else they know, but somehow do not. The term absence therefore refers to *conspicuous* omissions, things we might expect a person to believe. They are sometimes more readily identified from the outside, spotted from someone else's frame of reference.

Absences need to be carefully distinguished from injunctions. These latter terms are defined as a negative or prohibiting command which comes from the parent and is then replayed as a form of internal conflict (Berne, 1972; Steiner, 1974). Injunctions block the acknowledgement of fully realised impulses. The term is part of a wealth of transactional analysis concepts which seek to explain how we know something out of awareness but don't allow it to emerge into consciousness. By contrast, absence refers to circumstances where a belief has never had the opportunity to form let alone be blocked. They are things we don't and have never known. Clinically these two phenomenon can be hard to distinguish for attempts to fill an absence by bringing new information to someone's awareness can often result in wariness or confusion, but this should be distinguished from the specific, contentful anxiety which comes when we invite a forbidden impulse to emerge from under a prohibition.

141

Injunctions may turn progressively into absences across generations. If the same injunction is delivered to all children consistently across a community so that everyone is inhibited in the way, then the public expression and circulation of those ways of being vanishes. Gradually what was forbidden in one generation may become lost to the next one. Where there are gaps in the knowledge of the previous generation, either innocently occurring or the consequence of knowing prohibition (see Proctor, 2008), the experience handed down contains absences. Equally, where a younger generation faces new challenges unfamiliar to their predecessors then new absences in know-how have opened up which the latter have never known how to fill. People cannot teach you what they do not know or give you what they do not have. Current collective ingenuity will often ride to the rescue in the end, but it is certainly slower to appear in worlds that are not good enough.

Absences in our experience will often pass unnoticed because our frame of reference binds our worldview into a semblance of wholeness. We use the word impasse in transactional analysis to designate conflicts between ego-states which would lead to a divide in our frame of reference, but we lack a word for internal harmony leading to coherence. I will refer to a state of coherence and good fit between ego-states as an *accord*. When our ego-states appear to be in accord our world view feels settled, uncomplicated as though things just are as they are around here and nothing needs to be interrogated. When ego-states are in accord yet the frame of reference does not contain necessary knowledge then people won't understand the nature or origin of their distress. Horizontal problems cannot fully announce themselves in a way which might lead to resolution or understanding. For example, it is possible for a community to understand that they are oppressed whilst not fully understanding quite what this has cost them, for they have never yet had a chance to know what a life of freedom looks like.

One way in which our frame of reference is aroused from the comfortable slumber of accord to fill a newly announced absence is through fresh experience. At this point we are confronted with something we didn't previously know. When suitably disposed, our attention is then drawn into learning from the experience. Successfully filling an absence has the feel of revelation, as though it were obvious things were that way all along even though we didn't quite see it. The second way in which we can identify and rectify absences is through contact with someone whose frame of reference is sufficiently similar to ours whilst at the same time knowing something that we don't. A parent consoling their young child, distraught over a fight with a friend helps them to name their pain, to understand that the hurt will pass and that relationships can be repaired, all things the child does not yet know. In doing so they begin from the shared zone of understanding whilst adding their greater experience and knowhow to the child's knowledge repertoire. A person struggling with horizontal problems will lack people in their sphere of acquaintance whose experience is one step ahead of their own. They will live in a world where all are equally lost and no one can show the way.

Identifying and filling an absence is a precise and intricate business. Correctness of fit is paramount. In the clinical domain coming to notice a gap in a client's world view is rather like completing a jigsaw puzzle and sensing that some pieces are missing. The more complete the jigsaw, the more we can look at the overall shape and tell what ought to go there based on our knowledge of the surrounding pieces. Taking a panoramic perspective on a client's frame of reference we can notice that it follows naturally that if a person holds certain beliefs they are more likely to hold others as a matter of consistency. In Chapter 5 I argued that in dialogue we track both what the other person has said (committed to) and could have meant (entitled to): in exploring their frame of reference we similarly take in what they believe and what they could also believe. Filling an absence moves the person one step beyond their current comprehension, but only to the knowledge they should already have had.

Clinical vignette

Kenneth was born at a time when homosexuality was illegal in the United Kingdom. As a child he knew no other gay men and the ones he heard about were described in hushed and disgusted tones. He remained single and sexually inexperienced throughout life, his sexuality known but not acknowledged to himself. He did his best to build a dignified though loveless life by throwing himself into work. As the years passed he could not fail to notice the huge leap forward in social and legal esteem that gay people coming after him enjoyed. Stories of contented, respectful gay lives became commonplace. When he came to therapy in his mid-seventies he disclosed feeling an overwhelming sense of loss and anger linked to his current Adult reappraisal of his early years. If only he could have seen things then as he does now! Kenneth certainly was the recipient of multiple injunctions around his sexuality, but in those early years counterpoint narratives creating a sense of the possible were unavailable. His grief and anger were not waiting there all along to be unearthed, they were created by these new stories filling the absence in his understanding. Kenneth's story shows that finding out what you should have known all along can bring loss along with gain but he was emphatic that he would never give up the sharp pain of comprehension for the dull, gnawing ache of a problem he could never quite name.

It may seem that I am proposing the filling of absences with simple facts. It may also appear that I am in danger of underestimating disadvantaged people by claiming they are ignorant of things they know only too well. It should readily be conceded that the disadvantaged are graphically aware of their misfortune and knowing this has brought them neither relief nor a change in circumstance. These are strong objections but I believe they can be met by pointing out that knowing is a matter of degrees and kinds. A person either does or does not know that Madrid is the capital of Spain but this is a relatively simple kind of factual knowledge to which there is only one correct answer. The outcome of therapy rarely turns on simple facts. Yet there are other beliefs we might hold which emerge from a whole, complex attendant worldview. Aristotle refers to this as phronesis, a practical knowing about how to live which informs our daily interaction (Aristotle & Brown, 2009). This kind of knowing is less concerned with discovering of facts and more with the acquisition of what we might call wisdom.

We can meaningfully divide phronesis into degrees and thereby distinguish between what I will refer to as knowing and KNOWING. When we merely know something we have a bare command of the facts, a sketch rather than a picture. Knowing is a dry and distant knowledge of a form of life, something we have never embraced as central to our sense of self or our practice of living. It can prick our curiosity but rarely move us to change. It's the equivalent of flicking between webpages rather than extended, involved contemplation: it's information, not knowledge (Han, 2015). It's what occurs when you confront a client's contradictions and they greet it with a shrug. The gap between knowing and KNOWING can seem both inches and miles apart simultaneously yet the latter is only achieved when a way of seeing things snaps together and comes to life.

To understand how KNOWING differs from knowing, we might return to the metaphor of learning a language. Early on we know what words mean and assemble them somewhat mechanically into grammatically appropriate sentences. You can get by, but you are not a native speaker, you do not yet think or dream in this language, don't understand its flavour, you can't play with it or master its delicate inflections. It doesn't feel like home. KNOWING something is characterised by this deep familiarity, the ability to commit to the full meaning and resonance of something. At its best KNOWING isn't stale or habitual, for our sense of things is renewed with authority by daily experience. When we KNOW something we have a native grasp of how a belief hangs together with our overall world view, its full meaning and use in the course of life is effortlessly and immediately apparent. At its best, outsight is KNOWING which maps the contours, depths and possibilities of reality whilst maintaining an accord between ego-states.

KNOWING is linked to integrity (Chapter 2), inseparable from the overlapping stories of people and places where life experiences coalesce into an ethos. It isn't acquired overnight and it won't be abandoned swiftly. This recalls what constructivist psychotherapists call 'impermeable beliefs', aspects of a collective mindset which are so solid, so central, so deep rooted that new experience cannot easily dislodge them (see Chiari & Nuzzo, 2010). KNOWING is only replace by new KNOWING, it doesn't leave a vacuum. KNOWING only becomes problematic where familiarity bleeds into stagnancy, where changes aren't registered, where other necessary ideas get crowded out and where integrity turns into stubborn, unresponsive conformity (Barnett Pearce, 2007). Where our KNOWING draws too heavily from the Parent then authority cannot emerge from the consensus viewpoint to do the necessary work of reform. Where our

Child is ascendant then past experience impedes present understanding rather than enabling it.

New KNOWING begins life as knowing. It starts by peering curiously over the fence at unfamiliar horizons before the person dives in and substitutes uninvolved contemplation for committed learning. The challenge of working with horizontal problems is how to invite someone to step out of familiar, absence-ridden KNOWING when the new perspectives we encourage them to know in therapy can initially seem so foreign and insubstantial. The task of contextual transactional analysis is to take clients from knowing their disadvantage to the cusp of KNOWING it. They only KNOW they are disadvantaged once a complex, coherent picture of the myriad ways the world works against them meets up with a fully realised, experience-rich sense of what an improved life would be like. The final sting in the tale of disadvantage is that it is a familiar prison which may yet be clung to. If all we are offering struggling persons is rootless and disengaged outsight without KNOWING, then we risk asking our clients to leave their worldviews behind without an alternative. It is an invitation that many will refuse.

Vocabularies

I have focused so far on individual frames of reference, but there are also shared worldviews, an observably consistent and coherent body of cultural beliefs that are widely held by groups of people who enjoy ongoing relationships. An account is needed about the relationship between individual and the collective belief.

I am reluctant to follow others in referring to harmful cultural beliefs as 'cultural scripts' (see Roberts, 1975; Shivanath & Hiremath, 2002) since this seems to fall back into the trap of trying to understand the social through the psychological and the functional in terms of the dysfunctional. As a concept, script presumes the pathology of the individual psyche but contexts can't have scripts because they don't have minds, defences, unconscious processes or unintegrated parts. What we need is an appropriate recognition of both the enabling and disabling aspects of shared belief and a sense of the ways and reasons they come to be held that embraces social as well as psychological aspects.

Whilst the concept of oppression can sound rather like a social equivalent to script, the fit isn't precise and it doesn't explain all the problems a collective ethos might develop. Collective frames of reference can be as shambolic as individual ones. They can be inefficient, blind and error-prone be it in a tendency to favour settled habits over more adaptive knowing in periods of change, vulnerable to failures in communication and truthfulness amongst peoples leading to a degeneration of collective knowhow and inefficient at problem solving in ways that inevitably accompany complex social collectives (see Diamond, 2011). Calling something a script narrows and tidies things up when what we are searching for is a term which captures the amble and sprawl of ethos formation.

None the less, I agree with White and White when they suggest that collective beliefs arise and persist in part because common predicaments are likely to generate common experiences which will naturally converge over time (White & White, 1975). In addition to the principles of adaptation and naturally occurring convergence of individual experiences into a larger whole, people also organise to pool experience and knowledge in social collectives and make shared decisions about how they wish to run their lives. Cultural beliefs will usually feature this mixture of the planned and unavoidable as well as beliefs adopted and retained for historic reasons and those which represent a response to current reality. They are an ever changing motley.

Cultural beliefs don't stick around unaided. Within a relatively consistent context, we both inherit and hand on shared beliefs in the course of our transactions. I would suggest it is possible to split transactions into *circulatory* and *interrupting* subtypes as a way of understanding how this process of transmission works. Circulatory transactions refer to interactions where the background assumptions of the participant's shared worldview are simply taken as given. Our collective frame of reference is confirmed and handed on without challenge. In interrupting transactions usually unquestioned assumptions are brought into the foreground for fresh evaluation by both parties. Here the possibility of a local deviation from or revision of the collective frame of reference is made possible.

Most transactions will be circulatory because most daily interactions within a context aim at nothing more than uncomplicated co-operation, social agreeableness and the sustaining trickle of strokes (see Geis, 1995). In addition, either out of life choices or by virtue of circumstance, many people end up spending their life enmeshed in social networks with people like themselves. The more time we spend with similar people the more our frames of reference converge (see Crossley et al., 2015). Combined, these are powerful built-in buffers against the social disturbance of frequent contestation. It's easy enough to see how an uncritical acceptance of common ideas and a consequent cognitive drifting in a certain direction can result from the wider imperatives to get on with others, trust what they say and stay away from unnecessary complications. This is how we end up with that sense that things just are as they are around here.

Growing up and living in a particular context involves learning to think in the language of shared beliefs. I intend to refer to a collective frame of reference, the hanging together of a shared way of seeing things, a set of ideas, behaviours, dispositions and values generated from a collective experience and history as a *vocabulary*. A vocabulary will always somewhat reflect the varying circumstantial needs and aspirations of the people who make it as well as the inefficiencies that arise from collective belief formation. The term owes a conceptual debt to both Pierre Bourdieu's concept of the habitus (Bourdieu, 1984) and John Dewey's notion of habit (Dewey, 1922). Bourdieu stressed that shared beliefs tend to tug experiences back into conservatively familiar patterns. Habitus ensures orderliness and competence of action but at the price of nothing changing. Dewey emphasises the outward facing, responsive aspect of shared beliefs, that they allow us to achieve not merely a good fit to the world but also mastery and creative expression of interest. An optimal vocabulary will balance these aspect to be both fit for purpose and endowed with an aspirational thrust: a faltering one will leave us incapable in the present and unable to find a way to our futures. Against prior arguments (James, 1994), I propose that our individual frame of reference cannot be separated from the vocabulary, for it is the pen in which much of our singular experience is written.

A vocabulary may be formed and maintained for specific reasons but this does not mean they cannot have additional consequences for our understanding. Shared beliefs can be retained for reasons of nostalgia long after their initial purpose has been served, often being formally inscribed in custom and ritual. Since vocabularies are assembled somewhat loosely over time, an emergent product of a shared way of living, they constitute a collective form of memory, KNOWING more than knowing (Erll, 2011). After their original purpose has dwindled, vocabularies can stay on as relics of past struggles or valued connections with those who came before us. If they hang around, sometimes new purpose and meaning becomes attached to old ways of thinking. They are not wholly systematically assembled though to those who speak them they may have the appearance of complete unity projected on to them with hindsight. There may therefore be an irreducible tension between the historic richness of a vocabulary and its responsiveness to present circumstance.

We are not merely trapped within our vocabularies, we often lean upon them because when we swim with the social tide it can give our actions a sense of effortless meaning. In this way vocabularies support the condition of integrity which I have deemed essential for a good enough world. Yet some vocabularies provide a better support to meaningful, purposive and effective action than others. When they are not produced under 'good enough' conditions, a vocabulary may be characterised by absences awaiting fresh development. Often the best way to identify the absences of a vocabulary is to listen to the jokes told about it. A skilful comedian can identify exactly those absurdities of everyday action where we all do things even though they make little obvious sense, contradict our stated values and break with our preferred image of ourselves.

Within the communities identified in Chapter 2, people seem to make use of a vocabulary in which toughness and coping appear to be the organising ideas. Whether directly stated, or covertly expressed through demeanour and deportment, these ideas are circulated in every transaction from robust humour and readiness for confrontation to the dismissal of book learning, the slapping down of complaint or aspiration in favour of 'just getting on with it', the admiration for people who have it hard and get by and the suspicion of those from outside as 'posh'. This vocabulary has history, the texture of lived experience, effortless familiarity and is the object of some affection. It might also be said to limit the capacity to forge strong individual and collective identities in a radically changed, post-industrial landscape. We might take an absence of faith in the

147

changeability of things as its most striking omission. Perhaps it is hard to revise and reform the dead strands of thought in a vocabulary without somehow feeling that you are sacrificing something precious.

Working with our client's vocabularies is therefore a tightrope art of carefully focusing in on problematic absences without engendering a defensive recoil. Whilst we should concede that we have no basis to comparatively evaluated whole cultures against each other (see Habermas, 1986) this should not mean we feel helpless to propose small, necessary areas for reconsideration, particularly where we think it will make a vocabulary a better version of itself. A vocabulary may contain absences if a problem appears that a person does not appear to fully understand or know how to solve. The self-deception of script can be overcome by acceptance or insight, but gaps in cultures are true absences not conceal-ments. There simply isn't the KNOWING present to make something graspable. Opening up a space for revision and reform is the only way ahead.

Our individual scripts are often written in our most familiar vocabulary. Children always use shared stories and experiences as the starting point for their own narratives. Absences in vocabularies as much as more tangible cultural beliefs will ensure that individual scripts will be somewhat similar as they emerge from this background of shared assumptions. Put more simply, individual scripts are as much shaped invisibly by what isn't there, by what can't be thought as they are by what visibly is and can.

Conclusion

Calling something by a single term, either frame of reference or vocabulary, inevitably generates an expectation in the reader's mind, that you will be leaving them with a crisp, operative definition. Those expecting to emerge from this chapter with either a unified explanatory account of how a frame of reference works or sharp theoretical scalpel to help them cut away unhelpful cultural beliefs from the living tissue of relevant ones will be somewhat disappointed. These are expectations I am happy not to meet. An account can only be as unitary and explanatory as its subject allows. The search for a single key which unlocks the secrets of a frame of reference misunderstands that we are dealing with something profuse, mobile and subject to different interests or principles which may rise and fall in importance depending on context. I can help the reader to better describe a frame of reference but not completely explain it.

There is no substitute for respectful and curious immersion in the individual specifics of a frame of reference or a vocabulary. We don't need to find our way to common workings or general principles which cut across cases, we need to trace the specific history, patterns and priorities of the belief systems we are working with against the background of the context in which they emerged. We simply return endlessly to the question of why things are some way and not another way. If the reader is able to keep in mind the multiple interests and cognitive processes which feed into a frame of reference and recalls that those processes can shift with a change in context then the chapter may have been worthwhile.

It is neither desirable, necessary nor possible in most cases to pursue a whole-sale revision of a person's frame of reference. We seek productive, subtle reform rather than wholesale revolution. The therapist's challenge is to gain the best possible vantage point on the client's worldview so they might venture a guess as to what works and what doesn't, what might change and what will endure, whether to work with the grain of the frame or how best to cut across it, to care-fully explore the different ways in which a possible new 'piece' might fit an identified absence. We need to be awake to changes both intended and unin-tended, waiting to see how a whole constellation of beliefs shifts in the wake of a single alteration. The aim is new KNOWING, a way of seeing comprehensive, robust and detailed enough to support a viable re-engagement with the world.

References

Aristotle, Brown, L. (2009) *The Nicomachean Ethics.* Translated from Greek by D. Ross. Oxford: Oxford University Press.

Barnett Pearce, W. (2007) *Making Social Worlds: A Communication Perspective.* Malden, MA: Blackwell Publishing.

Berne, E. (1966) *Principles of Group Treatment.* New York: Grove Press.

Berne, E. (1972) *What Do You Say After You Say Hello?* London: Corgi.

Bourdieu, P. (1984) *Distinction.* Translated from French by R. Nice. London: Routledge.

Boyd, R., Richerson, P.J. (1985) *Culture and the Evolutionary Process.* Chicago: University of Chicago Press.

Brandom, R. (2000) Vocabularies of Pragmatism: Synthesizing Naturalism and Histori-cism. In R. Brandom, Ed., *Rorty and his Critics.* Malden, MA: Blackwell Publisher, 156–182.

Chiari, G., Nuzzo, M.L. (2010) *Constructivist Psychotherapy: A Narrative Hermeneutic Approach.* London: Routledge.

Childs-Gowell, E. (2000) *Reparenting Schizophrenics: The Cathexis Experience.* Lincoln, NE: iUniverse.

Clarke, J.I. (1996) The Synergistic Use of Five Transactional Analysis Concepts by Edu-cators. *Transactional Analysis Journal,* 26 (3), 214–219.

Clarke, S.L. (2014) Updated Frame of Reference. *The Transactional Analyst,* 4 (2) Spring, 12–16.

Cornell, W.F. (1988) Life Script Theory: a critical review from a developmental per-spective. *Transactional Analysis Journal,* 18 (4), 270–282.

Crossley, N., Bellotti, E., Edwards, G., Everett, M.G., Koskinen, J., Tranmer, M. (2015) *Social Network Analysis for Ego-Nets.* Los Angeles: Sage.

Dawkins, R. (2006) *The Selfish Gene.* 3rd edn. New York: Oxford University Press.

Dewey, J. (1922) *Human Nature and Conduct: an introduction to social psychology.* New York: Henry Holt and Co.

Dewey, J. (1998) *Experience and Nature.* New York: Dover Publications.

Diamond, J. (2011) *Collapse: How Societies Choose to Fail or Survive.* 2nd edn. London: Penguin.

English, F. (1988) Whither Scripts? *Transactional Analysis Journal*, 18 (4), 294–303.

English, F. (2003) How are You? And How am I? Scripts, Ego-states and Inner Motivators. In C. Sills, H. Hargaden, Eds, *Ego-states*. London: Worth Publishing, 55–72.

English, F. (2010) It Takes a Life-Time to Play Out a Script. In R.G. Erskine, Ed., *Life Scripts: A Transactional Analysis of Unconscious Relational Patterns*. London: Karnac, 217–238.

Erdelyi, M.H. (1985) *Psychoanalysis: Freud's Cognitive Psychology*. New York: W.H. Freeman and Co.

Erll, A. (2011) *Memory in Culture*. Translated from German by S.B. Young. Basingstoke: Palgrave Macmillan.

Geis, M.L. (1995) *Speech Acts and Conversational Interaction: Toward a theory of conversational competence*. Cambridge: Cambridge University Press.

Habermas, J. (1986) *Autonomy and Solidarity: interviews with Jürgen Habermas*. Edited by P. Dews. London: Verso.

Han, B.C. (2015) *The Transparency Society*. Translated from German by E. Butler. Stanford: Stanford University Press.

Haslam, N. (2016) Concept Creep: Psychology's Expanding Concepts of Harm and Pathology. *Psychological Inquiry*, 27, 1–17.

James, N.L. (1994) Cultural Frame of Reference and Intergroup Encounters: A TA Approach. *Transactional Analysis Journal*, 24 (3), 206–210.

James, W. (2000) Pragmatism and Other Writings. New York: Penguin.

Proctor, R.N. (2008) 'Agnotology: A Missing Term to Describe the Cultural Production of Ignorance (and its Study)'. In R.N. Proctor, L. Schiebinger, Eds, *Agnotology: The Making & Unmaking of Ignorance*. Stanford: Stanford University Press, 1–36.

Roberts, D.L. (1975) Treatment of Cultural Scripts. *Transactional Analysis Journal*, 5 (1), 29–35.

Rorty, R. (1989) *Contingency, Irony, and Solidarity*. Cambridge: Cambridge University Press.

Schiff, J.L., Schiff, A., Mellor, K., Schiff, E., Fishman, J., Wolz, L., Fishman, C., Mombs, D. (1975a) *Cathexis Reader: Transactional Analysis Treatment of Psychosis*. New York: Harper and Row.

Schiff, J.L., Schiff, A., Schiff, E. (1975b) Frames of Reference. *Transactional Analysis Journal*, 5 (3), 290–294.

Shivanath, S., Hiremath, M. (2002) The Psychodynamics of Race and Culture: an analysis of cultural scripting and ego-state transference. In C. Sills, H. Hargaden, Eds, *Ego-states*. London: Worth Publishing, 169–184.

Stich, S.P. (1990) *The Fragmentation of Reason: Preface to a Pragmatic Theory of Cognitive Evaluation*. Cambridge, MA: MIT Press.

Steiner, C. (1974) *Scripts People Live*. New York: Grove Press.

Summers, G., Tudor, K. (2000) Co-creative Transactional Analysis. *Transactional Analysis Journal*, 30 (1), 23–40.

White, J.D., White, T. (1975) Cultural Scripting. *Transactional Analysis Journal*, 5 (1), 12–23.

Wollheim, R. (1991) *Freud*, 2nd edn. London: Fontana.

7

GAMES ALONG THE HORIZONTAL AXIS

Introduction

Games are the part of transactional analysis theory where the link between intrapsychic and interpersonal, between our minds and our interactions, is most fully realised. It's also where Berne's attempt to explain the social through the psychological runs up most sharply against its inherent limitations. This chapter invites us to consider what a theory of games might look like if we understood at least some games as more social than psychological phenomena. Insisting that what happens between us structures and enables what happens inside us, even if the reverse relationship is sometimes more important, leads to a theory of 'horizontal games'. I am suggesting that we separate off a subset of games as arising less from covert motivations and more from either absences in collective KNOWING and vocabulary, from oppressive circumstances where our thinking is taken over by someone else's description of the world or times of overlap where previously fixed patterns of opportunity, permission and constraint have moved into flux. I hope to suggest the conditions under which horizontal games are likely to be played and the different responses they might require on our part.

My treatment of preceding theories of games is revisionist rather than corrective. Previous definitions here can only be a starting point rather than the inviolable parameters in which we must work because our existing definitions are both multiple and also strangely limited with regard to the social structuring of games. Berne's original game theory does not want for clear statements on what a game is, a representative example being '… sets of ulterior transactions, repetitive in nature, with a well-defined psychological payoff' (Berne, 1972, p. 43). A careful reader will observe however that a fair portion of what he wrote on the subject can't be completely reconciled with his own definition (see Berne, 1964). We are left with the dilemma of either following his arguments or his statements. This is a tension which requires resolution.

A theory which attempts to marry descriptions of recurring patterns of social interaction with a subtle, layered picture of psychological functioning will inevitably be ambitious. It reflects what I take to be Berne's belief that a successful theory must be comprehensive, broad in application and schematically formulated. Aiming for comprehensive integration as well as encompassing utility, his theory of games sometimes seems to juggle more ideas than it can successfully bring together. Zalcman's admonishment that subsequent revision of and addition to Berne's theories have muddied the waters further by leaving us with ideas which overlap without fully cohering is fair (Zalcman, 1990), but I suspect that a theory with so many different cogs to click into place will either be too complex to wield or prone to ambiguity and overspill. This leaves us with a second dilemma: tighten up the internal structure of our definitions too much and we will be left with a theory of greatly reduced explanatory range; become overly permissive and the theory becomes unclear.

I hope I have side-stepped some of these issues by breaking the presumed link between covert psychological dispositions and patterned social interaction of Berne's original theory and partly by my insistence that sometimes we have to start again rather than looking to a rejigging of past efforts for answers. The simplicity which comes from a more singular focus on social rather than indi-vidual causation of games meets both of these requirements. Nor am I con-strained by the need to mesh my findings seamlessly with pre-existing transactional analysis theory since I have already proposed a comprehensive revisionist architecture comprising self-and-world, cognitive vulnerability, absences and revised accounts of the ego-states and frame of reference into which my propositions about games can be embedded.

One consequence of my starting again is the liberty of being less concerned than some about drawing a crisp line between games and social interactions which share some common features with them. It is inherently difficult to carve out a distinct phenomenon like games whilst also acknowledging that individual examples will always exceed the formula in some way. It's also tricky to say that games are just one thing when they can result from a multitude of different moti-vations and rationales which aren't uniformly present in every example. A theory can only be as schematic as the phenomenon it is attempting to describe permits. In the interests of keeping the theory both broadly useful and meaningfully coherent, I suggest we need to be somewhat tolerant of 'nearly-games', inter-actions which have some but not all features of games proper and where the theory may still be largely useful to explain what is taking place. In this chapter the basic 'what?' of games, their delineation of repetitive, confused and prob-lematic social interactions, will retain an approximate core shape familiar to those acquainted with prior theory. The 'why?' and 'how?' of games, the wider reason we play games of the horizontal variety and how we end up in the same place again and again, will be introduced in line with the broader conclusions of the book.

Although I offer a brief consideration of why there are divergences and dis-agreements in game theory, the aim is less to deliver a magical, seamless inte-gration of all the conceptual pieces we have lying around and more to show how my revisions are at least somewhat warranted by the theory as it currently stands. Moreover, since I am not aiming to trace the same line from the mind's hidden depths to the patterns of social interaction above that Berne aimed at, I can afford to shed some assumptions and clarify the outlines of others without aiming at the same comprehensiveness. What follows is simply an argument fit for my expressed purposes.

The 'what' of games

Although some will be unsatisfied at the absence of unified consensus about what a game is, perhaps we should turn the question around and ask what we might all agree we are saying when we talk of games. Assuming this starting point is productive then we can additionally think about the things we ought to agree on, however minimally, if we think games are still worth talking about at all. I suspect we might all agree that games are interpersonal, requiring two or more people (Joines, 1982; Zalcman, 1990). We might go on to agree that games are a kind of process: they have a starting point and an end point reached via something happening both inside and between the individual players. We would probably concur in the end that the process is likely to be a pattern, meaning it has happened before to the participants and will happen again if not interrupted (although a dissenting voice might spoil things here by pointing out that every game has to be played for a first time ...). Finally, all participants would surely acknowledge that this patterned, interpersonal process was significant and meaningful for the parties involved. There is always something at stake in a game.

To agree this much about games is already to say something useful, but perhaps it is not yet enough to count as a theory of a singular phenomenon. In order to give the concept explanatory significance we must risk adding a little more. I would argue that games must feature some aspect of their process which is not fully understood by the participants. This has usually meant the game player's motivations or interests in playing are not fully present to them, an assumption that guides the theory inevitably in a psychodynamic direction. An alternative explanation, better suited to comprehending horizontal games, is that there is an absence in the person's frame of reference, perhaps a deficit in KNOWING, which renders certain alternative options for interaction unavailable and which therefore funnels the players towards a predictable and unsatisfactory outcome. We think of clients playing games when we perceive alternative options for living and are curious as to why the person themselves doesn't acknowledge them.

A further knot to be untangled centres on the complicating factor as to whether 'good games' should be included in the definition. Berne certainly thought so at points, and a small chorus of agreement has followed (Berne, 1964; Zechnich, 1973; Summers & Tudor, 2000). It's fair to say the matter is somewhat vague since a consistent case for them has rarely been made. Certainly, a person is unlikely to embrace the notion of good games unless they disagree with my proposition that games are played in lieu of superior options as a matter of definition. My position is that carving games up into distinct good and bad categories should be abandoned in favour of a nuanced tally of advantages and disadvantages on a case-by-case basis. It's a fair assumption that games would not persist if there were little to be gained in playing them. I'd also suggest we wouldn't be calling them games at all if we didn't think there was a better way of relating available. I will contend that to some degree games must conclude negatively, as opposed to a merely sub-optimally, for fear of surrendering the theory's clinical utility.

Berne seems to have concluded that good games must fit within his definition because they contain ulterior transactions (Berne, 1964), though I don't think he consistently maintained this position. This argument seems to confuse the meaningful distinction between autonomously withholding something from open communication for reasons of social convention or strategic self-interest, and communicating something unknowingly from another ego-state because our script compels us into indirect expression. If procuring indirect stroke benefits is the best that can be managed for reasons of genuine external constraint then I am not sure that there is enough common ground here for the theory of games to apply. Perhaps we could use the term good games to refer to repeated patterns of behaviour which result in obvious gains for the players but where there is still some sense that there are better ways of doing things.

I propose to work from a revised definition of games which identifies them as a repeated interpersonal pattern of significance, where alternative options for interaction are not recognised and which results in a generally negative outcome for the persons involved. This reworking strips back some of the psychological assumptions that Berne considered essential to make more room for the social structuring of games. It's a definition better suited to a starting point of self-and-world and my interest in horizontal problems. I cannot guarantee that my starting point will satisfy everyone but at least it prepares the reader for the case I will make in its favour.

The 'why' of games

The 'what' of games has been sketched; the 'why' has been hinted at but not fully supplied. Whilst horizontal games will be shown to have a particular cause, I don't believe games more generally are played for one reason alone. Berne accounted for the existence of games in three somewhat distinct ways which I shall call the economic, the structural and the dynamic principles. These three principles exist in varying degrees of priority across the course of his writing with the economic falling behind the dynamic in his later years though it's fairly apparent that he saw no fundamental incompatibilities at work and aspired to achieve complete harmonisation between them. Once we understand what each principle contributes to the original theory then its place in my revised, narrower account should become clearer.

The economic principle

The economic principle refers to the fact that during the course of a game a person will be engaged in an ongoing, tacit process of judgement about which values and interests are at stake in the encounter and what actions best further them. Economic here simply refers to the weighing of competing interests, the evaluation of risks and rewards and pursuing the course which seems to promise the desired outcome. There is usually more than one value in play in games and the most conspicuous is not always the most important. Berne used the language of primary and secondary gains to describe the ways in which, upon further discovery, someone's stated wants sometimes ran into direct conflict with values and hopes that were unacknowledged. Viewed through the economic principle, the game player is revealed as attempting to reconcile competing demands, caught on the horns of a dilemma, torn and ambivalent about which path to choose.

There is good reason to believe that Berne had the economic principle in mind when he first outlined his theory of games. Although he curiously denied significant similarity (Berne, 1964, p. 12), the economic principle along with the word game itself seem to have been derived from game theory, a body of ideas dedicated to mapping strategic interaction between people using mathematical models which emerged in the 1940s (see Colman, 1995). Were these influences more widely understood and agreed upon, I suspect some of our reservations about the judgemental pallor of the word game might ease. According to game theory, a player calculates and recalculates the overall balance of interests as an encounter progresses in the light of new information. They may aim at their goals in a straight line only to change course suddenly when the 'price' of a course of action suddenly alters. In the real world, estimating the outcome and corresponding value of an action is a matter of ongoing guess work. Situations are complex and we are rarely in full command of all necessary information which makes the whole calculation process somewhat haphazard. Berne's brief flirtation with the idea that games were homeostatic or tending towards a stable equilibrium would be a further example of the economic principle in action. (Berne, 1964; Bary & Hufford, 1990; Heath & Oates, 2015). As a prompt to focusing on what is at stake for the game player, the economic principle will continue to play a crucial role in the theory.

The structural principle

The structural principle refers to the subdivision of game sequences into standard components, a consistently arranged assembly of moving parts, similar in function and ordering across cases. It naturally lends itself to concise descriptions. The most commonly cited structural definition is Berne's pithy 'Formula G+' which proposes the unvarying sequence of 'Con + Gimmick = Response → Switch → Crossup → Payoff' (Berne, 1972, p. 43) with James' game plan (James, 1973) a further though less cited example. The structural principle finds favour with those pursuing strong, clear definitions. On several occasions Berne stated that his structural definition was the means by which games could be distinguished, a position sufficiently authoritative for some (Stewart & Joines, 2012) to insist that we take Berne at his word and thereby banishing those portions of his writings which stray beyond his self-imposed prescription (Berne, 1964).

As someone who finds Berne's breaking of his own rules more a source of interest than a frustrating inconsistency, I am quite content to treat structural principles as interesting guidelines rather than unbreakable laws. The bigger charge against the structural principle is that it describes but does not explain, lacking as it does any thought as to *why* things turn up in the same order each time. It divorces the structure of games from individual and collective motivation and meaning. The context-sensitive account of games offered here can justify the structural principle in new ways by highlighting how all social interactions make use of precedent. Unofficially established, recognisable and socially endorsed ways of doing things with others are frames for action we are inducted into, make use of and perpetuate in daily interaction (Goffman, 1974). Games have an identifiable social shape because our interactions make use of pre-laid social pathways.

The dynamic principle

The dynamic principle states that the peculiar, confused and unsatisfying interpersonal sequence of a game is best understood as resulting from psychological content outside of the participant's awareness. This idea has been taken forward most fully in recent times by practitioners keen to model games on unconscious, transferential relationship patterns (see Cornell, 2015; Stuthridge & Sills, 2016; Stuthridge, 2015). Although there would seem to be close alignment between dynamic and economic principles since they can both entail a disjuncture between overt and covert motivation, it is not a requirement of the economic principle that some motivations are concealed from conscious awareness. I might also argue that the economic principle can account for multiple, divergent interests at once whereas the dynamic principle typically rests upon either a single unconscious motive or a clash between a pressing urge to feel something and an equally urgent compulsion not to think it. The heady appeal of the dynamic principle is that it bridges games and scripts seeing the former as repetitions and reinforcements of a projected script narrative which tightens its stranglehold on our heart, mind and actions with each fresh occurrence.

Each of the three principles holds a particular explanatory virtue within game theory. The economic principle underscores the intelligibility of games. It draws our attention to the fact that players can be taken to be making fine-grained moment by moment and longer-range evaluations about the best way to achieve and balance a range of desired outcomes. The procurement of strokes, maintenance of life position and the precious continuity of viewpoint and identity can all be in jeopardy. In addition to providing clarity of definition, the structural principle brings to the fore the observability and predictability of games. We can sometimes spot them coming by their common features and make an informed guess as to where we are going to end up if things carry on uninterrupted. The dynamic principle both links the game to the individual's personal history and resultant script and offers a plausible explanation for why players end up stuck in such fruitless patterns, blindly recreating the same problems without perceiving other ways forward.

The structural principle looks at games 'from the outside', from the observable, social progression of interpersonal moves and their impact on the overall course of the interactions. It presumes that private dramas adopt the scaffolding of a recognisable public form. Our individual wants find their form and weave their way along socially established pathways of thought and action. Economic and dynamic principles approach things more 'from the inside' understanding games as unfolding out of the participant's complex motivations and values. These are psychological theories which take the individuals beliefs, desires, values and intentions as the best way of explaining what is going on. Any complete account of games must achieve a balance or reconciliation of these different dimensions or else show how one of them can be plausibly substituted for a different kind of explanation. The dynamic principle will have less hold over a contextual transactional analysis account which seeks to link games principally to problems in a frame of reference rather than the constrictions of script. It is here the attempted substitution might be made.

A contextual transactional analysis view of games

There are unresolved questions about the relationship between the psychological and the social dimensions of games. Previous theories have tended to see the social as simply the end product of the psychological in action. This proposed unidirectional influence from psychological to social might try to account for the fact that games take certain stereotypical forms by way of the following line of reasoning. It would start by indicating that all people possess certain common wants and needs. It would go on to note that they must get these wants and needs recognised and met in the same shared world. Psychological dispositions and ways of expressing them are generally responded to in similar ways by other people. Hence similar needs inevitably lead to similar real-world outcomes as sure as night follows day. That games end up having a common structure is therefore a matter of the unintended convergence of thousands of individual encounters pouring like tributaries into common cultural forms. We might call this a 'bottom-up' view of games which begins with a psychological picture of the individual in interaction and aggregates multiple examples into a social pattern.

This story needs to be complimented, though not entirely displaced, by a corresponding 'top-down' counterpart which adds necessary explanatory muscle to the structural principle. In a top-down account, social form exerts a correspondingly greater structuring influence over individual thought and action. Our minds make use of familiar social forms to structure and express our experience, some of them helpful, others more limiting. We play the same games because the world does not disclose a sense that things can be otherwise. Our self-and-world lacks the necessary authority over the shared ideas for Adult authority and originality to emerge. It is therefore dependent upon Parent ideas as a means of navigating interpersonal encounters. This happens most often in places where the world is not good enough to make authority possible. Deficits in resourcefulness, responsiveness, truthfulness and integrity eventually result in particular absences in our KNOWING, our vocabularies and our individual frame of reference. Alternative options for action within the game which might allow us to step out of it are rendered unavailable by absences. Our interactions inevitably swerve towards the same predictable, familiar but unhappy outcomes. To be clear, it's not always so much that alternative options are entirely invisible, more that they get passed over because they can't be reconciled with what the player KNOWS. This is an evolved, socially sensitive variant on the cathexis theory argument which states that games are begun and maintained by discounts (Schiff et al., 1975). Here discount is substituted for absence and the absence is likely to occur at the general, contextual level rather than individual one.

Hints of the top-down position can be found in Berne's writings. He observed that games were transmitted within families across generations. He also noted that different cultures played different games (see Berne, 1964, p. 151). He further proposed that games could become part of the social fabric if they turned up in sufficient numbers and hung around (Berne, 1968, p. 309). In addition, he showed how scripts could be communicated and modelled through parent behaviour though he showed no curiosity about whether such transmission might also take place outside the family home. He does not pursue these tantalising suggestions to their inferred end points – that socialisation runs deep. As a subscriber to the myth of internal sufficiency, whilst Berne was happy to point out that games emerge from the clash between a prohibiting social influence and our better homegrown natures, he was consistent in his belief that socialisation and context are not destiny. Berne only ever describes things as learned as a prequel to insisting they can be unlearned. He never takes the alternative, plausible view that games are primarily perpetuated, transmitted and acquired socially because game players lack the socially granted authority to see new horizons beyond old worlds. The ambivalences, confusion and torment which accompany games are as much a product of the social context as they are a cause of them.

Horizontal games are therefore those which are top-down in origin. They flourish in social conditions marked by absences in a vocabulary, a lack of Adult authority and deficits in KNOWING. They are equally probably under social conditions which are rigidly fixed and those dissolving into flux. Horizontal games also thrive in overlaps between worldviews where an old KNOWING is crumbling and the new has not yet taken root. Here alternative options to step out of games are green shoots, emerging social forms which are not yet well established. They are also inevitable under conditions of oppression where Adult authority is contextually withheld by the world. Here there is no opportunity to see the world clearly enough to transform our sense of it in the light of new experience.

Games are best played with someone who shares the same vocabulary. Under such circumstances, both participants will transactionally circulate a view of the world which neither challenges nor extends the vocabulary: this keeps the game on predictable rails. Games are familiar within a social context, but understanding and approval will be variable. Whilst games can emerge in times of flux as new opportunities begin to coalesce, convenience of habit plays its part in their survival as a form. Until a new ripple disturbs the existing order, the same games remain as transmitted and circulated forms of life, recognised by all without their workings being fully grasped. They make partial sense to their local players because their shared vocabulary ensures that the same sense of what happens around here is shared. Things get tied back to the same old stories, the same old way of doing things. When our particular corners of the world only teach us certain things then everyone who occupies the same place and time is more likely to have the same blind spots. We drift along in generally the same direction. We can't do and think what others won't understand or let us get away with in routine interaction. The more widely they are played in a social context, the more firmly rooted in that ethos games become. They become ingrained if unofficial ways of coping with and making sense of collective dissatisfactions. Whereas 'vertical' games (defined here as games which are script-driven) tend to stand out as unusual against the background consensus view of routine social behaviour, horizontal games are all too familiar. They consolidate the social fabric from which they emerge.

Whilst I am defining games in part by the absence of better options for living within a vocabulary, it's important to stress that adjustments to these absences can vary in their creativity and compensatory virtues. No matter the sour taste they can leave at the end, games are a way of doing things that are immediately available to us as ways of cushioning our fall. They add narrative familiarity to unhappiness so that we can feel a sense of kinship with those who share our predicaments, telling war stories to our friends for a consolation prize of strokes. This is what Berne referred to as the trap of becoming a more comfortable frog though this way of seeing things will not be obvious to those trapped within contextually restricted horizons (Berne, 1972).

Horizontal games are not always completely static edifices because they arise in a world which is itself in motion. They shift and change with the currents of use. The opportunities and constraints embedded in our vocabularies which produce games are always in motion, subject to the revisions of everyday living and in doing so may provide tantalising yet fleetingly insubstantial glimpses of new ways of doing things. At the same time, interactions can be economically invested with so many different kinds of meaning simultaneously that ambivalent and complex responses are sometimes inevitable. Horizontal games can be busy intersections of the old and new, of love and hatred, of opportunities and prohibitions. We can know and not KNOW what we are doing simultaneously.

Games which began in one time for a particular reason can gradually shed their previous advantages and yet the overall interactional form sometimes survives to be picked up and embellished for new reasons. Several decades later, the kind of 'marital games' Berne described (Berne, 1964) seem distinctly time-bound. The liberalisation of social mores around relationships including greater acceptance of divorce, the increasing economic emancipation of women, greater awareness and condemnation of sexual and physical violence and the increase of 'pure relationships' aiming at mutual sexual and emotional satisfaction to the exclusion of other considerations (Giddens, 1992) have increased opportunity to the point where yesterday's games have nearly dissolved. The reticence of his clients to embrace freedom represented in a game like 'if it weren't for you' only makes sense in an overlap between new opportunity and old prohibition and yet unmistakeably, even in clients long accustomed to new liberties, the ghost of old games, a form of life lingering in the collective memory, can continue to assert themselves even after the initial circumstances and rationale of their emergence has long passed.

Games draw our attention to the ambivalence that may accompany even mostly welcome changes. Traditional gender roles and relationships may provide a relief from responsibility and uncertainty. Living as others do can provide an easier place in a community than striking out on your own. As pre-given options recede in the era of chaos, young lovers are as likely to receive collective encouragement to leave an unsatisfying relationship than to stay together. The freedom of choice that was yesterday's dream has been accompanied by a range of greater uncertainties about how to find and retain relationships and what should be asked of them (Illouz, 2012). Today's dissatisfied couples living and loving in times of chaos (Bauman, 2003) are playing games we are only starting to recognise, games premised upon managing uncertainty and responsibility, around failing to live up to the cherished ideals they hold around relationships. The games sometimes look the same from the outside, but they are increasingly serving a different purpose, new wine in old bottles.

During lulls where social change has slowed to a trickle, the more often games are played and circulated the tougher they become to dislodge. As we get better at scraping the consolations out of failure, a kind of affection and nostalgia can set in, a fatal impediment to the development of better ways of living. The pluses begin to outweigh the perceived minuses. The pay offs attached to a game become strengthened, thickened into custom by the frequency of their appearance and the weight of collective experience they accumulate. Games become taught and modelled in social contexts as collectively used, somewhat successful ways of managing disappointment, of granting an excuse, a dignity, an ethos for familiar failures so that they can at least achieve social intelligibility, collective recognition and a settled place in the world.

The psychologically complex individual continues to play a crucial role in this process of game formation and consolidation. Game formation is bidirectional. Behind every story of how collective ways of thinking and being that were once available and went on to become forgotten over time lies countless private stories of uncertainty, shame, ambivalence, conformity and confusion. As I suggested in Chapter 2, things which don't get talked about eventually drift into things that can't be thought about. Large scale self-deception and insincerity, often born of the necessity of managing collective trauma, can inaugurate a process whereby ways of living are starved of public display and recognition. At the start of this decline the game player is always split between the demands of their public face and their unexpressed hopes, becoming more and more unreal as they fall into disuse. These moments when a different road could have been taken recede into history, never to be known by those who come after.

Paul Wachtel has written at length about how unhelpful interpersonal patterns or what he calls 'cyclical psychodynamics' (see Wachtel & Wachtel, 1986; Wachtel, 2008), are maintained because people become accomplished at recruiting others into confirming what they appear to be. Our outward face gets treated as our inward nature. What you pretend to be will be bought into by others until the gap between pretence and reality blurs. The man who is not offered the option to describe himself as sad or unhappy across the course of his life but instead is initiated into anger and complaining will be taken by others to be an angry man and responded to as such. The more he makes use of games to understand and communicate his predicament the more firmly entrenched they will become into his sense of himself and the way he is regarded. Over time he may forget that there were once paths he did not take, who he is cemented into place by a lifetime of action in one direction. He will come to extract as much pride and purpose from his pretence as he can manage and will find many allies in his quest to do so. Having nearly become the man he has always taken himself to be, he may hand on this form of life to his children with only the quietest nagging doubt at the back of his head that something has been lost. Finding your way back from such a path can be a mighty challenge. Small wonder the prospect of bringing a game to an end can seem a bewildering prospect with a price the person may not be sure they wish to pay.

Not so long ago, men from working-class communities were raised to be physically tough and emotionally undemonstrative. They were being prepared either for an existence of backbreaking and often dangerous physical work or to risk their young lives in military service. Putting aside feelings was an essential part of bearing such a burden though it too often resulted in men becoming remote fathers and unsympathetic husbands. Wars ended, peace was won and kept and heavy industry declined rendering the rationale for toughness increasingly obsolete, but by that point it had swung free of its initial utility and morphed into a badge of honour. Public brawling, street crime and steroid use took seed in this form of behaviour and flourished, keeping it animated after its original purpose has long since departed. A detailed social template for playing games where they end up in the persecutor position, one sufficiently robust and well-circulated to withstand social change, was firmly in place (Karpman, 1968).

As traditional male roles of breadwinner, husband and head of household were challenged by social changes, there was a simultaneous emergence of a new culture of emotional tolerance and expression which jarred with the expectations of yesteryear. These games now sit across an overlap between old and new senses of the world, the first where toughness and reserve reign supreme, the latter based on a new ethos of emotional openness. Games emerge from this unstable tension between a fragile, burgeoning and unsupported curiosity about embracing the fresh opportunities of the present and maintaining a useful embrace of the certainties and the pleasures of past ideals.

A contextual transactional analysis account of games would resist the urge to reduce this scenario down to a cautionary tale about teaching boys never to cry, for the ethos handed down from parent to child has a complex history lurking behind this simple message. People cannot see their way to a better future from a rootless present if the real lessons of history are lost to them. Rather than just shifting people from past to present opportunities, our task must be to reconstruct the whole story with all its secret pain, valiant effort and honest errors. We must open up the present truthfully so that all values and interests which converge on games can be reconsidered and reconciled in the light of the present and a new pathway to the future opened up.

Breaking out of horizontal games demands respecting the past whilst learning to think beyond current limits. This depends in turn on recognising that our sense of the world is imperfect, marred by absences and ripe for reform. We swerve towards the familiar because its worth is known, its tally of strokes already priced up, its consequences mapped out: by contrast the glimpse of the unfamiliar is a roll of the dice. A more complete autonomy can be hard to picture when a community lacks the resourcefulness of better narratives. The new option doesn't seem yet solid enough to offer necessary continuity of identity and sense. There is no guarantee that it will be understood and taken respectfully by others in our life. It can be hard to picture the whole form of life in which new options for living might naturally sit. Departing from a horizontal game entails being a pioneer, striking outwards whereas vertical games call upon us to venture inwards and know ourselves better. The resolution of horizontal games requires greater authority, progressive reform of vocabularies and the consequent imagining of better worlds.

The 'how' of games

So far, I have suggested that encrusted and absence-ridden frames of reference which govern interaction tilt the course of games back towards that same old familiar, hurt place. My suggestions so far have some bearing on the thorny and unresolved question as to whether a game player aims strategically at their unhappy ending from the beginning or whether things arrive in the same place without design. I don't doubt that some games can seem to advance a furtive masochistic or sadistic agenda, their intent present from the beginning and straight as an arrow. Where horizontal games are concerned, I agree with Fanita English when she states that the switch in a game, the moment when it fixes its course on the negative outcome, occurs when something goes wrong in a previously uncomplicated interchange (English, 1977). English correctly observes that a game shifts course when the balance of risk and reward alters for one or both of the players. The switch is triggered by a perceivable change in the encounter and with it the reduced likelihood of a favourable outcome.

In saying that games are socially structured I have not been claiming they are wholly socially determined. The stereotypic form of games is always something around which specific encounters dance and weave in the service of the player's interests. Since the game player can spy no clear and uncomplicated path towards what they want, their interactions walk a tightrope between risk and reward. In aiming at an uncertain outcomes, they flirt with danger. Games begin in a spirit of unformed and unacknowledged hope and end in damage limitation – a fluid economic principle in action. A contextual view of games follows English in seeing the switch and pay offs as a kind of safety net, an ever-ready strategy for rationalising, managing and compensating for fresh disappointments. The structure of games with their mix of flow and dramatic interruption is simply the pattern that emerges from these principles in action. They only become a game proper in hindsight when the outcome is confirmed. A masochistic theory of games which views them as ways of intentionally furthering a script or confirming a life position is politically uncharitable. It presumes that people are always in a position to know what they want and be capable of pursuing it, a conclusion this book has cautioned us against endorsing. I recommend a greater place in our ideas for due sensitivity to the force of circumstance in all its churning complexity.

Game players will impose a retrospective narrative order on things, an 'its-happened-to-me-again'. The story told shaves away the decisions not made, the things not said, the options not considered. The impetus to extract consolation means that possibilities are tidied up into a sense of the inevitable, a move that illegitimately uses the game to confirm the social template from which it draws. This is the biggest objection to the notion that games are planned in advance to consolidate our life position for who of us could seriously guarantee that interactions will work out exactly as we intend?

Our world is full of 'nearly-games' where people were veering close to a dramatic switch but something occurs to prevent it happening. They are best understood as an unsatisfying interpersonal sequence that lacks a dramatic denouement. We may all have stumbled towards the end of a game without realising it but nearly-games don't linger in the memory because near-misses lack drama and consequent effort to restore equilibrium. Games proper require a concentrated effort to piece together the payoff from the wreckage of events. To my mind, attempts to describe games in terms of transference struggle to fully explain this because they underplay the importance of conscious retrospective narration which bookends an unhappy encounter. Although Moursund and Erksine have usefully argued that consciously held beliefs work to rationalise the intrusion of unconscious experience in order to maintain psychological equilibrium (Moursund & Erskine, 2004), I would suggest that what is consciously concluded at the end of a game will inevitably affect the expectations governing similar future encounters. Perhaps interpersonal sequences governed mostly out of conscious awareness on a template forged by early experience are best considered as a type of nearly-game.

Horizontal game players remain stuck, going round in circles until they can name what is wrong and embrace a different path. So often they are feeling their way tentatively towards the apex of their confusion and curiosity, circling the place where new understanding should be but finding little there. I often refer to this in my clinical practice as a 'message in a bottle' moment because it can seem as though the client is waiting for someone around them to answer a secret call they didn't know they sent, to complete or supplement their understanding and show them a way out of their confusion. Working with vertical games we are often helping the person to know and embrace who they are and what they want: working with horizontal games involves introducing someone to who they could be and opening up new possibilities for meaningful action.

Clinical vignette

Lee slouches in the chair, legs splayed, peering out at me from underneath a baseball cap. He spends our sessions bragging about how he is the best mechanic at the garage he works at and how his boss knows it, the amount he spends on cocaine on a weekly basis and how little sleep he gets by on as a result, the number of women he has seduced including many of those belonging to his mates and the number of people he could beat in a fight if he wanted to. His contempt towards me is palpable; I feel pre-emptively dismissed as another middle-class do-gooder.

In spite of his disdain, Lee needs to change for his young son, the arrival of whom has impressed upon him new values and concerns which sit uneasily with his usual way of being. He tells me he is going to be the best dad in the world which could sound like a customary boast but I sense a more sincere voice speaking. Telling him I see a glimmer of something new, he retracts his earnestness in a flash, parrying my gestures of recognition and returns, snake-eyed, to his bragging. Lee has spent years being smarter and stronger than the other guys in the room. He isn't going to surrender these advantages until I can show him its worth doing.

In his teens, Lee was a bit overweight. He tells me that he knew he was funny so he kept the big kids off him by making them laugh and eventually was part of their crowd. Even so, Lee understood that in the pecking order, being the class jester ranked a long way below where he wanted to be. Being hard, sarcastic, rule-breaking, good with girls put you on the path to being someone. Quietly he cut down on sugar and began going to kick-boxing three times per week until he had hammered his body into the kind of shape that fitted the picture of himself he had in his head.

I have met enough young men like Lee to know that their vocabulary centres on street smarts and physical prowess. Other options for living are at best distantly available. Those who cannot live like this quickly recede into the background or get trampled underfoot. Like their fathers before them, Lee and his peers learnt to walk the daily walk of contempt for schooling, edgy competitive humour, scepticism towards tradition and authority, respect for risk taking and physicality and an attitude towards women some distance from respect. Lee's every gesture told me that he had lived up to these ideals, it just seemed like hard work to get right. He had pushed his social jousting as far as he could go but his friends found it hard to be around him. Lee seemed impressed that he had the power to drive people away but somehow couldn't quite work out how his friendships kept breaking down. It was always their fault, they couldn't keep up with him. It would be easy to read Lee's case in terms of cultural requirements to bury feelings of vulnerability behind his surface armour plating, but there was more to Lee than this. At points he was strikingly sincere: he genuinely couldn't understand why, having got to the top, things didn't seem right.

As work progressed, Lee admitted he was struggling to manage his relationship with his ex-partner and mother of his two-year-old son. They split after nine tumultuous months when she found out that he had been unfaithful. Both remained committed to raising their son well. Lee had readily agreed to his ex being his son's primary carer because it seemed the right thing to do, but he hated her having the upper hand in negotiations. Rows he tended to see as her getting one over on him Their arguments increased once she began a new relationship. Lee began calling her at all hours of the day to scream abuse at her and, at the culmination of one particularly venomous argument, he smashed up her house with a baseball bat. Here was the saving payoff to the game for the gesture that made him top dog again even as he risked losing access to his son. He struggled to reconcile competing senses of himself as king of the hill and slumped in the gutter.

We began to talk of fatherhood. Uncles had stepped in to look after him after his own father died in a car accident having been only fitfully present throughout Lee's early years. He wanted something different for his own son. Lee understood that he hated feeling in a one down position to his partner but couldn't see how he could reconcile being a dad with the sense of being a man that his vocabulary gave him. A criminal record on the cards, Lee found himself at the same crossroads so many of his male peers had traversed, how to reconcile their uncompromising, antisocial vision of manhood with the compromise and self-restraint necessary to raise children well. These men find themselves pressing at the limits of their vocabulary, unable to reconcile who they take themselves to be with what they want to do. This pressing question was the absence in Lee's frame of reference.

Working with Lee's games, his frequent breaking of relationships and pride in his refusal to back down, required a careful tracing and revising of the many components in his frame of reference. He was smart enough to take on board new ideas and keen to come out of therapy a changed man as long as I didn't rip him wholesale out of his way of being and leave him lost and disorientated. Sensing a means to extend his vocabulary in a way which might fill the gap, we talked about different ideas of strength, the one he had with his mates versus the strength his mum showed in raising him. I asked Lee to think about how it could seem smarter to step out of conflict than step into it: he said he felt he could call out the game as being stupid and say he had more important things to think about. It sounded right, but odd, a freshly minted way of seeing things he couldn't quite piece together. One session he reported that he had told his mate in the middle of banter that being a dad was the only thing he really cared about and that the fight was ridiculous. Once he had said it, he felt he believed it. New habits of mind seemed to be forming and growing spontaneously. Lee felt stronger and more grown up.

Lee started to KNOW what he previously only known – that he and his mates were wasting their lives and he felt none of them lived up to the standards men of previous generations had set. They were boys struggling to become men. At points I shared my sense of how I took things to have changed around there across the years, how several years ago his mates would all have had permanent, better paid work and a more central place in their children's lives. Over time something clinked into place in Lee's view of things, he noted how easily he and his friends slipped into the assumption that they would be deadbeat dads and how much a sense that they couldn't occupy their place in relationships with pride played a part. Inching towards new understanding, he talked about how often his friends had been denied access to their children by the courts or by ex-partners. He never denied that their behaviour played a part in their downfall, but he began to see his games as a symptom of a kind of social disintegration of which he knew but didn't fully comprehend. Once a man like Lee would have found a place in the world where strength and respectability could be reconciled. Things changed and it was no longer possible to choose both.

Conclusion

Working with horizontal games is premised on recovering and building what the world never gave us the chance to become. It is restorative, learning-focused, respectful of the past and oriented to the future. It honours the complexities and authenticities of both surface and depth and holds back from quick judgements about what is going wrong. It asks for a careful reconsideration of the player's whole worldview, turning over each element and exploring their interrelation until a new path forward appears. It doesn't look for unitary causes and suspends judgement about which interests may ultimately prove to be most important to the person. As such, it aims for a kind of completeness of feeling and thinking, enlarging the circle of understanding so that absences in the frame of reference are filled and sense of the possible duly expanded.

Seeking completeness rather than authenticity of feeling and understanding acknowledges that negative events will often bring up a complex bundle of different thoughts and emotions. Games unhelpfully simplify things into a unitary position at their conclusion. We draw the hidden feelings into the light not necessarily because they are more true than the surface ones, but because we want the client to see the whole picture, to understand what else they are feeling besides what is most present. When dealing with horizontal games played by entire communities, turning the game over too quickly to reveal what has been left out can risk being jarring and disrespectful. Horizontal games are best treated as matters of reform, taking the next step towards change but not jettisoning a whole way of life. Add things to the picture, increase the complexity, enhance the client's authority over the vocabulary they use, add some resourcefulness from the therapist's own frame of reference and hopefully options for doing things just a little differently will emerge.

In this the contextual approach to games bears some resemblance to Bary and Hufford's suggestion that therapist and client must carefully recalibrate the various interests maintaining a game, cautiously turning over one value and observing how the effects ripple out onto others (Bary & Hufford, 1990). Where the games are horizontal, the need is to go beyond the current frame of reference not behind it, fill in its absences, bring new and perhaps better ways of doing things to the client's awareness for exploration. The game is given up when a new path for action, crystallised in the mind's eye and workable in the world the client must return to, is capable of managing the tasks of living in all their complexity.

References

Bary, B.B., Hufford, F.M. (1990) The Six Advantages to Games and Their Use in Treatment. *Transactional Analysis Journal*, 20 (4), 214–220.

Bauman, Z. (2003) *Liquid Love*. Cambridge: Polity Press.

Berne, E. (1964) *Games People Play*. London: Penguin.

Berne, E. (1968) *A Layman's Guide to Psychiatry and Psychoanalysis*. London: Penguin.

Berne, E. (1972) *What Do You Say After You Say Hello?* London: Corgi.

Cornell, W.F. (2015) Playing at Your Own Risk: Games, Play and Intimacy. *Transactional Analysis Journal*, 45 (2), 75–90.

Colman, A.M. (1995) *Game Theory and its Applications in the Social and Biological Sciences*. 2nd edn. Hove, Routledge.

English, F. (1977) Let's Not Claim it's Script When it Ain't. *Transactional Analysis Journal*, 7 (2), 130–138.

Giddens, A. (1992) *The Transformation of Intimacy: Sexuality, Love & Eroticism in Modern Societies*. Cambridge: Polity.

Goffman, E. (1974) *Frame Analysis: An Essay on the Organisation of Experience*. Cambridge, MA: Harvard University Press.

Heath, L., Oates, S. (2015) To Change or Not to Change: Reflections on the Role Games Play in Maintaining Psychic Equilibrium. *Transactional Analysis Journal*, 45 (2), 91–103.

Illouz, E. (2012) *Why Love Hurts: A Sociological Explanation*. Cambridge: Polity Press.

James, J. (1973) The Game Plan. *Transactional Analysis Journal*, 3 (4), 14-17.

Joines, V. (1982) Similarities and Differences in Rackets and Games. *Transactional Analysis Journal*, 12 (4), 280–283.

Karpman, S. (1968) Fairy Tales and Script Drama Analysis. *Transactional Analysis Bulletin*, 7 (26), 39-43.

Moursund, J.P., Erskine, R.G. (2004) *Integrative Psychotherapy: The Art and Science of Relationship*. Pacific Grove, CA: Brooks-Cole.

Schiff, J.L., Schiff, A., Mellor, K., Schiff, E., Fishman, J., Wolz, L., Fishman, C., Mombs, D. (1975) *Cathexis Reader: Transactional Analysis Treatment of Psychosis.* New York: Harper & Row.

Stewart, I., Joines, V. (2012) *TA Today: A New Introduction to Transactional Analysis.* 2nd edn. Melton Mowbray: Lifespace.

Stuthridge, J. (2015) All the World's a Stage: Games, Enactment and Countertransference. *Transactional Analysis Journal*, 45 (2), 104–116.

Stuthridge, J., Sills, C. (2016) Psychological Games and Intersubjective Process. In R.G. Erskine, Ed., *Transactional Analysis in Contemporary Psychotherapy.* London: Karnac, 185–208.

Summers, G., Tudor, K. (2000) Co-Creative Transactional Analysis. *Transactional Analysis Journal*, 30 (1), 23–40.

Wachtel, E.F., Wachtel, P.L. (1986) *Family Dynamics in Individual Psychotherapy: A Guide to Clinical Strategies.* New York: Guildford Press.

Wachtel, P.L. (2008) *Relational Theory and the Practice of Psychotherapy.* New York: Guildford Press.

Zalcman, M. (1990) Game Analysis and Racket Analysis: Overview, Critique, and Future Developments. *Transactional Analysis Journal*, 20 (1), 4–19.

Zechnich, R. (1973) Good Games: Therapeutic Uses and Four New Ones. *Transactional Analysis Journal*, 3 (1), 52-56.

8

CONTEXTUAL TRANSACTIONAL ANALYSIS IN PRACTICE

This chapter was written with strong reservations. Therapy of any kind is poorly served by being thought of as the mastery of techniques. I had good reasons for setting out to write a 'why to' approach things differently book, not a 'how to' approach things differently book. The simple possession of new tools is far less important than learning to use them well whatever your chosen approach. Ideally, endowing clinicians with a comprehensive new picture about what is happening with their clients should be enough for help them to creatively reconfigure their existing skills for new jobs. This is a model which draws back from becoming a method.

None the less, I recognise that some people find it beneficial to have an outline of practice from which to begin, like the kind of parental scaffolding I described in Chapter 3, a simple temporary structure in which the more robust edifice of a unique therapeutic take on these ideas can be erected. I therefore offer tentative suggestions here as starting points for the reader's own understanding: these are guidelines not rules. I impose no restrictions on the kinds of things that a therapist might do to achieve the right ends, I merely offer up some thoughts on what I take to be the novel aspects of these ideas. Some of what I suggest will be no more than new rationales for old ways of doing things. Considerations of space mean I must be brief and skim over details. I hope the reader will understand the obligation to exceed my starting point. In handing these ideas over I am designating them as 'ours' not merely 'mine': My own working practices are constantly evolving. I don't have a monopoly or a final say on what constitutes a good practical application of the ideas introduced in this book.

Recall that contextual transactional analysis is offered as supplementary rather than stand alone theory. Making frequent and appreciative use of other approaches, particularly those which have guided us best in working with early experiences and the Child ego-state, remain central to my own practice, particularly where a client presentation has a strong vertical problem aspect. I agree with Hargaden and Sills' suggestion that therapy often cycles between decontamination and deconfusion (Hargaden & Sills, 2002), between moments of quiet, empathic inward reflection on what is and focused interludes of Adult outsight. Whilst I don't advocate rapid switching between models, for those looking to incorporate contextual ideas into their customary way of working I have found that sometimes a clearly delineated segment of time within a larger engagement, contracted and mutually agreed, can represent a satisfactory addition to a more 'vertical' therapy process.

The clients' own views on their difficulties and what kind of help they want and expect will be an inevitable factor in the viability of the work. The extent to which any therapist seeks to change a client's understanding of the reasons they are struggling and the best ways to change are dilemmas which can only be resolvable by contingent judgements Not everyone can dive into an active, change-focused approach immediately or consistently. Gentle persuasion is encouraged, dogmatic persistence in the teeth of palpable displeasure is not.

Basic foundations

This approach presumes a sufficiently developed capacity to hear clients' stories with a contextual ear. We must be able to hear the relationship between the fore-grounded individual against the background of their lives. We must learn to notice the authoritative Adult voice emerging from and falling back into the Parent, when they are uncritically speaking with the common voice and when they make that voice their own. This is a variation on Berne's diagnostic criteria for recognising ego-states (Berne, 1963) and calls for knowledge beyond competence in theory. Contextual transactional analysis in practice is not possible without sufficiently detailed familiarity with the vocabularies and forms of life around us: clinical training usually provides this only fitfully. We must be able to hear the local rhythm and cadence of life to the point where its blind spots and subtle contradictions, its strengths and continuities emerge. We must be able to walk alongside our clients as though their life might be ours whilst retaining the productivity of our differences brought into dialogue, hearing what is and hinting at what might yet be. Social and cultural competence is built from adopting an outward-looking sensibility that embraces both specialist clinical knowledge and general practical wisdom harvested from wider engagement with life.

It will be difficult for a practitioner to help a client achieve their own political identity if their own is untended and underdeveloped. There is more than one possible vision of a good life, and there is no sense here that a therapist simply shares their own conclusions with the client. A contextual practitioner must adopt a political sensibility, not political conclusions. Fostering political identity in ourselves and our clients entails becoming disposed to seeing the myriad ways in which we are irreducibly self-and-world and that current social arrangements are chosen and changeable leading us to imaginatively commit to plausible revisions of the world. We are not just self-and-world, we are also therapist-and-citizen. Our work takes place behind closed doors but this makes the activity private, not separate from the lives we lead outside. If we see our clients as self-and-world too then we will see our work less as separating the person from the world to better help them and more returning them to life with more authority.

This opens up permissions and requirements to broaden the topics of a therapeutic conversation.

A contextual practitioner will risk being more active because they will not subscribe to the myth of internal sufficiency. We can't always wait for politics to turn up in the session because our clients often won't always take this turn unprompted. Neither imposing political awareness nor hanging back from it, the practitioner will consider with all due care and humility what seems the best thing to do next, to work with what is there or to add something new. There is simply the most open, constructive response we can manage in the light of the values we take to be most important against our background sense of how we generally take things to be. Submit our honest actions to the test of experience and be willing to change course if occasion demands it.

Aims

Contextual transactional analysis aims primarily to resolve horizontal problems by helping the person achieve a position of Adult authority. Carefully considering the overall drift of an individual frame of reference or vocabulary, the therapist seeks to identify absences, things that could have been thought and aren't as starting points for discussion and learning. The approach will see horizontal problems as often resulting from deficits in resourcefulness, responsiveness, truthfulness or integrity in the wider context. Therapeutic work which seeks to support authority is fruitfully led by a focus on the relationship between the client's Parent and Adult ego-states though due sensitivity to the overall frame of reference and the living memory of the Child must also be present. The achievement of authority will return people to an OK-OK (Berne, 1966) relationship with their community. In contextual transactional analysis, an OK-OK position entails acknowledging that existing in a common world with others is an irreducible part of existence, that other people are in principle as entitled to occupy the world as we are, that social formations are not inevitable, that things could have been another way and that political sensitivity aims both at individual benefit and more satisfying and just ways of living for all.

A helping relationship should not exclude any feasible options for decreasing deficits in resourcefulness, responsiveness, truthfulness and integrity that can be practicably combined with therapy without tarnishing its distinctive contribution. A responsible therapist should develop a keen knowledge of available resources outside of the consulting room which might be accessed. They will most often have only limited control over the absence of material resourcefulness, but greater KNOWING and outsight are the resource which therapy might plausibly increase.

Responsiveness may be enhanced where the work can support a client to find new ways to participate meaningfully and with greater impact in the common life. Opportunities for interpersonal solidarity, resistance and more productive adjustment should be encouraged. I usually make a point of finding out who the client routinely interacts with during the course of an average week. Sometimes a different kind of conversation with friends and family can be all that is needed to keep hope kindled.

Acquiring a clearer picture of the world requires honesty and a willingness to pursue and try new ways of thinking in a spirit of curiosity. Since horizontal problems are characterised precisely by pessimism and incredulity at the prospect of things being different, truthfulness can take time to get going. Like any good teacher who understands that engagement must precede learning, the therapist's responsibility is to proceed slowly, creating the conditions under which curiosity can flourish and new ideas can be considered, learned and pursued without coercion, fear, confusion or shame. Invite clients to be interested in their own minds, histories and lives and the process will slowly unfold in the right direction.

If the world around the client is confused through a deficit of integrity, then an initial process of piecing things back together, of understanding how people got here and what matters to them may be an essential first step. Loving restoration of integrity, a piecing together of who we have been, is sometimes the necessary precondition for coming to realise who we might be. These four conditions fulfil the same function that protection and permission do in classical ways of working (Crossman, 1966) and the notion of support does in gestalt therapy (Joyce & Sills, 2014). Providing solid information, greater efficacy in action, the safety to explore and the opportunity to live and learn more truthfully may open up the new and needed pathway.

Ethics in contextual transactional analysis

Insight and outsight are essential preconditions of autonomy, personal efficacy and civic participation (Tudor & Hargaden, 2002). Knowingly depriving or failing to provide people with the means to understand their circumstances and themselves constitutes what Miranda Fricker calls 'hermeneutic injustice' (Fricker, 2007). As clinicians we must acknowledge an ethical call to right this wrong. Since we are all prone to cognitive vulnerability it's fair to assume that hermeneutic injustice is widespread. Our professional ethos states that everyone 'has the capacity to think' (Stewart & Joines, 2012, p. 6); we need to add the caveat that thinking only achieves authority under good enough contextual conditions. Therapy sometimes offers new ideas about things not just to relieve suffering but because there is an ethical imperative not to withhold that which is essential for someone to take an equal, authoritative place amongst others. Authority is its own reward, it needs no further justification. Fear of imposition needs to be temperate. Unless we subscribe to the myth of internal sufficiency, there should be no general ethical or clinical impediments to introducing ways of believing. A person can only reject a belief if they know that it exists.

The concept of cognitive vulnerability reminds us that authority is not a pre-given quality of isolated individuals: hermeneutic injustice would be a redundant concept if we all just knew things irrespective of circumstance. The therapeutic space must provide some conditions for authority as it temporarily becomes part of the client's self-and-world. The therapeutic process should aim to provide what Habermas calls an 'ideal speech situation' (Habermas, 1986, 1997, 1998), where as much as is possible, the client is granted the knowledge, experience, freedom, support, security and loving respect necessary to achieve an authoritative grip on their situation. These conditions are never met perfectly nor in the same way each time, so it's perhaps best to understand this as a short-hand for saying that the therapist will aspire to ensure that all known barriers to authoritative expression will be reduced to their minimum.

Contextual transactional analysis holds it likely that a client may need to change the 'partial-explanation' of their suffering to a more social and political one as a precondition of change. Since it rejects the myth of internal sufficiency, we cannot presume that a better understanding hovers preformed under the mind's surface. We have nothing more secure than our own heart-felt, experientially informed and carefully thought-through sense that there are better ways to see things. This is an awkward but unavoidable place to reach: presuming that a person already tacitly has what is needed is a great comfort, for it allows us to hope that we can simply facilitate the emergence of authority rather than actively contribute towards its construction. Neither contracting nor emergent process can provide the guarantees we are looking for in contextual work. The matter is even more sensitive when the therapist is working with a client from a cultural background very different than their own. It may prove much harder to understand the strengths and deficits of a different cultural vocabulary.

I can offer no universal guidelines or magical solutions to these dilemmas. Risks of unwanted imposition are real. Experienced therapists will recognise that there is little about their training which makes them uniquely qualified to pronounce on social and cultural questions. Practical reasoning about what is right is always a necessary alchemy to turn abstract principles into specific judgements. Hopefully as therapists we are quicker to spot misjudgements and more willing to correct our mistakes when we make them. In the end we can do no better than advise the therapist to presume neither the correctness of their judgements, nor their inadequacy. Whether we are more active or elect to hang back there is no firmer foundation than what seems right in the moment. Humility coupled with a refusal to evade responsibility for saying what you think might need to be said is the best that we can do.

Let us hold open the possibility that sometimes we *might* have good reason to think that we know some things better than our clients (just as they sometimes know more than we do) and that it might be a good idea to make use of that information in our work. Let's agree that our minds are never complete, that partial and occasional deficits in understanding are inevitable and that we might sometimes be grateful for the chance to see things differently. Let's also concede, however tentatively, that not all social contexts can be presumed in advance to uniformly provide good enough conditions for their members and that this will lead to deficits in a person's capacity to know themselves. Not speaking out means sometimes we stand to one side and let the old injustices play on.

There are two caveats to the requirement to alleviate hermeneutic injustice which are sufficiently strong to count in most cases. Where a client actively refuses a social and political retelling of their difficulties or is likely to become more distressed by our insisting upon this then the principle of first do no harm must win out. Second, where the client belongs to an oppressed group where there are good reasons to suspect that efforts by a majority-culture therapist to suggest alternative ways of seeing things will be perceived as a further slight then the greater good is served by working within their existing vocabulary even if this constricts the work.

The position I am laying out is that a therapist should be *charitable* but not *respectful* towards a client's worldview. Being charitable entails an appropriate minimum presumption that people are generally disposed to solve problems and organise their collective existence in favourable ways until we have specific grounds to presume otherwise. Charitability is automatically extended in advance of specific knowledge of the individual or their culture but it is not a final verdict. Respectfulness by contrast entails an informed and knowing judgement about the value, worth and viability of a worldview. As therapists, if we are initially charitable rather than respectful then we reserve the right to question a worldview at the point at which we have some supportable ideas about potential limitations and what could be thought instead.

Contracting

Walking a tightrope between respecting the client's pre-existing resources and needing to open the invisible cage of their horizontal problems can render contracting a challenging business. Even if the therapist sincerely believes they can see something that the client can't, how and why this is communicated and received is as important as what is said. As Paulo Freire observed in his work on the education of the oppressed, a learning that is done *to* people rather than *with* them merely exchanges one oppression for another (Freire, 2000).

The client should be informed at the beginning of therapy that your way of working may include a significant, socially-sensitive focus on what is happening around them. It's an essential frame to explain at the earliest opportunity that the client may find their understanding of the problem changing as we go through therapy and that you may have some thoughts about what a different understanding might be. The therapist should be keen to stress that a different viewpoint is not a better one until the client owns and accepts it. Borrowing and adapting from systemic practitioners who will sometimes allow clients to overhear live supervision of their work by an observing colleagues (Burnham, 1986), I stress that I can be and often am somewhat mistaken in my ideas and that they only work if they make sense for the client in the end. Engaging in a process of confessing our mistakes risks being off-putting if the client harbour fantasies of our protective omnipotence, or irritating if it feels they are being asked to forgive us for our sins, yet there are opportunities here to disrobe the therapist of their mystique and validate the client's discrepant opinions as a way of boosting their competence. Mistakes are seen as opportunities to share what new thing we have learnt about the client; it makes these moments win-win. Showing that occasional errors are merely necessary steps in experimentation on the path to better answers secures the optimism necessary to keep going.

Contracting is responsiveness in action. Clients who live in socially and politically unresponsive contexts may be unaccustomed to being treated as the kind of people who can say what they want and having others take that seriously. The risk of privately resentful over-compliance with a powerful professional must be taken seriously. It's crucial to treat clients as the kind of people who have the power to say no whilst at the same time holding open the possibilities that they can become better versions of themselves. This sometimes means reaching in and digging out disagreements buried under reticence to show that the space can and should contain their dissatisfaction. The contracting process is not just the gateway to therapy, its inseparable from the formation of the relationship and the space for experimentation in new ways of living which the therapy aims to provide.

Contracting in this way of working is a tentative, rolling, experimental process rather than something tied down before therapy gets under way. There are already well-articulated precedents for this within transactional analysis (see Lee, 2006; Widdowson, 2010) but this approach differs slightly in continually looping back to stress the emerging difference between the starting definition of the problem and present understanding, helping the client to keep track of and approve the emerging changes. The contracting process here also makes more room for the therapist to occasionally suggest new thoughts or directions for living the client might try on the understanding that the experimental process itself endows the client the authority to ultimately reject the suggestion. Contracting and the therapy process align and mutually support each other, rather like trying to find the right focus on a camera lens, clarity emerging and disappearing as new experience arises for consideration.

Promoting authority

Horizontal problems dissolve when the client has achieved the capacity for authoritative outsight. The therapy leaves the client with a clearer view of the changeability and contingency of the world, the present configurations of opportunity and constraint, and the consequent picture of a self-and-world inseparable from circumstance. If the therapy process has been successful, this outsight will lead to an underlying sense of why things are as they are and an enhanced possibility of valued action. Achieving this new plateau is premised upon embracing an ethos of truthfulness in conduct matched with a commitment to seek out and honour the lessons of new experience. In principle, all parts of a frame of reference can potentially be placed in jeopardy unless there are strong cultural prohibitions against doing so.

The route to outsight isn't a straight line nor is it achieved in a single leap. Political worldviews are broad, summative products of a whole host of thought processes and experiences. In keeping with the conclusions of Chapter 6 we shouldn't expect to unlock a worldview with a single key. A therapist needs to respect and understand the different sub-components of the frame of reference, their varying purposes and consequences: different components may require different responses. Whatever the therapist does to promote curiosity, encourage rational appraisal, enhance empathy or soften resistance there is a circular movement between focusing in on the part and periodically drawing back to understand the relationship between part and whole, a structure to therapy which needs to be explained and contracted for. After each significant reconsideration there is a requirement to envisage what consequences it might have for the wider frame of reference.

The approach therefore departs from an emphasis on either challenging individual thoughts or unearthing the hidden script mechanism which keeps everything in place in favour of subtly shifting a whole worldview segment by segment. In common with the pioneers of CBT (Ellis, 1985; Beck, 1976), Berne worked on the assumption that thought was atomistic and therapy could hone in on the particular problematic belief to the mind's overall benefit. His metaphor for this was the plucking out of a splinter and watching the whole diseased body right itself as a result (Berne, 1971). Change was often portrayed as a frequently dramatic explosion of insight, driving the client's attention onto a single point until realisation breaks through (Berne, 1966; Goulding & Goulding, 1979). Later generations of transactional analysts began to speak openly about achieving only limited clinical success with these ideas: too many cases resulted in merely a listless revelation without transformative release (Oates, 2016; McNeel, 2015). The end result was a renewed interest in affect above thought and the frequent conclusion that only a lengthy engagement with the earliest stirrings of script would be enough.

Contextual transactional analysis takes a different response to these challenges, working at 'breadth' across the undulating, varied surface of the worldview rather than plunging into 'depth' behind it. Proceeding from the view of language and thought introduced in Chapter 5, the approach is holistic rather than atomistic, seeing our world views not as collections of individual thoughts but an interconnected and complex constellation, ever shifting and reforming in the light of new experience. Rather than presuming a conflicted split between thought and feeling, I endorse the position that emotion itself is a complex evaluative process with an irreducible cognitive component (see Nussbaum, 2001). Focused, rational re-appraisal has its place, often as a catalyst of a wider process of new knowing, but we are less interested in detached contemplation than passionate and committed engagement that comes from or produces KNOWING.

Novel contemplations must descend from their bird's eye view to meet up with the viscera of experience. We ultimately want heart and mind to march together even if the former sometimes takes the lead.

Since we can't address a whole frame of reference at once, we will still bring our focus to bear on a particular portion of belief at any one time. Reworking Berne's metaphor about the splinter, I would argue that even if the problem starts with a single injury the subsequent pathologies which develop as a consequence of the whole body's response may not be curable simply by healing the original wound. We are interested in both the original hurt and the way it ripples through the system, tracing the impact, the lasting consequences, the ways the constellation of mind and being compensates, succumbs and resists.

The revised ego-state model provides a partial guide in mapping the frame of reference as it unfolds and shifts in session. We may witness old ways of being (Child) jostling with new, borrowed, consensus beliefs (Parent) rubbing up against a more flexible authority (Adult), dogged realism and vivid imagination seesawing in and out: all is welcome. The living memory of the Child can appear as bright shards of raw experience gripping us temporarily without leaving a lasting trace or as stories which say more about our lives and worlds than simple facts can convey. Our Parent beliefs, inherited by necessity from others and used without full authority may sometimes yield a taken-for-granted quality, a sense that other ways of seeing things are not available. The trick is to notice the shifting pattern of response as new ideas are introduced.

Contextual therapy is Adult-led therapy for it is in the crucible of authority that new beliefs are likely to be entertained, grasped, tested and accepted. The clamour for Adult authority is not austere; it must be tempered with realism about the extent to which people can or will cut themselves adrift from their history of experience. It must also acknowledge that cognitive vulnerability is unavoidable and that some things will continue to be taken on trust until compelling reasons to think differently are offered. Perhaps they cannot be eliminated. A perfect accord between ego-states or omniscient view on reality is beyond us; we aim only for a slightly more authoritative drift. This calls for careful, reforming work of the surface and an understanding that multiple, overlapping changes are necessary to change course. It's not a process that has an end point as such, but we may begin to suspect the work is done when thoughts begin to drift fairly naturally in a slightly modified direction and when curiosity and responsibility have developed their own momentum. The intended outcome is a better process, not an improved product. We are not simply interested in getting people to change their thoughts, we are interested in turning them into thinkers.

The course of therapy outlined above will neither be set on a straight and true course through a binding initial contract nor via the inherent integrity of following the process. It's more like piecing together a jigsaw than following a story, intuitive and experimental jumps, sometimes following the client's lead, sometimes the therapist's hunches. The picture we seek to build of the world and the self within it must come to life in the process of assembly, periodically stopping to notice how things bind together. Speculation must take root. Since we are keen to turn initial knowing into KNOWING, the basic unit of our work is what I will call a 'scene'. These are defined as recalled narrative memories which may be retained in the mind for more than one reason. An individual life course will be made of thousands of individual scenes but many of these will have been long forgotten and only those retained by memory provide a workable starting point.

Scenes are detailed and overdetermined, a nexus for a host of different meanings and values. They are often brought forward to justify or support a frame of reference. They seem to express and tie together most of its underlying drift and content. Most of us can recall scenes which compress a lifetime's meaning into an episode, a vision of the world into the every day. When prompted we can usually notice lesser scenes which echo aspects of these compressions, however faintly. It is these moments where the particular provides a window into the general that we seek here.

Scenes knit our KNOWING together, relics of our whole, embodied movement through the world. The use to which they are put in maintaining our sense of things means their composition and conclusions can seem self-evident. They are often the memories we lean on the most. At the same time scenes are highly concrete. They describe events, things that happened not just what we thought of them. They can be productive sites of contestation and revision for the basic narrative spine of facts will often support different meanings. A scene can be explored from multiple angles, diving into the feelings and experience or soaring into the distant overview provided by reason and rethinking. The point of working with scenes is to reconcile both aspects, immersion or distance depending on what seems to be needed. If we send ripples through the frame of reference at is most central and knotted points then the kind of broad but small changes we are looking for may appear.

Scenes are the places where meaning and absence sit side by side. Even though a scene is told from our own perspective, the events relayed are not necessarily about us. Things could always have been seen from another perspective. In contrast to a therapy focused on the resolution of vertical problems which always centrifugally draws events back to the client's own patterning perspective, scenes can show us glimpses of the roads not taken. The cognitive vulnerability that guarantees the existence of our Parent ego-state means we aren't always the sole authors of our own stories. The drift of our frame of reference means that our stories are only partially organised. There will always be plenty of absences, cracks and discontinuities in a scene in which new understandings might flourish. One aim of contextual therapy is to subtly, sensitively retell the procession of scenes so that an alternative view, one which includes greater social and political awareness begins to fill in the absences, weave around the existing elements, anchor fresh thinking in the parts of life most valuable to us and bring them to life in a new and coherent way. The approach owes a debt to Vittorio Guidano's constructivist therapy approach which recommends building up a range of explored scenes with common threads, the therapist cinematically zooming in and out like a camera to reveal patterns and hidden orders which gradually change their overall sense (Guidano, 1987, 1991).

A therapy focused on scenes will get the client used to sometimes tuning out of the flow of their own process and stopping to saying more about what happened. Some scenes will be visited once, others will be return destinations, held in client and therapist's memories and revisited with each fresh outsight that takes root. Scenes will tend to fall into two categories, the most meaningful and the most recent. Meaningful scenes are the nexus points identified above where established sense can be revised, but recent scenes have the value of representing life in its still-molten state. A scene from contemporary life shows not merely the overlooked possibilities but the still-live opportunities, the open potential for thought and action yet to be embraced.

Working with scenes depends upon the kind of dialogic, language-based sensibility introduced in Chapter 5. As they listen to the scenes the therapist hears areas of agreement, places where they need to understand more and occasions where they are sure some other viewpoint could have been reached. Questions are asked for clarification and tentative suggestions for what could have been meant are offered as a starting point for discussion. The accumulation of things that could have been meant but weren't adds up progressively to enhanced social and political awareness. This enhanced consciousness isn't thrust at the client in one gesture, it is lightly threaded through the overlapping scenes, pausing to hear each doubt, extending present meanings in new directions, leaving what is valuable undisturbed, encouraging the client's digestion, reflection and ownership. Jarring challenges are a last resort. We seek informed, careful, enabling agreement not over-adaptive compliance.

The kind of political and social awakening which results in a new drift of the frame of reference will not take seed immediately. It should be explained to the client that therapy may at points have a meandering quality where it must be a gesture of faith that a new sense will eventually emerge. In common with some systemic practitioners, I tend to view such acts of reframing not as ends in themselves but things volunteered by the therapist as the starting point for new understanding (see Nicholls, 1987). We seek to stimulate as much as to transmit, to share our truths not to impose them, to foster ownership and authority, not blank agreement. The client should be prepared for and supported through instances of confusion and uncertainty, advised that this is not evidence of inadequacy, and reminded frequently of their right to disagree. The role of the therapist is not to think legalistically, building a case for a new thought so it feels as though they are closing down the client's chances for escape. Instead the therapist and client return to thoughts again and again as the focus expands across more and more scenes to consider if the view has changed. The reframing has an initial 'as if' quality which will turn into KNOWING if ultimately acceptable to the wider psyche.

Our frames of reference, like the lives they are part of, are unfinished. When we take political reframing and link it to the daily substance of the client's life, their memories, embodied values and yearnings then we have bridged the person and the world in a way which returns people to events with an enhanced sense of possibility. I don't believe in pushing concrete outcome goals or behaviour changes mechanically, but I am interested in foregrounding the interconnection between a person still authoring their life in real time and the scenes they have yet to write. If we allow our clients to imagine, to taste and smell what a different world might look like they may yet fall in love with the possibilities they have only just seen.

At some point if the work has taken the client will begin not merely to question but to actively learn something new. The revision of old scenes is all well and good but new scenes from a life better lived will strengthen and consolidate a new self-and-world. Sometimes in transactional analysis we have assumed that change in action follows from change in internal structure, that external doing consolidates internal redecision (see Woollams & Brown, 1979). Contextual transactional analysis emphasises thinking and action as forms of experimentation, a trying out of new ways doing things. Experimentation is a way of acknowledging that all freshly-minted beliefs must be held lightly until they pass the test of experience. We are interested in whether something new and emergent helps the person to get a better grip on the world, whether it leads to greater accord between their ego-states and whether it allows the person to imagine different orderings of the world. If we look closely the client will often be doing something useful without acknowledging its wider significance. We must do our best to exploit these happy coincidences and enhance their potential.

The kind of contracts for specific change recommended by the classical tradition (Stewart, 1996) are useful tools for focused, motivated action to realise agreed goals. I favour a more exploratory approach with someone just ambling into a general new direction of travel, trying to feel their way into a new way of thinking and living. Acceptance into the general drift of a frame of reference can feel like a subtle, intuitive business. Experimentation presumes that we will revisit a new thought again and again and notice the unintended consequences both positive and negative as it fans out across the frame of reference. When a client's mind has really taken a thought and run with it we should expect to be surprised by what turns up.

There are sound reasons for pursuing experimentation tentatively. Human beings are not as good as they think they are at anticipating what things will mean to them (see Gilbert, 2006; Paul, 2014). In addition, the world is complex and fluid; our minds aim at multiple moving target. Sometimes unexpected consolations have to be taken in place of expected victories, we have to swerve as often as we continue straight. As long as something useful is learnt, something which can inform the future direction of life, then things are not lost. Clients who have been deprived of resourcefulness, responsiveness, truthfulness and integrity need every opportunity to gain valuable new experiences, to see that some doors will open if you push them in the right way and that the habit of thinking brings new things to light. All lives will have unassuming moments where the social and political can be subtly brought into view. Experimentation doesn't have to be grand or aim at a big pay off. It's not the end point that matters so much as that the client has got there by meeting the test of experience and becoming the kind of person who is willing to try things. In the process they have partially reclaimed authority over their minds.

The therapeutic relationship

The kind of work advocated here requires the periodic co-creation of a very specific kind of relationship. Nothing that falls within the bounds of commonly accepted therapeutic practice is definitively ruled out, but the ideas presented in this book about will inevitably mean that some things might have to be done differently. Transactions are ideally Adult to Adult, where Adult is understood in the sense introduced in Chapter 3, an authoritative context-dependent state of being where at least some of the things that are needed for autonomous living are provided by a good enough environment. It is an irreducible part of doing this kind of work that as assumptions become unsettled in the light of new experiences, we come to realise we were actually acting in the light of Parent beliefs all along.

The relationship is periodically structured with the central aim of helping the client to gain outsight. This requires learning and a willingness to explore, to consider, and to entertain new ideas. It demands we see ourselves and our clients as a capable co-pilots still needing to chip away at their cognitive vulnerability, helping each other out along the way. In this the approach comes close to the collaborative relationship stance endorse by CBT and systemic approaches (Gilbert & Leahy, 2007; Minuchin & Fishman, 1981).

The relationship is therefore structured by these expectations rather than ones which anticipate an emergent process. Transference-sensitive therapies keep attention focused on the self coming together in the relationship, whereas I am interested in the relationship being used as merely the starting point for a more socially literate, outward facing and capable self-and-world. In our customary way of thinking, this comes close to describing how we decontaminate the Adult from Parental limitation. Inevitably the client's immediate needs and capability to undertake a potentially demanding reorientation should be carefully appraised: hearing and healing must sometimes precede changing. Transferential callings should be acknowledged if their clamour is overwhelming and nothing else will get through, but I don't go looking for them by default. An ideal contextual stance sits between faith in new possibility and realism about the often cautious and faltering steps clients will take to get there. Periods of stillness, reflection and empathy are welcome, but they are not the final destination.

Where the client can lead, the therapist should be one step behind; where we sense that the client might wish to consider another way of thinking the therapist may temporarily take one step ahead of the client – but no more than one step. Finding the optimum point between faith and realism recalls Vygotsky's zone of proximal development (introduced in Chapter 3. See Vygotsky, 1962). If our faith in the client is too far ahead of their present development they may feel shamed and overwhelmed: if we are too conservative, we sell them short. Modifying the useful lessons of some systemic practitioners (Seikkula & Arnkil, 2006), a contextual therapist should ideally treat a client as though they were at the limits of their current potential and then wait for them to grow into that space before reviewing their expectations.

As with any learning process, trying and failing sometimes precedes competence. We seek to provide the conditions for people to be capably interested in their own minds, to give them the permission to explore, to speculate, to be wrong and for it not to matter, to have confidence that they can come to have better ways of seeing things: whilst the therapist must always appear capable enough to instil confident and provide security, we need to model the virtues of fallibility in our conduct.

Ideally as therapists we would have gained all the wisdom necessary to be one step ahead of the client in every direction they might take: in practice this won't always be possible. Whilst therapy training often provides an excellent space for developing reflective capacity and open habits of mind, it does not do much to reduce our general cognitive vulnerability. Perhaps the best we can do is turn the negative of our deficits into the positive of humility and willingness to be responsible for educating ourselves. We can't be all-knowing but we can always be willing to learn. We must embrace this responsibility as the best that can be managed.

The curious upside to humbly acknowledging the cognitive vulnerability we share with our clients is that we only have to regard their frame of reference charitably rather than respectfully. We are both stumbling towards the light together. This leads necessarily to greater permissiveness about importing social and political ideas into the therapy room. Whilst a therapist should acknowledge particular responsibilities, restrictions and privileges when entering the therapy space, a contextual practitioner should be less likely to see a radical distinction between therapeutic and wider, personal know how. At the end of the session we walk out onto the same streets as our clients. We continually draw upon ideas from all areas of our life in our work. A contextual practitioner does not fetishize therapy as inherently different to the kinds of useful relationships we might form elsewhere. We need to be careful and responsible but there is no urgency to trace what we do back to esoteric theories to guarantee its efficacy. We have ideas, we think they might be useful, we can intelligibly account for why we think they might help, let's not hold back unnecessarily from introducing them appropriately. Sometimes simply saying what anyone else could say is what is needed most.

Introducing social and political ideas to a client carries an obligation to be 'outsightful', informed, reflective and humble. I can only hear from the place in the world I usually occupy, but this does not mean my current horizons are unchanging or that my differences cannot be of use. I must learn from my client about their world to get a sense of what they might want to learn from me. In Chapter 5 I outlined how such a dance of understanding might work, how dialogue is premised on a link between understanding what a person is saying against our background sense of how things are. Smooth passages of uncomplicated understanding will give way to moments where our worldviews pull apart in a way that demands either contestation or revision. A contextual transactional analysis relationship is thus one where learning, contesting, reinforcing and revising our assumptions are the preconditions for understanding.

A contextual transactional analyst warmly supports the centrality of accurate, empathic understanding to the therapeutic endeavour though the addition of a social and political dimension means that empathy is understood a little differently. We see ourselves less as a mirror and more as an echo. We understand the client's experience as uniquely theirs, but not without precedent for we live as part of the same world and stand alongside them, echoing their distress from the flesh and bone of our shared predicament. Add social and political awareness to empathy and you get solidarity, a *standing with* our clients rather than just a relating to them.

It's tempting to write about the ideals of the therapeutic relationship whilst downplaying the often gritty reality. Living in a condition of persistent and pervasive environmental disadvantage can impoverish a collective vocabulary to the point where any prospect of escape or fight back has almost entirely evaporated. Whilst suffering recognised as unjust can spur resilience and defiance, clients often arrive in the consulting room confused, wounded and defeated. The confidence, energy, willingness and optimism to explore new perspectives can be hard to kindle when you have little sense that things can change. There is an understandable wish for the gnawing tooth ache of psychological pain to be simply removed. In addition, the ethos of therapy with its emphasis on empathy and mutual respect may be a welcome relief from business as usual but it can also jar heavily with cultures which have developed a protective rind of unfeeling harshness to manage their predicament. Add into these the thorny questions of the therapist's perceived greater cultural prestige and we have identified several large hurdles for any therapeutic relationship to clear.

The ideals must be made to work on the ground and therefore the relationship must begin where the client starts from. It's crucial that you anticipate where possible what clients from your working context might think about sitting with a professional like you. Inviting a questioning attitude towards widely shared habits of belief is a sensitive matter that can be experienced as unsettling or disrespectful unless the groundwork has been laid carefully. As a therapist develops a sense over time of the kinds of people who end up in their clinic, it's useful to establish how people are used to interacting with others and in particular how disagreement, exploration and differences in opinion are regarded and managed. If you get the sense that the client does not come from a place where respectful dialogue about important matters is possible, then being in therapy itself will be a kind of experiment which needs to be managed carefully.

Cast iron cultural prohibitions on diverging from a majority culture position are steep barriers to most kinds of therapy. If cultural vocabularies repel discussion and reform of cultural norms outright then client work may simply not get off the ground. How to respond to such situations is a matter of case-by-case practical judgement though the dilemma is sharper if the client's perceived needs and the requirements of the cultural vocabulary are fundamentally antagonistic. Although there are now a number of publications which advocate bringing differences of power and viewpoint out into the open within the therapy space (e.g. Lago, 2006) there are considerable risks here. Whilst this strategy respects the condition of truthfulness, some of my clients seem to find it both abruptly exposing and a distraction from what they want to talk about.

It is consistent with the ideas I have presented in this book for the therapist to be initially more 'parental' in terms of anticipating and providing what they take the client to need as preconditions for their burgeoning authoritative participation. I hope I have shown due sensitivity to the risks of this without undermining the more active stance I think is often the right path to take. Contextual therapists only grant themselves this privilege of greater know how on the assumption that they also accept greater responsibility for owning mistakes and changing their mind.

Concluding remarks

I have done my best in this chapter to outline the ethos and the kinds of conditions necessary for meaningful change in outsight and belief structure. My vision is of gradual and incremental change rather than Olympian leaps of outsight. This is a reformist rather than radical approach to increasing knowledge and enhancing authority though proceeding cautiously does not prevent the client eventually reaching radical conclusions about their corner of the world. The approach acknowledges the likelihood of fumbling down dead ends on the way to finding the right path, of multiple small changes coalescing into one rather than finding the Achilles heel of a worldview and hoping it brings the whole edifice down in one motion, of qualified optimism laced with patient realism. Inevitably, the success of such an approach in practice is dependent upon developing the right sensibility and awareness in the therapist as much as any specific technical skill. In this I think my ideas are not much different than any other kind of therapy. Hopefully the book has gone some way to engendering the same competence and optimism to have a go in the reader that we seek to instil in our clients.

References

Beck, A.T. (1976) *Cognitive Therapy and the Emotional Disorders*. New York: Meridian.
Berne, E. (1963) *The Structure and Dynamics of Organisations and Groups*. New York: Grove Press.

Berne, E. (1966) *Principles of Group Treatment.* New York: Grove Press.

Berne, E. (1971) Away from a theory of the impact of interpersonal interaction on non-verbal participation. *Transactional Analysis Journal,* 1 (1), 6–13.

Burnham, J.B. (1986) *Family Therapy.* London: Tavistock.

Crossman, P. (1966) Permission and Protection. *Transactional Analysis Bulletin,* 5 (19), 152–154.

Ellis, A. (1985) *Reason and Emotion in Psychotherapy.* 2nd edn. New York: Citadel Press.

Fricker, M. (2007) *Epistemic Injustice: Power and the Ethics of Knowing.* Oxford: Oxford University Press.

Freire, P. (2000) *Pedagogy of the Oppressed.* Translated from Portuguese by M.B. Ramos. New York: Continuum.

Gilbert, D. (2006) *Stumbling on Happiness.* London: Harper Press.

Gilbert, P., Leahy, R.L., Ed. (2007) *The Therapeutic Relationship in Cognitive Behavioural Therapies.* Hove: Routledge.

Goulding, M.M., Goulding. R. (1979) *Changing Lives Through Redecision Therapy.* New York: Grove Press.

Guidano, V.F. (1987) *Complexity of the Self: A Developmental Approach to Psychopathology and Therapy.* New York: Guildford Press.

Guidano, V.F. (1991) *The Self in Process.* New York: Guilford Press.

Habermas, J. (1986) *Autonomy and Solidarity: Interviews with Jürgen Habermas.* Edited by P. Dews. London: Verso.

Habermas, J. (1997) *Between Facts and Norms.* Translated from German by W. Rehg Cambridge: Polity.

Habermas, J. (1998) *On the Pragmatics of Communication.* M. Cooke, Ed. Cambridge, MA: MIT Press.

Hargaden, H., Sills, C. (2002) *Transactional Analysis: A Relational Perspective.* London: Routledge.

Joyce, P., Sills, C. (2014) *Skills in Gestalt Counselling and Psychotherapy.* 3rd edn. Los Angeles: Sage.

Lago, C. (2006) *Race, Culture and Counselling.* 2nd edn. Maidenhead: Open University Press.

Lee, A. (2006) 'Process Contracting', in C. Sills, Ed., *Contracts in Counselling and Psychotherapy.* London: Sage, 74–86.

McNeel, J.R. (2015) The Heart of Redecision Therapy: resolving injunction messages. In R.G. Erskine, Ed., *Transactional Analysis in Contemporary Psychotherapy.* London: Karnac, 55–78.

Minuchin, S., Fishman, H.C. (1981) *Family Therapy Techniques.* Cambridge, MA: Harvard University Press.

Nicholls, M.P. (1987) *The Self in the System: Expanding the Limits of Family Therapy.* New York: Routledge.

Nussbaum, M.C. (2001) *Upheavals of Thought: The Intelligence of Emotions.* Cambridge: Cambridge University Press.

Oates, S. (2016) Are we, can we, should we all be relational? *The Transactional Analyst,* 7 (1), 19–22.

Paul, L.A. (2014) *Transformative Experience.* Oxford: Oxford University Press.

Seikkula, J., Arnkil, T.E. (2006) *Dialogical Meetings in Social Networks.* London: Karnac.

Stewart, I. (1996) *Developing Transactional Analysis Counselling.* London: Sage.

185

Stewart, I., Joines, V. (2012) *TA Today: A New Introduction to Transactional Analysis*. Melton Mowbray: Lifespace.

Tudor, K., Hargaden, H. (2002) 'The Couch and the Ballot Box: The Contribution and Potential of Psychotherapy in Enhancing Citizenship' in C. Feltham, Ed., *What's the Good of Counselling and Psychotherapy: The Benefits Explained*. London: Sage, 156–178.

Vygotsky, L. (1962) *Thought and Language*. Translated from Russian by E. Hanfmann, G. Vakar. Cambridge, MA: Massachusetts Institute of Technology.

Widdowson, M. (2010) *Transactional Analysis: 100 Key Points and Techniques*. London: Routledge.

Woollams, S., Brown, M. (1979) *TA: The Total Handbook of Transactional Analysis*. New Jersey: Prentice-Hall.

Part IV

OUR PRESENT AND FUTURE

9

THE INSEPARABILITY OF THERAPY AND WORLD

Talking therapies themselves exist in a social context. Their institutions, theories and practices are as real, as much a part of the world, as rocks and stones. Therapy isn't just something that is present behind the closed door of the consulting room, it's also part of the background context of the world outside. It partially creates the general context in which the therapy work takes place. Therapy is therefore as shaped, enabled and created by wider, ever-changing social forces as the psychological problems it seeks to address. Nothing in this picture stands still. A transactional analysis which degenerates into a museum or shrine will fail tomorrow's clients for they will not be quite the same as today's. I'd like to propose we think a little harder about the particular ways as a profession we both create and are created by our context. There are pressing difficulties and barely visible opportunities in our current context which would benefit from closer attention.

As Jerome Frank has persuasively argued, therapeutic treatments and psychological problems emerge together symbiotically from the same circumstances. The clients seeking help and the therapists delivering it share common assumptions about how people are and why they suffer (Frank, 1991). The ritual of therapy only works to the extent that it conveys a helpful message to people in an already-familiar vocabulary. Much as I regard the myth of internal sufficiency as untenable in many ways, there is no doubt that it draws powerful sustenance from deep roots in the Romantic/Christian heritage of the west. Thinking in these terms can feel as natural as breathing because most of us will have absorbed these ideas as part of the overall cultural drift we inhabit. A therapist who circles in on someone's childhood unhappiness or unconscious feelings will likely be met with confusion by a client from a context where psychological pain is thought to be the work of evil spirits: without a background of shared assumptions, the therapeutic conversation simply couldn't get started. Client and therapist would talk passed each other. Assuming therapy is successful, both client and therapist leave with their background stories about why the work has helped confirmed. If Frank's argument is correct, then successful therapy will work both because it draws upon established background understandings of the world and because it becomes an established background understanding itself.

It would be unnecessary to contemplate this as long as the same kinds of people with the same kinds of problems were helped by the same kinds of therapists. Our ideas would be for all seasons. I have argued that this view is not tenable not just because our theories are imperfect or because idiosyncratic cases always turn up but because both people and their problems change with the world around them. Reform and revision of our ideas and practices are inevitable as a matter of ongoing necessity. As long as therapy remains alert, mobile, critical and responsive to the flux of the world, then the symbiotic relationship between clients and therapy has a chance of remaining relevant.

I am concerned that this is not happening enough. Therapy is not just a response to clinical problems, it is a social artefact in its own right, built and maintained by a constant stream of newly trained practitioners, published works, training institutions, governing bodies and clinical services. It is also afflicted with the inevitable conservatism that such professional success entails. Energies that were once focused outwards on developing a new, living practice fitted to the needs of the moment get turned inwards onto the perpetuation of traditions, the consolidation of rather than radical, ongoing questioning of practice, the pursuit of institutional success and a regrettable squabbling over minor differences between discrete professional groupings. Yesterday's ideas find their way into today's practice as therapists too often uncritically map their client's experience back onto the theories they have been trained to adhere to without question. The standard trajectory is for a once raw and innovative burst of ideas to settle into a comfortable rut.

The impact of this conservatism extends well beyond the bounds of our professional sphere. Therapy ideas have percolated into the vocabularies of the common life. Countless novels, films and TV shows replay, in however vulgarised a form, the link between childhood unhappiness and current incapacity. The idea that our minds have hidden depths which best explain the trajectory of our lives is similarly unavoidable. We raise and educate children in the light of therapeutic ideas with the avoidance of emotional hurt now a guiding ethos in the mindset of parents and teachers. Children raised in this context inevitably find their sense of self emerging from the unavoidable contextual background these ideas create. Once we had to help clients build narratives about kinds of hurt they did not know how to name: now they turn up 'pre-therapied', having built these stories all by themselves from the readily available therapeutic vocabularies that everyone has to hand. It's fair to say that as a profession we haven't merely responded to the world, we have changed it by adding our ideas to its general drift.

Of course, Berne explicitly intended to prise his theories from the hands of professionals and make them available to his clients for their own use. The social changes which therapy has been part of inaugurating have indeed often resulted in people coming to understand themselves more, like themselves better and live more freely and intimately amongst others. The downside is that the therapeutic infiltration of identity formation has often been so complete that whilst we have helped people to become accomplished at telling 'psychological' stories about themselves this has crowded out an equally necessary capacity to tell 'sociological' or 'political' ones. The contention of this book has been that at times these kinds of stories may represent a better way forward. Too many therapists are practicing in a way which illegitimately persuades their clients that their problems are entirely vertical in nature because they do not know how to do otherwise.

So often I am confronted with people who complain of being 'unable to trust' their partners as though this were a personal defect in need of correction without accounting for the increasingly transient and transactional nature of romantic relationships. I meet clients telling me that they need to 'boost their confidence' at work when their employment conditions are unstable and their manager is an unapologetic bully. Some people tell me they are suffering from something called 'low self-esteem' when further discussion reveals they have nothing in their life in which they can take pride and no-one who values them. This book became necessary as the uneasy sense grew that there were more useful ways of accounting for our lives which had either been lost or not yet found (see also Efran et al., 1990).

Since unhappy families and damaged children are unlikely to disappear any time soon, old theories will retain their frequent relevance: if you cut us, we still bleed. Yet there remains a tendency with therapy models of various stripes to assume that once you have established what you take to be an unvarying, comprehensive picture of human functioning that the clinical practice which results from this is fit for all occasions. By introducing the notion of horizontal problems, this book has shown at least one way in which this notion runs up against limits. The danger of not periodically reminding ourselves that all ways of doing things have limits is that we can drift into unwittingly indoctrinating our clients into believing they have a vertical problem because we lack the means, permission and confidence to see things horizontally. (Therapy has never quite managed to entirely escape the accusation that clinical practice only seems to confirm the validity of the practitioner's approach because the therapy process itself coaxes the client into seeing things the way the theory claims they are. See Abroms, 1968; Grünbaum, 1984; Rubovitz-Seitz, 1998.) If we fail to acknowledge that suffering requires a wider range of conceptions and solutions than we currently entertain, if we lack the capacity to meet our clients as social and political as well as psychological beings, if we cannot see that distress itself and our theories about it have transient and contingent aspects then we risk leading our clients away from the best available understanding of what is happening to them. In persuading them, however innocently, that their problems are something that they are not, we risk falling well short of the aims and obligations of helping to which we aspire.

We have come so far in a particular direction that making these changes can seem hard to imagine. Having collectively done a great job of persuading people that their difficulties are best understood vertically, it can be a hard task to talk them back out of this in favour of a horizontal explanation. We risk immediate disengagement by disappointing people's expectations. Recommendations to develop outsight can seem hard work when you are fervently hoping for a more personal relief. The approach I have introduced here requires a skilful sleight of hand to simultaneously engage the client at the level of their expectations whilst subtly shifting the understanding of the problem into a more social and political vein. The temptation to conduct therapy within the confines of the client's existing understanding will be strong and at least partially defensible. Many people leave the therapist's consulting room for the last time very contented and relieved having been told something which confirms their underlying assumptions even when better understandings may be available.

Clients such as these come believing that the therapeutic process can find something in them which will free them to flourish in spite of their circumstances: sometimes we can, sometimes we can't. It's the automatic assumption that this is the best way to understand the problem which should trouble us. To the best of my knowledge no therapy model, including transactional analysis, satisfactorily draws an operative distinction between the kinds of suffering that may respond to psychological help and those that may require an alternative solution. There is not enough room in our profession for recognition that certain kinds of suffering are appropriate and inevitable given what is happening to the person (see Watzlawick, 1983; Hari, 2018). I am troubled that too often our first thought when we hear of a rising tide of misery is to book a first session at the expense of calling for a better world. I am mindful that in the efforts to help and heal as best we can we may sometimes leave clients with the intimated view that they have to change to fit within current social arrangements and not the other way round.

The argument that therapy has over-reached by illegitimately psychologising the social has been made before and more fully by others (Furedi, 2004; Morrall, 2008; Kaminer, 1992; Illouz, 2007; Smail, 1996). That therapists have largely carried on as before is not a sign that these arguments have been countered but that they have been ignored. It would be a failing on my part if I left the impression that I had shown a way for social and material difficulties to always be solved psychologically. I have merely argued that we might be of help with a specific kind of secondary injury which accompanies social and material disadvantage – a much smaller claim. The reach of our work only goes so far. Occasional modesty about what we can accomplish becomes us better than attempting to raise our spirits through a misplaced eulogising of the power to change.

I hope the identification of horizontal difficulties has somewhat expanded the scope of our potential efficacy but the call here is as much for therapy to be humble about its limits as it is to go beyond them. Some voices heralding certain kinds of therapy as the only radical path to liberation may disagree (Jacoby, 1997) but paradoxically, sometimes the best and most useful thing we can do is to help our clients see that their difficulties aren't psychological in the sense they may think. A fully ethical response to horizontal problems requires that therapy does not seek to monopolise support options for beneficial change. Here then is another call for a refresh of the symbiosis, a clear vision of ourselves as a useful but incomplete response to our client's distress with an attendant requirement to make productive links with people and organisations fighting the same fight on different fronts. Some may protest that there is always something they can do as therapists to help, yet even if this is true, we surely have an obligation to advise when we sincerely believe another solution might be better.

The failings I am raising the alarm about are a sign of neither negligence nor questionable motives. They are simply the unintended outcome of good people trying to do the best job for their clients whilst losing sight of other options. Unfortunately, therapy ideas have not remained in our hands alone. Our refusal to draw a distinction between times where therapy can make a meaningful differ- ence and those where it cannot, between our circumscribed domain and the wider task of collective struggle, has been ripe with possibilities for the oppor- tunistic relocation of social and material problems to inside the mind. When elected officials piously wring their hands proclaiming the need to do more about 'mental health difficulties' whilst simultaneously doing nothing to change the social and material conditions which make suffering inevitable, then our ideas are being co-opted and wielded against the very people we are pledged to help. Without a more zealous guarding of our own professional borders, we may increasingly find ourselves on the horns of a dilemma, torn between our desire to help the person in front of us and the squeamish feeling that we are merely adjusting people to fit within an inhumane society. Some have pursued this reali- sation to the point that they have turned on therapy as a useless, compromised endeavour (Smail, 1996, 1993), a disenchantment that I hope I have drawn back from. The promise of the contextual approach offered here is that it takes the position that therapy can do something but not everything, it can take people to the point where they can envisage the changed world they want, but not neces- sarily have all those changes come about. The theoretical revisions proposed in this book should ideally be accompanied by a useful clarification of our profes- sional boundaries, our relationship to our own traditions and our ongoing engagement with the world outside the consulting room. We can – and often do – obviously make our own local adjustments but these need to be accompanied by the profession coming together and acting as one. Contextual ideas have been ventured in spirit which sits between reformist realism and utopian energy. Those who take the book as an invitation to adjust their own ethos and practice will hopefully gain much even if it sometimes feels as though the tide of circum- stance is overwhelming.

The future of our practice

Therapy remains a busy enterprise. There are no shortage of books, articles and publications refining and moving the profession forward but I don't believe I am being unfair in describing much of this literature as the minor adjustment of settled assumptions. There are too few voices observing that social changes are rendering our usual ways of doing things decreasingly pertinent (see Verhaeghe, 2007, 2008 for a notable exception). I went out into the world post-qualification and found horizontal problems hiding in plain sight. I assume there are therapists elsewhere who are similarly perturbed by the discrepancy between what they have been taught to see and what they are actually finding. In order to thrive and prosper in changing times, the therapy profession must dedicate a greater portion of its energies to the ongoing reform of practice in the light of fresh experience. I don't think it's too fanciful to say that locating our professional blind spots will go hand in hand with noticing what our clients are also missing.

Nothing can guarantee that we will not unwittingly perpetuate the innocent errors of our age. From the vantage point of hindsight, it has been easy enough to see that at least some of the early ideas of transactional analysis emerged from the cultural drift of post-war America. Understood in context, such boundless faith about human potential and personal responsibility may be better understood as reflecting the spirit of the age rather than a timeless discovery of the consulting room. Perhaps it took a therapist from the United Kingdom, born at the twilight of transactional analysis heyday and raised in a country where the iron grip of class runs furlongs-deep in the soil to understand that a therapy assembled from such gilded optimism might over-emphasise the exceptionalism and internal resourcefulness of the isolated self. In common with everyone else, I cannot see round corners. If all ideas need to be held lightly and revised in the light of new experience, then I cannot guarantee that my own theory will not one day fall into increasing irrelevance. This would not mean however that I did not have good reasons for holding to it now. Whatever the course, I welcome debates that challenge assumptions right down to the roots. As a pragmatist I speak as truthfully as I know and am willing to change my mind as new ideas come in. I can think of no better way to go about things.

Tomorrow's practitioners will bear responsibility for solving tomorrow's problems. If transactional analysis is to meet those clinical challenges, training courses must embrace outward-looking criticality as well as inward looking reflexivity. To our three-cornered training ethos of theoretical learning, personal therapy and clinical practice I'd like to make space for an emphasis upon worldly engagement and awareness. Take this book as a starting point for imagining a therapy of place to compliment a therapy of people. Can we envisage creating invigorating spaces in our professional lives where practitioners old and new can build, discover and share knowledge which lays bare the complexity of the social and the resulting self-and-world? Can we develop the intellectual and interpersonal competences necessary to help our clients to learn as well as to become? Transactional analysis has been better than most models at admitting a plurality of ideas through the gates from elsewhere but our culture often remains problematically hierarchical. Everyone brings something about their corner of the world to the profession that their trainers don't know. This is distributed cognition in action, vast reservoirs of experience which can feed professional excellence if we tap into it. Let's welcome the next generation as pioneers as well as apprentices.

Appealing on behalf of increased knowledge of the social risks running headlong into a bracingly deep shibboleth that we should see through what the client has in common with others to find what is most particular, unique and separate about them. Although I have argued that this belief needs to be qualified, a secondary objection – that therapists do not have the time or the opportunity to become intimately familiar with the social fabric of their client's lives on top of everything else – needs careful consideration. Initially perhaps our outsider's eyes see little, but over time as we have met with a significant number of clients from the same walk of life we will come to know a great deal about the local vocabulary. Our clients tell their stories in a way they don't tell anyone else. Therapists are keepers of community secrets. We occupy a uniquely advantageous vantage point. Granted, we should be cautious about taking people seeking psychological support as generally representative of their communities, but if we can only give ourselves permission to notice the patterns and cadences of meaning as they fan out across overlapping individual stories then the kind of detailed knowledge which underpins contextual working will coalesce over time. Granting myself the permission to become an 'ethnographer of convenience' made this book possible. The addition of more voices from different communities would be a welcome way of strengthening our collective resourcefulness.

John Dewey argued convincingly that the goal of learning is not the transmission of ideas but the creation of learners (Dewey, 1916). Yesterday's findings are not to be tossed aside carelessly but nor are they to be the recipient of undue reverence. Every experienced practitioner will be aware that the further away they get from their training the more they start to do things which depart from their models. The scaffolding of strict theory falls away to reveal the artful intuition of responsible improvisation. This parallels the move often discussed in this book between a 'your truth' and 'our truth' position. We may arrive at therapy training in a 'your truth' position as theorists, but this shouldn't obscure the fact that we may be have great authority in other areas. Transactional analysis will stand or fall on whether it recruits and nourishes creative, thoughtful practitioners capable of responding to the individual and local circumstances they find themselves in. Its validity should be called to the tribunal of experience in each generation and in every place: it has no automatic right to survive on the basis of yesterday's accomplishments.

This book is a starting point, a framework of some basic ideas about the social and political but intentionally some way short of a model to explain. Just as no psychological theory will ever account for every aspect of a client so no social and political theory will fully capture or explain the living, breathing forms of life in which we participate. The urge to categorise and generalise is understandable but must be moved passed. I ventured out into the wilderness beyond the bounds of current sense and have brought back some useful ideas but no precise map for other terrains. I hope it will support people in their own productive immersion in the world around them for lived authority rather than theory is what will succeed in the end. This is one way of understanding what Berne was pointing at when he told us to think Martian (Berne, 1972), that we might couple an insider's lived familiarity with how things work with an outsider's sense how things can be different. If we can balance on this tightrope then we will find ourselves in the best position to be of some use in restoring the dignity and capability which accompanies fully rounded social and political identities.

Venture beyond the gated enclosure of theory. Allow client's stories to speak to you in different ways. Notice as your ear becomes keener in picking out the background pulse of the common life. Go out and notice the buildings and streets, how people live and love around here. Be patient in your endeavours. When you have harvested enough observations, however fragile and uncertain, allow them into your work in the ways outlined in this book with all the due diligence, respect and care which your calling demands of you. And when your work is less faltering and your mistakes and misjudgements fewer, come back to us and share the stories of the place and the people where you live and work, for this book is merely knowing and what we need as a community of therapists is KNOWING. Help us to thicken and strengthen the braid of our experience in working with horizontal suffering, for our task is hard, the need is great and collecting our strengths and ideas together represents our best hope of success. If we do well enough then perhaps today's clients will respond to our better efforts and whilst tomorrow's therapists may find reasons to leave practices and conclusions behind, they may be grateful that the ideas we prepared today helped to make the outsights of tomorrow possible.

References

Abroms, G.M. (1968) Persuasion in Psychotherapy. *American Journal of Psychiatry*, 124 (8), 98–105.

Berne, E. (1972) *What Do You Say After You Say Hello?* London: Corgi Books.

Dewey, J. (1916) *Democracy and Education*. Hollywood, FL: Simon & Brown.

Efran, J.S., Lukens, M.D., Lukens, R.J. (1990) *Language, Structure and Change: Frameworks of Meaning in Psychotherapy*. New York: W.W. Norton & Co.

Frank, J.D. (1991) *Persuasion and Healing: A Comparative Study of Psychotherapy*. 3rd edn. Baltimore, MA: Johns Hopkins.

Furedi, F. (2004) *Therapy Culture: Cultivating Vulnerability in an Uncertain Age*. New York: Routledge.

Grünbaum, A. (1984) *The Foundations of Psychoanalysis: A Philosophical Critique*. Berkeley: University of California Press.

Hari, J. (2018) *Lost Connections: Why You're Depressed and How to Find Hope*. London: Bloomsbury.

Illouz, E. (2007) *Cold Intimacies: The Making of Emotional Capitalism*. Cambridge: Polity Press.

Jacoby, R. (1997) *Social Amnesia: A Critique of Contemporary Psychology*. 2nd ed, New Jersey: Transaction.

Kaminer, W. (1992) *I'm Dysfunctional, You're Dysfunctional: The Recovery Movement and Other Self-Help Fashions*. Reading, MA: Addison-Wesley.

Morrall, P. (2008) *The Trouble with Therapy: Sociology and Psychotherapy*. Maidenhead: Open University Press.

Rubovitz-Seitz, P.F.D. (1998) *Depth-Psychological Understanding: The Methodological Grounding of Clinical Interpretations*. Hilldale, NJ: Analytic Press.

Smail, D. (1993) *The Origins of Unhappiness: A New Understanding of Personal Distress*. London: Constable.

Smail, D. (1996) *How to Survive Without Psychotherapy*. London: Constable.

Verhaeghe, P. (2007) '"Chronicle of a death foretold": the end of psychotherapy', Conference presentation at Health4Life, Dublin, DCU. Accessed at: www.paulverhaeghe.com/lecturesandinterviews/DublinHealth4life.pdf. [Accessed 20 December 2014]

Verhaeghe, P. (2008) 'A combination that has to fail: new patients, old therapists', Lecture in Dublin, EISTEACH, accessed at: www.paulverhaeghe.com/lecturesandinterviews/Dublineisteach2008.pdf. [Accessed 6 October 2017]

Watzlawick, P. (1983) *The Situation is Hopeless, but not Serious: the Pursuit of Unhappiness*. New York: Norton.

GLOSSARY

This book introduces a number of new terms into the transactional analysis theoretical lexicon. It also revises some previously established and commonly used ideas which it inherits from pre-existing theory. Most of these terms are introduced and defined at their first time of appearance in the book but they are often then used in subsequent sections of the text without reminder. This glossary has been produced to help the reader hold in mind what those terms mean as they progress through the book for fear that otherwise they would have to disrupt their reading experience by flicking backwards and forwards trying to locate the initial definition. This glossary may also be of assistance to future inquirers who may wish to cite these ideas in their publications and presentations.

Where a term has been inherited from the pre-existing transactional analysis lexicon without being revised then standard definitions laid down elsewhere can be consulted. I have not included those terms here. In keeping with the wider argument of the book that knowledge is co-owned and produced I have no ultimate authority to fix the way these terms are used indefinitely. Readers who take themselves to be able to improve on both my ideas and the resulting definitions cited here have my blessing to do so.

Absence The conspicuous lack of knowledge in someone's frame of reference. It will be the absence of either something the person might be expected to know given what else they know or alternatively something they can be taken as needing to know in order to live successfully.

Accord A state of harmony between ego states leading to a broadly coherent frame of reference.

Adult ego-state Defined in contextual transactional analysis as the emergent product of a confluence between our innate capacity to think, a resourceful frame of reference, a personal disposition to be accurate and sincere, and shared cognitive resources which underwrite the authority to reach the best view of the world currently possible.

Authority The capacity and opportunity to make optimum use of beliefs or words we have learnt from and share with others. Authority is the defining attribute of the Adult ego state.

Chaos   A sub-type of horizontal problems. Chaos is defined by an over-whelming profusion of options and possibilities for living. Its likely impact on the self is a state of confusion and a sense of being overburdened with both choices and responsibilities.

Child ego-state   States of being which either recall periods of developmental immaturity or previous versions of selfhood which have been superseded by subsequent experience.

Circulatory transactions   A sequence of interaction where the background assumptions of the participant's shared world view are taken as given and not challenged.

Cognitive drifting   The sense that our worldviews develop cumulatively in a certain direction without there being any one underlying explanatory reason for this.

Cognitive opportunity   The extending of our knowledge and cognitive capacity made possible by borrowing and sharing beliefs with other people. The term is conceptually linked to cognitive vulnerability.

Cognitive vulnerability   Our ongoing social dependence upon other people to provide us with necessary knowledge about the world via testimony. It specifically refers to beliefs and knowledge which we can use competently but over which we don't have full authority. The term is linked to cognitive opportunity.

Disorders of opportunity   A kind of psychological distress which can emerge in contexts characterised by abundant opportunity and an accompanying sense that if you could do something then you should do it. Disorders of opportunity are often characterised by indecision and exhaustion. The term is linked to chaos.

Frame of reference   Defined in contextual transactional analysis as a variable ordering of our collected knowledge and experiential content, shaped by a changing assortment of cognitive habits from which a somewhat stable core of beliefs and processes emerge as a by-product of our largely consistent life paths and environments.

Games   Defined in contextual transactional analysis as a repeated interpersonal pattern of significance where alternative options for interaction are not recognised and which results in a generally negative outcome for the persons involved.

Good enough world   A large-scale social context characterised by sufficient levels of resourcefulness, responsiveness, truthfulness and integrity.

Horizontal games   A subtype of games where the non-availability of options is linked to absences in the frame of reference or vocabulary.

Horizontal problems A sub-division of psychological distress which occurs when the person's context either deliberately withholds or fails to provide something necessary for the person to become autonomous, to understand the nature and origin of their problems and to successfully resolve them.

Integrity A pre-condition of the good enough world. Integrity is the state reached by a social context when it attains sufficient coherence, character and intelligibility.

Interrupting transactions A sequence of interactions where one or both parties place a usually presumed and unquestioned assumption into the foreground for fresh evaluation by both parties.

KNOWING A knowledge of how to live supported by significant individual or collective lived experience. KNOWING will enjoy strong confluence with the overall frame of reference.

Language-led understanding A way of understanding people which prioritises the words they use in thinking or acting but does not deny that embodied or emotive dimensions will be part of any complete picture.

Liberal scepticism A political and philosophical position typical amongst therapists which presumes that attacking or undermining power, truth and dominant ideas automatically leads to an increase in freedom resulting from pluralism of viewpoint.

Myth of facilitation A therapeutic axiom which presumes that the job of therapy is to facilitate the emergence, integration or acceptance of what is already present in the client. This will usually encourage a therapeutic practice which is maximally attentive and minimally intrusive.

Myth of internal sufficiency A belief common to many therapeutic approaches which stipulates that people already have inside them the resources necessary to flourish and solve their problems irrespective of their life experiences and current circumstances.

Nearly-games An interpersonal sequence of significance which has some features of a game but does not fulfil all the criteria for inclusion. Often a nearly-game will not reach the negative outcome of the game sequence.

OK-OK Within contextual transactional analysis this life-position entails acknowledging that existing in a common world with others is an irreducible part of existence, that other people are in principle as entitled to occupy the world as we are, that collective change is possible and that we are aiming at more satisfying and just ways of living for everyone.

Oppression A sub-type of horizontal problem. Refers to a social configuration where one individual or group of people exploits, controls or restricts another individual or group of people often with an intent to hoard resources and power. Oppression may be either covert or overt. The psychological mechanism of oppression is best understood as a symbiosis whereby the oppressor forces the oppressed to live under an imposed description of reality which leaves them disorientated and powerless.

Our truth position Where a person has as much authority over the shared ideas and beliefs they hold as the people with whom they share them or from whom they learnt them. Occupying an our truth position is a precondition for the Adult ego state.

Overlap A sub-type of horizontal problem. An overlap occurs in a time of marked social transition when two quite distinct senses of how the world is will be simultaneously present for people. Overlaps may lead to increased instances of internal conflict.

Parent ego-state In contextual transactional analysis the Parent ego-state is defined as the emergent product of the successful functioning of our innate capacity to think and where efforts to be accurate and sincere may be present, but under social conditions where, due to deficits in our current frame of reference and the conditions necessary for a good enough world, we cannot hold beliefs in full authority.

Partial explanation An explanatory story which a person tells about their distress which, whilst somewhat informative, excludes or obscures a more accurate and useful explanation.

Resourcefulness A pre-condition of the good enough world. The capacity of the world to provide for people the things they need to live successfully so that a required level of security and satisfaction can be achieved with a level of effort which falls within the spectrum of human capability. Resourcefulness can be material but social roles and cultural beliefs and practices are also included within the definition.

Responsiveness A pre-condition of the good enough world. Defined as the capacity and willingness to recognise an individual or a community's identified wants and to respond appropriately to them. Responsiveness covers both individual and collective or state action.

Scenes A segment of narrative memory which may support multiple levels of meanings. A scene is often a pivotal aspect of the person's frame of reference.

Self-and-world A way of thinking about selfhood which suggests we emerge but never fully separate from the world. A complete understanding of our identity will always consider self and context in unity.

Truthfulness A pre-condition for a good enough world whereby people's dealings with each other are sufficiently accurate and sincere for the individual to understand themselves and their environment.

Vocabulary   A term used to describe a collective frame of reference. It is the hanging together of a shared way of seeing things, a set of ideas, behaviours, dispositions and values generated from a collective experience and history.

Vertical games   A subtype of games where the sequence and negative outcome result from the game player's script.

Vertical problems   A kind of psychological problem best understood in terms of the person's ongoing individual disposition to think, feel and act in a certain way. These patterns of response will be consistent across contexts and are often understood longitudinally as being linked to the person's psychological development.

Your truth position   Where shared beliefs we hold can be used competently but not with full or equal authority to others who hold them. The your truth position is a precondition of the Parent ego-state.

INDEX

Page numbers in *italics* denote figures

contextual transactional analysis in
    practice 7–8, 169–84; aims 171–2; basic
    foundations 170–1; contracting 174–5;
    ethics in 172–4; experimentation 175,
    180–1; promoting awareness 175–81;
    scenes 178–80; therapeutic relationship
    181–4
contracting 173–4, 180–75
Cornell, William F. 133
Craig, Edward 55
creativity 94
critical therapies 11
cultural beliefs 145–8
cultural script 145
cultural vocabularies 173, 184
cyclical psychodynamics 161

Darwin, Charles 72
Dawkins, Richard 135
deindustrialisation 46–7, 49–50, 58
democratic deficits 58–9
descriptive cognitive pluralism 135
Dewey, John 27, 71–2, 146, 147, 195
dialogue 117–22, 179
discounting and discounts 30–1, 51, 133,
    158
disorders of opportunity 37–9
domestic violence 32, 53–4
Durkheim, Emile 48
dynamic principle of games 154, 156,
    157

Eagleton, Terry 101
economic principle of games 155, 156–7,
    163
ego-state theory 63–5, 136, 177
ego-states: accord between 142, 144, 152,
    177, 180; frame of reference and 136–9;
    and neuroscience 65; recognising 170;
    splits within 35; two ego-state model 73;
    see also Adult ego-state; Child ego-
    state; Parent ego-state
emergence 27–8, 70
Emerson, Ralph Waldo 78–9
emotions, formation and expression of
    74–5
empathy 112, 183
English, Fanita 54, 163
Erskine, Richard 69–70, 164
ethics 172–4
ethnic minority communities 67
experimentation 175, 180–1
exteropsyche 66, 70, 77

families: oppression in 31–2; social
    changes 66–7
Feltham, Colin 97
feminist movements 47, 53–4
fish and ocean metaphor 25–6
Foucault, Michel 99–100
frame of reference 19, 30, 131–49, 152,
    176; absences in 140, 141–4;
    charitability towards 173, 182; clinical
    vignettes 139–40, 143; cognitive drifting
    135–6, 137, 146; collective 145–8;
    defined 133–9; ego-states and 136–9;
    horizontal problems and 133, 136,
    140–5; injunctions 141–2; knowing and
    KNOWING 144–5, 147, 149, 178–80;
    scenes 178–80; script and 131–3;
    vocabularies 145–8
Frank, Jerome 189
Fraser, Nancy 12
free or natural child ego state 93, 94–5, 106
freedom, language and 123–6
Freire, Paulo 174
Freud, Sigmund 74, 94
Fricker, Miranda 52, 172

games 151–67; bottom up view 157;
    clinical vignette 164–6; contextual view
    157–62; dynamic principle 154, 156,
    157; economic principle 154–5, 163,
    156–7; good games 153–4; 'how?' of
    162–4; nearly-games 152, 163; shared
    vocabulary and 159; social changes 160,
    161–2; structural principle 155–8; top-
    down view 157; and transference 163–4,
    181; vertical 159, 162, 164; 'what?' of
    153–4; 'why?' of 154–7
gaslighting 32
Giddens, Anthony 24
Gillett, Grant 74
Goffman, Erving 53
good enough mother 44
good enough world 43–59, 75–6, 80, 146;
    integrity 56–8, 59, 76, 80, 144, 147,
    171, 172; resourcefulness 46–9, 50,
    54–5, 58, 76, 80; responsiveness 49–53,
    58, 76, 80, 171, 171–2, 175; truthfulness
    53–6, 58–9, 76, 80, 104, 171, 172
Gopnik, Alison 72
Guidano, Vittorio 178–9

Habermas, Jürgen 51, 105, 115, 117, 173
habitus 28, 146
Hacking, Ian 34–5

Made in United States
Troutdale, OR
12/20/2023

16278256R00126